FOREIGN POLICY BEHAVIOR

FOREIGN POLICY BEHAVIOR

The Interstate Behavior Analysis Model

Jonathan Wilkenfeld,
Gerald W. Hopple,
Paul J. Rossa, and
Stephen J. Andriole

SAGE PUBLICATIONS   Beverly Hills   London

For information address.

SAGE Publications, Inc.
275 South Beverly Drive
Beverly Hills, California 90212

SAGE Publications Ltd
28 Banner Street
London EC1Y 8QE, England

Printed in the United States of America

Library of Congress Cataloging in Publication Data
Main entry under title:

Foreign policy behavior.

   Bibliography: p.
   1. International relations—Research.
I. Wilkenfeld, Jonathan.
JX1291.F665   327'.07'2   80-13161
ISBN 0-8039-1476-8

FIRST PRINTING

CONTENTS

LIST OF TABLES AND FIGURES

ACKNOWLEDGMENTS

An unusually large number of individuals contributed to the Interstate Behavior Analysis Project; we gratefully acknowledge their advice, assistance, and support. Graduate research assistants Robert McCauley, Lilymae Fountain, and Robert Stoker deserve thanks for their efforts, as do Mark Allen, Calvin Jillson, and Dan Crawford. A corps of undergraduate research assistants and data collectors—including Dorette Feit, Merle Feldbaum, Bill Goodwin, Janna Itzler, Michele Lane, Stuart Perry, Helene Rubinstein, Lee Ann Taylor, and Patricia Waldron—contributed immeasurably to our research. We also wish to acknowledge the efforts of project secretaries Molly Parker, Amy Favin, Nancy Hett, and Judy Bilberry. A number of foreign policy and international relations scholars have offered valuable critiques of various portions of our work over the years; we will thank them anonymously, since the list would be excessive in length. Terri Coleman of the Defense Advanced Research Projects Agency Cybernetics Technology Office (DARPA/CTO) rendered invaluable assistance in the completion of this volume. Thanks also to John Correnti, Edward Billheimer, and Phillis Hutchinson for the design and production of the figures and tables. Dr. Robert A. Young, former Director of the Cybernetics Technology Office, initially supported this research and provided continuous encouragement. Special thanks go to Amy Favin who typed various drafts of this volume. The computer time for this project was supported in part through the facilities of the Computer Science Center of the University of Maryland.

The coauthors share equal responsibility for this volume. Robert McCauley contributed to the analysis sections and introduced us to the PLS approach developed by Herman Wold, to whom we are also greatly indebted.

This research was supported by the Advanced Research Projects Agency of the Department of Defense and was monitored by ONR under Contract No. N00014-76-C-0153. The views and conclusions contained in this book are those of the authors and should not be interpreted as necessarily representing the official policies, either expressed or implied, of the Defense Advanced Research Projects Agency or the U.S. government.

PREFACE

The purpose of this volume is to present the major findings of the Interstate Behavior Analysis (IBA) Project, which was designed to construct, refine, operationalize, and derive testable models from a framework for the comparative analysis of foreign policy. The final step in this sequence—which is the focus of the concluding chapters of this volume—is the actual testing of a series of increasingly more sophisticated models of foreign policy behavior.

Scientific foreign policy analysis now constitutes an established field of inquiry within the disciplines of international relations and political science (see McGowan, 1976). The relative adolescence of the field becomes clear when we list the landmark dates in the "infancy" of the movement:

1966—the publication of Rosenau's (1966) seminal "pre-theories and theories" article

1969—the formation of the Inter-University Comparative Foreign Policy or ICFP Project (Rosenau et al., 1973)

1973—the publication of a compendious inventory of tested empirical and comparative propositions in the field of foreign policy (McGowan and Shapiro, 1973), as well as the ICFP Meeting on the Future of Comparative Foreign Policy Analysis, Ojai, California, June 1973 (Rosenau, 1976).[1]

The appearance of propositional inventories and the proliferation of edited volumes, journal articles, conference papers, and panels at professional meetings are all among the indicators inferring that a subfield has "taken off." These signals of intellectual vigor—as well as the evidence of extensive work in the realms of data collection and analysis, hypothesis-testing, conceptualization, and framework construction—all demonstrate that the comparative or scientific study of foreign policy has emerged as a viable field of research and analysis.

Three deficiencies, however, pervade inquiry in the scientific foreign policy community. One is the absence of sophisticated analytical strategies. A second is the theoretical poverty of the subfield; ad hoc hypothesis-testing and exploratory empiricism have prevailed until recently. The last is the chasm between the research and policy communities.

The IBA Project was explicitly designed to develop, refine, and apply a relatively sophisticated analytical strategy for the study of external behavior. In the process, we have hopefully contributed to the articulation of a skeletal theoretical edifice which can be built into a genuine theory of foreign policy. We pursued a course between the extremes of narrow inductivism and avid deductivism; the explicit emphasis was on the promotion of a "dialogue" between data and theory.

Analytical strategy specification and theory construction are tasks which mesh well with the IBA Project's explicit basic research orientation. The nexus between this volume and the sphere of "applied research" is less obvious and should be illuminated. When the IBA research was initiated in the fall of 1974, we confronted massive obstacles to the goals of conceptualizing the focus of our inquiry and constructing, refining, and operationalizing a general framework for the analysis of foreign policy behavior. These objectives have since been accomplished. After we converted the framework from an abstract to a testable model, we conducted a series of model specification and analysis activities. These myriad tasks were completed between 1974 and the early fall of 1978. In the course of this effort, our own emphases and those of the sponsors of this research at the Cybernetics Technology Office (CTO) of the Defense Advanced Research Projects Agency have become increasingly applied in nature.

How can basic research contribute to the policy process? We would assert that high-quality basic research by its very nature can enlighten the policy maker—by clarifying premises and making assumptions explicit, by generating a set of interrelated, verified propositions, and by yielding explanations of patterns and predictions of trends. In a more direct sense, basic and applied research are related in a symbiotic fashion. The *variables* which we specify and operationalize in this volume can be (and in some cases have been) converted into *indicators* for monitoring and forecasting behavior. The *causal models* which we delineate later in the volume can be viewed as explanatory and predictive systems of variables (from a basic research perspective) and as *tools* for conducting such policy-relevant operations as conflict and crisis *warning* and *management.*

We recognize that there is an ineradicable core of dynamic tension between basic and applied research (not to mention basic and applied researchers). But the two are also inextricably linked in a dialectical relationship. In fact, a number of observers maintain that the positing of a basic/applied dichotomy is both false and misleading. Regardless of the actual or putative relationship, we maintain that basic research of the kind described here can have indirect and direct payoffs for the processes of policy-making and policy evaluation.

NOTE

1. For a more extensive "chronology" of significant events in this field, see Kegley (1979).

Chapter 1

Introduction

In the subfield of scientific foreign policy analysis, the tempta-
tion to examine phenomena in a random or ad hoc fashion has
always been irresistible. Increasingly in recent years, both the
policy and academic communities have recognized the intrinsic
complexity which characterizes foreign policy processes and
behavior and have highlighted the need to delineate
systematically the field's scope of inquiry as an aid to productive analysis. The construction and application of an analytical
framework is viewed as an essential prerequisite for cumulating
reliable foreign policy knowledge.

Social scientists are hardly unfamiliar with such a strategy. By
the very nature of their work, they must employ analytical
strategies which are often markedly inferior to those employed
by physical scientists. Although the understanding of human
behavior is the primary objective, controlled experimentation is
frequently ruled out. Instead, researchers must undertake the
systematic analysis of past events. Social scientists are seldom in
a position to generate comprehensive explanations of human

AUTHORS' NOTE: *Several sections of this chapter constitute expanded versions of
material which originally appeared in Andriole et al. (1975).*

behavior without the aid of such a strategy. Since they must base their conclusions upon a much less precise portrayal of the process of cause and effect, many social scientists have resorted to the strategy of organizing their analyses around the construction of analytical models or frameworks. When properly constructed, such frameworks serve to structure speculation concerning "cause-and-effect" relationships. In so doing, frameworks facilitate the identification of specific research hypotheses.

A number of issues must be confronted in the course of constructing analytical frameworks. Initially, framework architects should be concerned with the comprehensive and coherent portrayal of their independent and dependent variables. Second, the ideal framework ought to cluster distinctly those variables which are analytically and conceptually interrelated. The analyst can subsequently extract, organize, and test hypotheses which pertain to similar or competing independent variables. Third, it may be necessary to specify intervening variables. Fourth, there should be conscious coordination between the chosen method of inquiry and the specification of the units of analysis. Without such coordination, it would be difficult to extract hypotheses and virtually impossible to test them.

The Interstate Behavior Analysis (IBA) Project was developed with the primary goal of constructing an analytical framework for the comparative analysis of foreign policy behavior. While similar objectives have guided other inquiries during recent years, few universal generalizations have been derived and foreign policy phenomena have remained embarrassingly mysterious. An examination of the major published inventories of findings in the relatively young field of comparative foreign policy analysis reveals that research has been disparate, uneven, and noncumulative (McGowan and Shapiro, 1973; Vasquez, 1976). One of the first tasks of the IBA Project was to conduct an exhaustive review of these earlier efforts in an attempt to categorize both their strengths and shortcomings and to use the prior work as a guide for the development of a new analytical framework.

Before we can offer our analysis of the existing literature, it would be useful to specify the scope of inquiry of the field. If the area lacks clearly defined research boundaries, as is often the case in the social sciences, the analyst must attempt to locate such boundaries or confront the prospect of producing disparate and noncumulative knowledge. Without a clearly specified scope of inquiry, we do not have "any very reliable classificatory or mapping system by which to tell what terrain is being covered or left unexplored" (Van Dyke, 1966: 1).

Perhaps the most useful way to delineate the scope of inquiry in foreign policy analysis is to introduce the vantage point of levels of analysis. These levels refer to the general areas from which certain behaviors are generated and at which these behaviors occur. For our purposes, five "causal and effectual" levels have been identified: the individual, group, state, inter- and/or multistate, and global. These levels of analysis represent the universe of causal and effectual analytical areas. As Figure 1.1 shows, foreign policy behavior normally occurs on effectual levels three and four and results from factors or conditions arising from one or more of the five causal levels of analysis. Thus, Figure 1.1 provides the conceptual foundation on the basis of which the field's scope of inquiry may be ascertained.

With the recognition that foreign policy behavior occurs at the state and interstate levels of analysis, we can differentiate between two distinct approaches to foreign policy analysis. The first type of behavior refers to that which results from the impact of certain internal and/or external stimuli. Such behavior suggests the need to conduct inquiry into what may be conceptualized as the *sources* of foreign policy.

After a state decides to respond to a set of stimuli, its decision-making apparatus is set in motion. This occurs when a state is initiating a foreign policy action as well as when it is reacting to the foreign policies of another state. This suggests the need to investigate what may be conceptualized as *initiative* and *responsive* decision-making. The scope of foreign policy thus requires analysts to conduct inquiry into the *sources* and *processes* of decision-making.

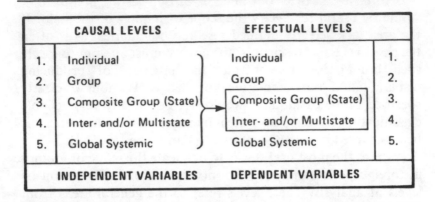

Figure 1.1: Comprehensive Foreign Policy Analysis

One final issue must be confronted in this introductory section. We must formulate a definition of the core concept in our research: *foreign policy*. For our purposes, foreign policy may be viewed as *those official actions (and reactions) which sovereign states initiate (or receive and subsequently react to) for the purpose of altering or creating a condition (or problem) outside their territorial-sovereign boundaries.*

EVALUATIVE CRITERIA

As noted earlier, a systematic evaluation of earlier conceptual work in the field of foreign policy analysis provided the initial impetus for this work. In order to be productive, such an evaluation must be guided by clear evaluative criteria. We selected the following criteria as useful evaluative dimensions.

Comprehensiveness

The first criterion requires that the ideal framework treat its subject matter comprehensively. While this criterion certainly does not require that the analyst deal with every conceivable factor in the domain of foreign policy, it does dictate the comprehensive treatment of the aspect of the subfield which will constitute the focus of inquiry. Regarding the sources of policy, this criterion requires that the analyst account for all possible sources of action; that is, the research must isolate, identify, and provide for the eventual ranking of both internal and external source variables.

Internal source variables refer to those which are instrumental in actually generating a national decision occasion; among these are the ideological, psychological, economic, social, and political factors which may contribute to the enunciation and adoption of a particular foreign policy position. External source variables refer to those which arise beyond a state's boundaries and may also lead to specific external action.

As for analyses of the processes of policy formulation and implementation, the comprehensive criterion is no less stringent. Process frameworks must isolate and identify all of the factors which are demonstrably crucial to the operation of a state's foreign policy machinery after a decision to act has been made; that is, after an internal, external, or intermix of sources requires a state to initiate or respond to an external action.

Comparability

The comparability criterion requires that the foreign policy analyst provide the means by which foreign policy behavior may be differentiated according to the type of state involved and the type of foreign event with which the state must deal. Failure to specify type of state and type of foreign policy event is equivalent to positing that states in general generally act in certain ways. Real-world decision makers respond differently to the actors (states) at hand; similarly, foreign policy analysts must construct frameworks which are explicitly comparative in nature.

The comparative criterion requires that various adjustments in its parameters will enable the ideal framework to yield insight into a variety of relational, temporal, and decisional settings. Obviously, this guideline assumes that a framework will take into account the differences between states as well as salient differences in the types of events which states confront. The comparative criterion may be applied either cross-sectionally, as in the study of a number of states at a single point in time, or longitudinally, as in the comparative study of the behavior patterns of a single state over time.

Operationalizability

This criterion requires that the foreign policy analyst carefully develop concepts and ensuing variables so that they may be adequately operationalized. We view this criterion as the key to the development of a framework which is capable of yielding foreign policy explanations; measures should thus be developed so that consensus can be achieved on the extent to which they accurately reflect theoretically significant concepts. At the same time, it should be emphasized that adequate operationalization does not result solely from careful planning and execution. Many of the seemingly most critical internal and external variables are precisely the ones which are most resistant to conversion to data-based variables. Nevertheless, through the imaginative synthesis of hard and soft data, important steps may be taken toward the development of an empirically based theory of foreign policy behavior.

Public Policy Relevance

The final criterion requires that the analyst engage in analysis for the purpose of contributing to the effectiveness of real foreign policy making. This involves research into the actual needs of policy makers and, second, into how such needs might be satisfied. Central to our perspective is the conviction that policy-oriented social scientists can enhance both the awareness and understanding of the factors which account for the significant trends in the international behavior of states. Since few contemporary writers have conducted this type of research activity,[1] this criterion will not be actively applied in the following review and critique. We would assert, however, that the proper conduct of social scientific analysis is in itself policy relevant.

REVIEW AND CRITIQUE OF EXISTING FRAMEWORKS

The criteria specified above can function as guidelines for the evaluation and critical appraisal of current and recent efforts at framework construction in the field of foreign policy analysis. The criteria are also useful to the extent that they link some of the more abstract concerns of social scientific inquiry to some of the specific problems of foreign policy research and analytical framework construction. Our review will concentrate on those analysts who have attempted to construct genuinely social scientific frameworks. While we are therefore excluding from our review the work of several important postwar analysts such as Morgenthau (1948), London (1949), Gross (1954), Organski (1958), Modelski (1962), and Frankel (1963), we readily acknowledge that many of their insights have had substantial impact on the works to be reviewed below.

An early effort at framework construction in foreign policy analysis was undertaken by Synder et al. (1962). In seeking to isolate and identify "some of the crucial variables that determine...responses to concrete situations," the emphasis of Snyder and his colleagues was essentially internal and attempted to provide insight into the decision-making process (Snyder et al., 1962: 2). Three internal variable clusters were emphasized in their approach to foreign policy decision-making: (1) spheres of competence, or "the totality of those activities of the decision-maker relevant to the achievement of the organizational objective" (Snyder et al., 1962: 106); (2) communication and information, which refers to the nature, quality, quantity, processing, and flow of information; and (3) motivation, defined as "the psychological state of the actor(s) in which energy is mobilized and directed toward aspects of the setting" (Snyder et al., 1962: 140).

The identification of a host of internal process variables, and the accompanying neglect of external factors, created an imbalance in the framework and obviously violated the comprehensive criterion. While the variable categories might be susceptible to comparative analysis, the failure to specify either type of state or type of decision seriously attenuated the comparative capability of the framework. Finally, operationalization, while certainly not precluded, would tend to be quite cumbersome. Indeed, it is significant that the framework has been completely operationalized for only one decision (Paige, 1968).[2]

Rosenau (1966) has also inquired into the nature of foreign policy analysis. In his well-known pre-theory, Rosenau identified what he viewed as crucial explanatory variables of foreign policy: (1) idiosyncratic (or individual); (2) role; (3) governmental; (4) societal; and (5) systemic. The idiosyncratic cluster included "all those aspects of a decision-maker—his values, talents, and prior experience—that distinguish his foreign policy choices or behavior from those of every other decision-maker." Role referred to the "external behavior of officials that is generated by the roles they occupy and that would be likely to occur irrespective of the idiosyncracies of the role occupant." The governmental cluster refers to "those aspects of a government's structure that limit or enhance the foreign policy choices made by decision-makers." The "nongovernmental aspects of a society which influence its external behavior" were included within the societal variable cluster, while all the nonhuman aspects of a society's external environment or any actions occurring abroad that condition or otherwise influence the choices made by its officials were subsumed under the systemic cluster (Rosenau, 1966: 46).

With the sources of foreign policy behavior presumably categorized in an exhaustive fashion, Rosenau then attempted to assess the relative potency of the variable clusters according to type of actor and issue area. States were classified according to size, economic development, and political accountability. To these dimensions was added degree of penetration. The issue areas included status, territory, and human and non-human resources.

Rosenau's pre-theory was a major improvement over its predecessors in terms of the extent to which it satisfied the comprehensive and comparative criteria. He was explicitly conscious of the distinction between internal and external source variables. Moreover, he alluded to the two basic typologies—of states and events—which are preconditions for thoroughly comparative foreign policy analysis.

Nevertheless, a number of problems remained. First, the boundaries among the variable clusters were not clearly demarcated, with a resulting tendency for the clusters to overlap. With regard to the systemic cluster, Rosenau failed to differentiate between external interstate- and/or multistate-level factors and truly systemic—that is, global-level—factors. This results in difficulties at the operationalization stage; while the categories of economic development and political accountability appear to be analytically sound, size and degree of penetration are misleading to the extent that they imply capabilities.

Wilkinson (1969), another noteworthy framework architect, began by constructing a typology of foreign policies, or a "role" typology, whereby first-, second-, and third-party states were identified. The bases for comparing states were not the dimensions of size, wealth, or governmental structure, but the roles to which states had been assigned.

In his discussion of foreign policy, Wilkinson emphasized three variable clusters: (1) capabilities; (2) will and prescription; and (3) residuals. Capabilities, in effect, were Morgenthau's (1948) elements of national power, while will and prescription referred to the psychological dimension of leadership. Political institutions, culture, and processes were all grouped in the residual category. In general, Wilkinson felt that a state's capabilities more accurately explain how and why it acts than its leadership, political culture, governmental processes, or political institutions. In fact, capabilities also determine a state's role. As in all essentially single-factor explanations, a certain amount of imbalance and distortion was introduced.

The Wilkinson framework thus fails to satisfy the comprehensive criterion and distorts the comparative criterion by attempting to fuse the categories of states and events. Since Wilkinson stressed the preliminary nature of his work, its potential for operationalization will not be assessed at this point.

The Brecher et al. (1969) framework focused on inputs, processes, and outputs in a systems analysis of foreign policy behavior. Foreign policy inputs were defined as phenomena which arise from an operational and/or psychological environment. The operational environment was composed of both internal and external variable clusters. The internal clusters included such variables as military and economic capability, political structure, and competing elite and group influences. The external cluster was comprised of an intriguing set of international subsystems, on the basis of which individual member states can be expected to modify their behaviors.

The psychological environment consisted of two sets of data: the attitudinal prism and elite images. The attitudinal prism was composed of psychological predispositions of the decision makers, while elite images referred to the cognitive distances between images and reality. Finally, the process of foreign policy decision-making referred to the formulation of strategic decisions in four issue areas: (1) military-security; (2) political-diplomatic; (3) economic-developmental; and (4) cultural-status.

The framework constructed by Brecher and his colleagues satisfies the comprehensiveness criterion to the extent that it at least implicitly accounts for all source and process variables. The comparative criterion is partially satisfied with the identification of issue areas, but the framework fails to type states aside from positing the dichotomous developed/underdeveloped category. In this regard, then, the Brecher framework seems to be most suitable for single case study analysis and has in fact been skillfully operationalized for the case of Israel (Brecher, 1972, 1973, 1974a, 1974b, 1974c). Operationalization on a quantitative, cross-national basis, however, would be much more difficult to accomplish.

Coplin (1974) has proposed a number of variable clusters which can serve as guides to understanding and analyzing both the sources of foreign policy behavior and the processes of foreign policy formulation. These are: (1) the behavior of the decision makers, which refers to the intellectual, psychological, and organizational aspects of decision-making, defined as nonrational problem-solving; (2) the policy influence systems or the structure of the domestic environment, categorized as interest, mass, partisan, or bureaucratic, with the influence varying according to the nature of the foreign policy problem; (3) economic and military conditions, consisting of such variables as GNP, international trade and finance, and pure military capability; and (4) the international context, which refers to the geopolitical, economic, and political realities to which decision makers must be responsive.

While Coplin's work appears to satisfy the comprehensiveness criterion, there are problems regarding its comparative capability. Coplin identified three types of foreign policy decisions—general, administrative, and crisis—and predicted that decision makers would be likely to behave quite differently depending on the nature of the decision to be made. However, in his discussion of the operation of the policy influence system, Coplin shifted his comparative focus to form the new categories of national security, ecomomic, ideological-historical, and procedural issue areas. This shift in comparative focus from decisions to issue areas precludes a consistent comparative analysis.

In their survey of scientific findings in the comparative study of foreign policy behavior, McGowan and Shapiro (1973) presented a framework which attempts to integrate many of the previously tested hypotheses in this domain. They identified eleven independent or causal variable clusters: individual, elite, establishment, political, governmental, societal, economic, cultural, linkage, external policy and action, and systemic. McGowan and Shapiro view the decision-making process as the equivalent of an intervening variable cluster. Regarding comprehensiveness, it can be concluded that the framework fulfills this criterion. However, with respect to the comparative criterion, the framework fails to classify either foreign policy actors or events.

A further difficulty with the McGowan and Shapiro framework concerns the positing of the decision-making process as an intervening variable cluster. This appears to raise the levels-of-analysis problem; by conceptualizing decision-making behavior as an intervening variable while retaining foreign policy as the dependent variable, they are implicitly attempting to investigate behavior which occurs on two absolutely and mutually exclusive levels of analysis. This "crossing" distorts the impact of their independent variables.

A recent and sophisticated approach to foreign policy analysis has been offered by Lentner (1974). The construction of his comparative framework began with a description of the units of analysis, which are grouped into three broad categories: (1) the actors who participate—to varying degrees—in the process of foreign policy formulation and execution; (2) the international environment; and (3) multidimensional situations. This was followed by a discussion of how internal and external determinants operate and affect foreign policy behavior, and a discussion of the process by which foreign policy is formulated and executed. Here Lentner identified: (1) decisions; (2) mobilizations; and (3) applications of instruments and techniques. The resulting foreign policies were grouped into the categories of insulatory, engaging, and expansive.

By including lengthy lists of both source and process variables, Lentner satisfies the comprehensiveness criterion. At first glance, the comparability criterion seems to be satisfied by the delineation of a whole host of classificatory schemes. In fact, the large number of such schemes may inhibit a structured comparative analysis. Some of these might be eliminated, while those which deal particularly with the situational dimension and types of states may require further refinement. Additionally, operationalization would be an extremely difficult task, given the excessive number of internal determinants.

The Comparative Research on the Events of Nations (CREON) Project is certainly one of the major efforts within the subfield. Begun in 1970, its principals, notably Charles F. Hermann, Margaret G. Hermann, Maurice A. East, Stephen A. Salmore, Barbara G. Salmore, and Linda P. Brady, are still pursuing the project's goals which include, among others, multi-causal explanations of foreign policy behavior and the inductive design of empirical maps "of previously unrecognized patterns and underlying dimensions of foreign policy behavior" (C. F. Hermann et al., 1973: 13).

The explanations were and remain some hypothesized function of the following variable clusters: (1) personal characteristics of political leaders; (2) bureaucratic aspects of governmental decision-making; (3) political features of regimes; (4) national attributes of societies; (5) transitory qualities of the situation; and (6) properties of the international system.

From this theoretical perspective, the CREON investigators selected 35 countries to examine. They then collected data on the foreign policy behavior (as suggested by their six perspectives) of these 35 countries on a random quarterly basis for the period 1959 to 1968.

The various perspectives and data sets have provided the basis upon which a whole series of analyses has been conducted (for a bibliography of CREON Project studies, see East et al., 1978) and the impetus for the continued development of the subfield. Also, it should be noted that the CREON Project represents the first comparative foreign policy research project explicitly designed to proceed from preconceived theoretical notions (expressed in a coherent design or framework) to concept/variable operationalization, data collection, and actual hypothesis-testing. With reference to our evaluative criteria, then, the CREON Project is perhaps the most important project which we have evaluated here.

It is, however, not without flaws. First, it is difficult to establish the intended cause-and-effect relationships from the six variable domains. For example, are the six domains presumed to be potentially equal in terms of potency? Are there inter-relationships among and within the domains that might affect the identification and organization of the variables and variable clusters? Finally, there is no explict recognition in the CREON scheme of the potential impact of (nonglobal) interstate variables, such as a nation's alliance commitments or the actions of another nation directed toward the nation under investigation.

There are more serious problems with the data set. Since data were collected for random quarters for the period 1959-1968, analyses of foreign policy behavior over extended periods of time cannot be conducted; and since the selection of nations was not made according to any geographical, behavioral, or categorical criteria, it is difficult to conduct truly comparative analyses and difficult, therefore, to hypothesize the impact of nation types as intervening variables.

Overall, the CREON framework is in our view internally comprehensive. It is, however, not truly comparative primarily because of the operationalization and data-collection procedures. Finally, the policy-relevance criterion is not satisfied by the CREON framework since it is directed toward the conduct of extremely basic theoretical research.

Table 1.1 "scores" the various frameworks on our four evaluative criteria and provides a convenient synopsis of the review and critique. It will be noted that each of the analytical frameworks—while certainly often worthy of pioneering praise—fails to satisfy at least one of the criteria. The IBA framework, which will be presented below, attempts to build upon these earlier works. In the process of charting the development of this framework, we will explicitly consider these evaluative criteria.

THE IBA FRAMEWORK FOR
THE COMPARATIVE ANALYSIS OF
FOREIGN POLICY BEHAVIOR: AN OVERVIEW

Having chronicled the various strengths and weaknesses of the major contemporary efforts at framework construction, we

TABLE 1.1
An Evaluation of Frameworks for Foreign Policy Analysis

	COMPREHENSIVENESS		COMPARABILITY		OPERATIONALIZABILITY		POLICY RELEVANCE
	INTERNAL	EXTERNAL	STATES	FOREIGN POLICIES	SINGLE CASE STUDIES	CROSS-NATIONAL	
Snyder et al. (1962)	X				X		
Rosenau (1966)	X	X	X		X	X	
Wilkinson (1969)	X		X				
Brecher et al. (1969)	X	X		X	X		
Coplin (1974)	X	X		X	X		
McGowan and Shapiro (1973)	X	X					
Lentner (1974)	X	X		X			
Hermann et al. (1973)	X	X	X		X	X	

now present the Interstate Behavior Analysis (IBA) framework. More elaborate discussions of each of the elements of the framework will be provided in subsequent chapters; the purpose here is to offer a brief overview of the overall scheme. A schematic representation of the entire IBA framework appears in Figure 1.2.

As Figure 1.2 illustrates, the IBA framework consists of three interrelated sets of variables which correspond to the standard social scientific designation of independent, intervening, and dependent variables. The source variables—the postulated determinants of foreign policy behavior—include a variety of internal and external factors. For purposes of analytical clarity, such factors may be grouped into components, which may be defined as vertically arranged sets of variables of the same type.

There are five distinct variable areas or components within which researchers can identify specific variables, such as decision-maker values (psychological component), public opinion (political component), economic indicators (societal component), international trade (interstate component), and international organization memberships (global component). Eventually, foreign policy analysts should attempt to rank variables and components in the contexts of varying types of states and foreign policies. In addition to this assessment of relative explanatory power, the causal configurations which characterize the interrelationships among components should also be specified.

The framework also posits that relatively static state characteristics intervene between the source factors and the dependent variable cluster of foreign policy behavior. Generalizations about the behavior of all states would be of very limited value to either policy makers or social scientists. States must be grouped; the state typing scheme represents a filtering screen which mediates between the source factors and foreign policy behavior. The classificatory scheme consists of static state characteristics which are subdivided into the general realms of economic structure, governmental structure, and capabilities.

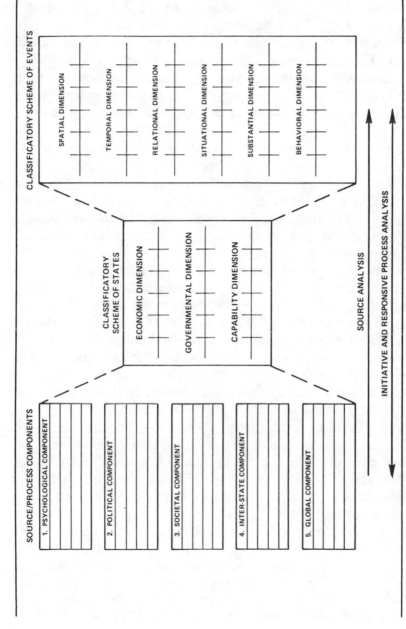

Figure 1.2: A Framework for the Comparative Analysis of Foreign Policy Behavior

35

Finally, foreign policy behavior constitutes the dependent variable cluster. The empirical study of a state's behavior requires that the action element of foreign policy behavior be given sufficient emphasis. In operational terms, actions may be equated with events; an event is a discrete portion of reality (Riker, 1957: 58-59). For purposes of the present framework, foreign policy events can be decomposed into six dimensions: spatial, temporal, relational, situational, substantial, and behavioral. Operationally, foreign policy behaviors may be classified in terms of *"who* does *what* to *whom, where, when,* and in what immediate *context?"*

We maintain that a single analytical framework can accommodate both source and process analyses by simply reversing the postulated causal chain. Responsive decision-making or process analysis views foreign policy behavior as the independent variable. Component factors become dependent variables rather than sources or determinants. A classic example of responsive process analysis is the case study of the decision of the United States to intervene in the Korean War (Paige, 1968). Another state's action (the perceived stimulus and independent variable) provoked changes in such component variables as elite attitudes and public opinion. In responsive process analysis, the type of state continues to function in an intervening fashion.

Initiative process analysis refers to those occasions when a state is involved in the formulation of a foreign policy action. The factors which give rise to the "decision-occasion" (or source factors from the components) have already set the stage for a series of decisional phases. In this case, the state is not responding to an input from another actor but is involved in the process of formulating its own output. Component factors may be both independent and dependent in initiative process analysis.

The framework described above is obviously indebted to its predecessors in the comparative study of foreign policy behavior. At the same time, several innovations distinguish the framework from earlier formulations. One is the explicit

distinction among the concepts of source analysis, initiative process analysis, and responsive process analysis. Thus, the
framework highlights the need to distinguish consistently and
unambiguously between the sources of foreign policy behavior
and the processes of foreign policy initiation and response.

A second innovation is the clusterting of static state
characteristics into a separate and intervening variable realm. It
is our contention that standard attributes do not directly determine or "cause" foreign policy behavior. A state's foreign
policy behavior is the product of immediate and more dynamic
factors. Long-term structural characteristics should be used to
classify states.

Before concluding, we shall deal with the general issues of the
state sample and temporal span which were analyzed by the IBA
Project. It was clear at the outset that the collection of extensive
cross-national data on all states in the international system
would ᴗe well beyond our scope and capabilities. The actual
criterion for inclusion stipulated that the state initiate 40 or
more foreign policy actions during the five-year period from
1966-1970.[3] This particular criterion ensures that only those
states which are major actors in the international system will be
represented. The choice of years was dictated by the data
available at the beginning of the project. All geographical
regions are represented in our sample of 56 states, and we can
conclude that it constitutes a reasonably heterogeneous "sample" of the international system. The states in the sample are
listed in Table 1.2. All subsequent analyses in this volume will
be based on data on these 56 states for the years 1966-1970. The
appendix to this chapter discusses the current status of the IBA
data set.

In subsequent chapters, each of the five source components,
the three state classificatory attribute clusters, and the six
behavioral dimensions will be discussed and specified at some
length. They will also be operationalized, and data will be
presented on each of the segments of the IBA framework. This
volume will conclude with a set of analyses which are designed

TABLE 1.2
List of 56 States

STATE	LETTER CODE	STATE	LETTER CODE
Western Hemisphere:		Middle East:	
1. United States	USA	33. Algeria	ALG
2. Canada	CAN	34. Iran	IRN
3. Cuba	CUB	35. Turkey	TUR
4. Brazil	BRA	36. Iraq	IRQ
5. Chile	CHL	37. United Arab Republic	UAR
		38. Syria	SYR
Europe:		39. Lebanon	LEB
		40. Jordan	JOR
6. United Kingdom	UNK	41. Israel	ISR
7. Netherlands	NTH	42. Saudi Arabia	SAU
8. Belgium	BEL	43. Yemen	YEM
9. France	FRN		
10. Spain	SPN	Asia:	
11. Portugal	POR		
12. West Germany	GMW	44. China	CHN
13. East Germany	GME	45. South Korea	KOS
14. Poland	POL	46. Japan	JAP
15. Hungary	HUN	47. India	IND
16. Czechoslovakia	CZE	48. Pakistan	PAK
17. Italy	ITA	49. Thailand	TAI
18. Albania	ALB	50. Cambodia	CAM
19. Yugoslavia	YUG	51. Laos	LAO
20. Greece	GRC	52. South Vietnam	VTS
21. Cyprus	CYP	53. Malaysia	MAL
22. Bulgaria	BUL	54. Philippines	PHI
23. Rumania	RUM	55. Indonesia	INS
24. USSR	USR		
25. Sweden	SWD	Oceania:	
26. Denmark	DEN		
		56. Australia	AUL
Africa:			
27. Ghana	GHA		
28. Nigeria	NIG		
29. Zaire	COP		
30. Kenya	KEN		
31. Ethiopia	ETH		
32. South Africa	SAF		

to assess the relative potency of various source variable clusters in explaining foreign policy behavior.

We should note at this point that this research deals exclusively with what we have referred to as source analysis, with foreign policy behavior as the focus of our analytical attention. We have stressed throughout that a truly comprehensive and comparative framework for analyzing foreign policy behavior must include both source and process analyses. That task simply proved to be too amibitious for the present effort, thus dictating our decision to concentrate on source analysis. Subsequent work will hopefully be undertaken in an effort to illuminate the nature, determinants, and effects of foreign policy decision-making processes.

APPENDIX TO CHAPTER 1—THE IBA DATA SET

As we indicated above, the data base upon which all analyses in the present volume are based covers the period from 1966 to 1970 for the 56 states shown in Table 1.2. While these analyses were under way, data collection for the IBA Project continued. As a result, virtually all IBA Project data sets now span the entire period from 1966 to 1975. In addition, the original state sample was expanded to include 77 states. This expanded sample represents an intentional balance between our own research needs, strictly objective criteria,[4] and research capabilities. Table 1.3 presents the expanded list of IBA states, with asterisks indicating the new states. The entire data set is available with documentation from the Interuniversity Consortium for Political and Social Research at the University of Michigan.

NOTES

1. For interesting studies which begin to address this issue directly, see *International Studies Quarterly* (1977) and Singer and Wallace (1979).

2. For a different perspective on his own previous work on the Korean crisis, see Paige (1977).

3. World Event/Interaction Survey (WEIS) data were used to identify this set of states.

4. In generating the actual list, it was determined that the optimum criterion for inclusion of a state was for it to account for at least .15 percent of all World Event/Interaction Survey (WEIS) events for the 1966-1975 time span. It should be noted that 12 of the original 56 states failed to meet this new criterion; however, they are retained in the sample of 77 to facilitate the examination of trends and patterns over time.

TABLE 1.3
List of 77 States

State	No. Code	Letter Code	State	No. Code	Letter Code
Western Hemisphere:			40. Ethiopia	530	ETH
1. United States	002	USA	41. Zambia *	551	ZAM
2. Canada	020	CAN	42. Rhodesia *	552	RHO
3. Cuba	040	CUB	43. Mozambique*	555	FRE
4. Mexico*	070	MEX	44. South Africa	560	SAF
5. Panama *	095	PAN	45. Angola *	561	ANG
6. Venezuela *	101	VEN			
7. Brazil	140	BRA	Middle East:		
8. Chile	155	CHL			
9. Argentina*	160	ARG	46. Morocco *	600	MOR
			47. Algeria	615	ALG
Europe:			48. Libya *	620	LBY
			49. Sudan*	625	SUD
10. United Kingdom	200	UNK	50. Iran	630	IRN
11. Netherlands	210	NTH	51. Turkey	640	TUR
12. Belgium	211	BEL	52. Iraq	645	IRQ
13. France	220	FRN	53. United Arab Rep.	651	UAR
14. Spain	230	SPN	54. Syria	652	SYR
15. Portugal	235	POR	55. Lebanon	660	LEB
16. West Germany	255	GMW	56. Jordan	663	JOR
17. East Germany	265	GME	57. Israel	666	ISR
18. Poland	290	POL	58. Saudia Arabia	670	SAU
19. Austria*	305	AUS	59. Yemen	678	YEM
20. Hungary	310	HUN	60. Kuwait*	690	KUW
21. Czechoslovakia	315	CZE			
22. Italy	325	ITA	Asia:		
23. Albania	339	ALB			
24. Yugoslavia	345	YUG	61. China	710	CHN
25. Greece	350	GRC	62. Taiwan*	713	CHT
26. Cyprus	352	CYP	63. North Korea *	731	KON
27. Bulgaria	355	BUL	64. South Korea	732	KOS
28. Rumania	360	RUM	65. Japan	740	JAP
29. USSR	365	USR	66. India	750	IND
30. Sweden	380	SWD	67. Bangladesh*	765	BGD
31. Denmark	390	DEN	68. Pakistan	770	PAK
32. Iceland*	395	ICE	69. Thailand	800	TAI
			70. Cambodia	811	CAM
Africa:			71. Laos	812	LAO
			72. N. Vietnam*	816	VTN
33. Ghana	452	GHA	73. S. Vietnam	817	VTS
34. Nigeria	475	NIG	74. Malaysia	820	MAL
35. Zaire	490	COP	75. Philippines	840	PHI
36. Uganda *	500	UGA	76. Indonesia	850	INS
37. Kenya	501	KEN			
38. Tanzania *	510	TAZ	Oceania:		
39. Somalia*	520	SOM			
			77. Australia	900	AUL

Chapter 2

Determinants of Action
and Reaction

As noted in the previous chapter, the IBA framework for the comparative analysis of foreign policy behavior consists of three major elements: a classificatory scheme for foreign policy actors; a classificatory scheme for foreign policy behavior; and a set of source-process components. These components constitute the sources of foreign policy behavior in source analysis and the dependent variable clusters in process analysis. Since this study will concentrate on source analysis, we will emphasize the determinative characteristics of the components in our treatment of them here.

It has become a virtual truism to point out that an actor's foreign policy actions and reactions are linked to a complex structure of internal and external factors. Recently, social scientists have attempted to construct frameworks which feature an array of variable areas for the comparative analysis of foreign policy behavior. But even the most potentially comprehensive pre-theories and frameworks—including those developed by Rosenau (1966), Brecher et al. (1969), and East et al. (1978)—have failed to achieve the goal of comprehensiveness in their delineation of the significant variables or variable areas.

In our framework, components represent a near-exhaustive collection of variable areas for foreign policy analysis. Factors which are similar in nature are grouped within the same component. Specifically, the five social scientific levels of analysis which were discussed in the previous chapter (see Figure 1.1) constitute the sources of five distinct components, labeled psychological, political, societal, interstate, and global.

Comprehensive foreign policy analysis requires an exhaustive specification of the universe of potentially relevant source and process variables. The voluminous recent literature in this field has been regrettably uneven in its coverage of this universe. While many researchers have identified some, if not all, of the five major clusters, most earlier work has failed to map out the scope of each cluster. This has resulted in the presentation of partial and ad hoc lists of variables within general categories. Unfortunately, comprehensiveness cannot be achieved in a post hoc fashion; the exhaustive specification of variables and variable clusters should precede data collection and analysis.

The eventual goal of inquiry is the ranking of variables within components and the determination of the relative potency of each component in the contexts of varying types of states and foreign policies. With this ultimate goal in mind, we can now offer a more extended discussion of the conceptualization of each of the five variable realms.

THE PSYCHOLOGICAL COMPONENT

During the past several decades, a considerable amount of research has been undertaken in the area of psychology and politics. More recently, the linkage between psychology and foreign policy behavior has been an important focus. Large numbers of variables have been scrutinized in empirical research. The extensive—albeit unsystematic and all too frequently case-specific—research has been based upon the premise that the individual actor can influence foreign policy behavior (see M. G. Hermann, 1977, 1978; O. Holsti, 1976; Hopple, 1980).

Students of foreign policy analysis would readily concur that the psychological domain is the most elusive and least amenable to systematic empirical analysis. Even more fundamental is the question of the relevance of the psychological component for source and process analysis. It can be argued that at the foreign policy behavior level of analysis, depth-psychological, intraindividual factors cannot be dismissed. Affective and distorting characteristics of human behavior can impinge on the process of policy formulation; irrational or nonrational factors may influence the search for, selection, and use of data (Costello, 1970: 161). Other types of individual-level variables undoubtedly exert considerable impact. In fact, it has been asserted that the beliefs of decision makers account for more variance in foreign policy behavior than any other single factor (Bonham and Shapiro, 1973: 56).

Three levels of analysis, or variable domains, have been identified by prior research in this area: psychodynamic factors, personality traits, and belief systems. The domain of psychodynamic causality is the most remote level of psychological inquiry. While repressed conflicts and other depth-psychological phenomena may not account for an event per se, such influences can affect the style or mode of response. Given the realities of politics and ideology, the conflict between President Woodrow Wilson and Senator Henry Cabot Lodge over the League of Nations was undoubtedly "inevitable." But Wilson's inner conflicts and personality needs shaped his uniquely rigid style of response and thereby transformed a serious partisan clash into a bitter and ultimately insoluble personal conflict (George and George, 1964). Idiosyncratic or actor-specific dispositions are thus potentially significant—at least for top-level elites who confront the fewest constraints from role and structural parameters—but these characteristics apply more to the qualitative features of a decision than to the actual content (Kelman and Bloom, 1973: 271).

Personality traits or dispositions represent the "intermediate concepts" level of analysis. Such characteristics as nationalism, belief in internal control over events, cognitive complexity, and dogmatism can affect policy outputs (M. G. Hermann, 1974). The personality traits which are identified are then employed as predictors of a decision maker's foreign policy choices.

The belief system approach has been employed extensively in prior research; examples include the work of Brecher (1968), George (1969), McLellan (1969), Burgess (1968), Winham (1970), and Axelrod (1972b). A decision maker's belief system consists of a potentially infinite number of discrete elements. By definition, a belief system contains a set of propositions (statements about reality, predictions about the future, preferred events and outcomes, basic goals); the set ranges from specific and verifiable beliefs ("the United States is allied with Great Britain") to a higher-order preferred end-state ("national security is essential"). The various elements of a belief system are organized into interrelated subsystems (Rokeach, 1968a). Operationalization of the belief system variable area will involve content analyses designed to yield belief, attitude, and value subsystem profiles for foreign policy elites.[1]

As Figure 2.1 indicates, ego-defensive and other psychodynamic forces are related to personality traits or dispositions. These traits interact with such sociological factors as subcultural learning of norms to shape the decision maker's belief system. Such personality dispositions as psychological rigidity, authoritarianism, and anomie may be precursors of at least some attitude and belief components of a belief system (McClosky, 1967). The belief system per se consists of attitude and belief subsystems (affective dispositions, cognitive-probabilistic propositions, and behavioral predispositions) and a temporally prior and causally primordial value subsystem. Value rankings and preferences, which structure attitudes and beliefs, flow from basic personality needs. These needs are intertwined with psychodynamics and personality traits. Decision occasions—which can be attributed to domestic and/or external inputs—are perceived by the actor or elite unit and filtered through the belief system. The foreign policy decision to act or react, the first link in the chain, is a function of the belief system(s) and other pertinent variables from other components.

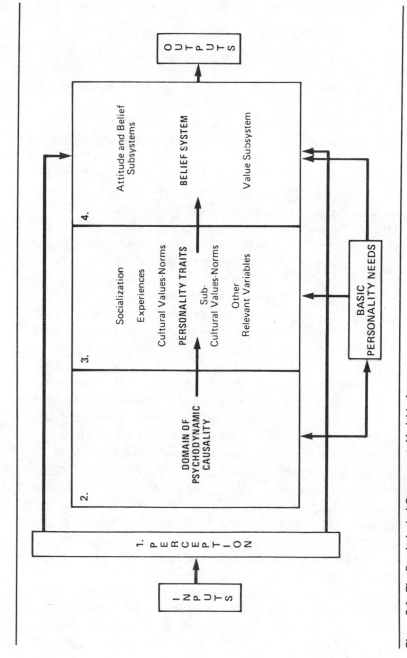

Figure 2.1: The Psychological Component: Variable Areas

OPERATIONALIZING THE
PSYCHOLOGICAL COMPONENT

Our intention has been to be explicitly operational in the development of our concepts. However, constraints precluded the total operationalization of all aspects of the framework. This problem was particularly relevant to the psychological domain, for which few data sets are currently in existence and for which data collection on a cross-national basis is both costly and time consuming. Therefore, we decided to concentrate our efforts in this particular domain on belief systems.

One of the more noteworthy aspects of a belief system is that it exhibits at least some degree of organization. An ideological belief system is tightly and coherently organized or constrained (see Converse, 1964). The structuring is deductive in the sense that knowledge of higher-level elements (such as the decision maker's position on the liberal-conservative continuum) permits the observer to infer lower-level phenomona (such as specific policy preferences) with a degree of accuracy that departs very significantly from chance expectations.

In order to analyze decision-maker belief systems, we selected content analysis as the most appropriate technique, given the nature of the available data. In cross-national research, only official, public documents can be employed in attempting systematically to reconstruct decision-maker belief systems. While public articulations may not always reflect a state's real intentions, such statements often limit a state's future freedom of action. Official and public foreign policy doctrines may exert this impact in at least two distinct ways—by shaping expectations of behavior within the state and among other actors and by influencing the basis upon which other actors make their decisions (Brodin, 1972: 195).

Progress in cross-national research on belief systems depends on the selection of a coherent framework. Such a framework is provided by the belief system and value system research of Rokeach (1960, 1968a, 1973, 1979).[2] In a very abbreviated fashion, each of the elements of a belief system can be defined as follows (see Rokeach, 1968a: 112-114, 125):

(1) A *response* is a verbal or other physical reaction to a stimulus on a survey or questionnaire; responses may reflect random reactions, opinions, attitudes, beliefs, or values.

(2) An *opinion* is a verbal expression of a belief, attitude, or value.

(3) A *belief* is "any simple proposition, conscious or unconscious, inferred from what a person says or does, capable of being preceded by the phrase, 'I believe that...' " Beliefs may be descriptive or existential, evaluative, or prescriptive. Beliefs have cognitive or knowledge, affective, and behavioral components.

(4) An *attitude* can be defined as "a relatively enduring organization of beliefs around an object or situation predisposing one to respond in some preferential manner." Attitudes are often elicited operationally by assessing affective reactions to a stimulus; this procedure is satisfactory if the assumption that the responses also reflect underlying beliefs is not tenuous.

(5) A *value* is a specific type of belief: "A *value* is an enduring belief that a specific mode of conduct or end state of existence is personally or socially preferable to an opposite or converse mode of conduct or end-state of existence. A value system is an enduring organization of beliefs concerning preferable modes of conduct or end-states of existence along a continuum of relative importance" (Rokeach, 1975: 5).

Research on mass or elite belief systems will yield only incomplete and distorted maps if the topography is not adequately described. The following guiding generalizations can be offered at this point: All individuals have belief systems; all belief systems include belief, attitude, and value subsystems; these subsystems are interrelated.

The value subsystem of a belief system emerged as a logical focus for cross-national content analysis. Values can be measured fairly easily; Rokeach's list of terminal values can be applied in diverse contexts. Values and value rankings can be obtained from *individuals* (through questionnaires and surveys) and from *institutions* (through content analyses of pertinent documents and sources).

As Rokeach (1979: 58) points out, extensive research by Eckhardt (1965, 1967) and White (1949, 1951) has demonstrated that "the values contained in various historical and political documents can be reliably extracted by content analysis." A content analysis of the writings of ideological leaders uncovered distinctive value profiles for Lenin, Hitler, Goldwater, and Norman Thomas (Rokeach, 1973). In another content analysis, Rokeach et al. (1970) concluded that the value pattern which characterizes the disputed *Federalist Papers* was more similar to James Madison's than Alexander Hamilton's; the evidence that Madison was probably the author of these papers has been independently confirmed by historical evidence and other research.

Rokeach (1979: 58) notes that the material analyzed in such content analyses is typically ideological and thus exhortatory in nature. He offers three general assumptions which will also guide the research reported below:

(1) The purpose of any exhortatory material is advocacy of one or more means or ends values.
(2) It is possible to uncover the values so advocated by content analysis.
(3) Exhortatory material originating with different social institutions will emphasize different values.

For purposes of measuring the value subsystems of foreign policy elites, the *Daily Report* of the U.S. Foreign Broadcast Information Service (FBIS) is perhaps the only readily available public source with appropriate data for a significant number of states. The *Daily Report* consists of material which is obtained through U.S. monitoring of foreign broadcasts. As would be expected, the source does not report on all states in a systematic, comprehensive (or even random) manner. Certain states—such as the Soviet Union, China, and most Middle Eastern and Eastern European states—receive an unusual amount of coverage, while some other states are virtually ignored. The source for the United States is the Department of State *Bulletin*.

Given the nature of the FBIS *Daily Report*, it was necessary to make a determination concerning the specific states to be included. After identifying the foreign policy elite (head of state or foreign minister) for all 56 states in the IBA set, we decided to include all states for which there were three or more cases (speeches) for a given year.

Table 2.1 provides the yearly state "samples." It should be noted that the state samples vary from year to year, with an N ranging from 31 in 1966 and 1967 to 20 in 1969. Table 2.2 highlights the states which appear with the greatest frequency: 14 states appear in all five yearly samples; this core group will obviously yield the most useful data for such research questions as value subsystem stability across time. The 14 states include many which were of direct interest to U.S. policy makers during the 1966-1970 period (e.g., Cuba, Czechoslovakia, the USSR, Egypt, Jordan, Israel, China, and South Vietnam).

For the value content analysis of the FBIS material, the list of 13 terminal values from Rokeach et al. (1970) was employed. During the exploratory phase of the content analysis effort, additional potential values were identified; these included terminal end-states which political elites tend to emphasize. Five such values appeared with sufficient frequency to warrant their addition to the basic list of 13: progress, unity, ideology, cooperation, and support of government. The 18 terminal values and their respective definitions are listed in Table 2.3.

The actual coding process assumed that the speech was the basic coding unit; within the speech, the sentence was the operational coding unit. A given sentence could contain no values, one value, two values, and so on. For each speech, the total for each value category was recorded.

As an initial training exercise, two coders content analyzed the values in twelve of the *Federalist Papers*. In a previous study, Rokeach et al. (1970) reported identical content analysis results. As noted, Rokeach and his colleagues were concerned specifically with the applicability of value analysis to the

TABLE 2.1

TABLE 2.1
Value Data: State Samples (1966-1970)[a]

STATE	1966[b]	1967[c]	1968[d]	1969[e]	1970[f]	TOTAL
1. United States[g]	171	62	69	92	87	481
2. Cuba	20	10	6	10	11	57
3. Chile	4	9				13
4. France	13	7		8	7	35
5. West Germany	5	11	3		27	46
6. East Germany	20	15	11	22	26	94
7. Poland	4	9	11	12	14	50
8. Hungary	4	10		5	10	29
9. Czechoslovakia	7	11	41	52	19	130
10. Yugoslavia	15	19	30	20	41	125
11. Greece	12	8				20
12. Cyprus		4			4	8
13. Bulgaria					9	9
14. Rumania	9	7	16	17	26	75
15. U.S.S.R.	38	49	32	36	62	217
16. Ghana	12					12
17. Nigeria	7	21		6		34
18. Kenya	9					9
19. Algeria	8	8			6	22
20. Iran		4	3			7
21. Turkey	3	4				7
22. Iraq	21	16	11			48
23. United Arab Republic	18	16	20	14	37	105
24. Syria	10	14	5		5	34
25. Lebanon					6	6
26. Jordan	18	28	8	11	30	95
27. Israel	5	33	21	9	60	128
28. Saudi Arabia	7	3				10
29. Yemen		5				5
30. China	30	26	20	9	27	112
31. South Korea			7			7
32. Japan	4		9			13
33. India	24	4		7	4	39
34. Pakistan	27	6				33
35. Thailand			4	4		8
36. Cambodia	42	19	16	5	10	92
37. Laos					7	7
38. South Vietnam	46	4	13	10	3	76
39. Indonesia	42	3		6	4	55

a. The figure is the number of speeches.
b. N = 31.
c. N = 31.
d. N = 21.
e. N = 20.
f. N = 25.
g. The source for the United States is the **Department of State Bulletin**.

TABLE 2.2
Value Data: Most Frequently Included States

STATE	ALL YEARS (1966–1970)	FOUR YEARS	THREE YEARS
1. United States	X		
2. Cuba	X		
3. France		X	
4. West Germany		X	
5. East Germany	X		
6. Poland	X		
7. Hungary		X	
8. Czechoslovakia	X		
9. Yugoslavia	X		
10. Rumania	X		
11. U.S.S.R.	X		
12. Nigeria			X
13. Algeria			X
14. Iraq			X
15. United Arab Republic	X		
16. Syria		X	
17. Jordan	X		
18. Israel	X		
19. China	X		
20. India		X	
21. Thailand			X
22. Cambodia	X		
23. South Vietnam	X		
24. Indonesia		X	

"disputed authorship" question: Were the papers authored by Alexander Hamilton or James Madison?

In order to assess reliability (between the IBA coders and among the coders and the Rokeach coders), the rankings in Rokeach et al. (1970) were compared with those of the two IBA coders. The Spearman's rho results were:

.78 for the rankings reported in Rokeach et al. (1970) and IBA coder A (statistically significant at .01)

.89 for the rankings reported in Rokeach et al. (1970) and IBA coder B (statistically significant at .001)

TABLE 2.3
Values for Content Analysis

1. A comfortable life (a prosperous life; economic stability; economic security, raising living standards).

2. A world of peace (free of war and conflict).

3. Equality (brotherhood; equal opportunity for all; impartiality; free from extremes).

4. Freedom (democracy; independence; free choice; liberty; absence of coercion).

5. Happiness (felicity; contentedness).

6. Governmental security (stability of government; sufficient governmental control).

7. Honor (feeling honorable; having self-esteem).

8. Justice (state of just dealing or right action; people receiving their due).

9. National security (protection from attack; sovereignty; serving national interests; integrity of borders).

10. Public security (protection of the rights of the people; law and order).

11. Respect (worthy of high regard).

12. Social recognition (admiration as a result of social status).

13. Wisdom (mature understanding of life).

14. Progress (goal achievement; economic/social/cultural development).

15. Unity (absence of opposition).

16. Ideology (balance; struggle; references to Marx or Mao).

17. Cooperation (friendship; coexistence).

18. Support of government (sacrifice for government; patriotism; loyalty).

NOTE: The first 13 values are adopted from Rokeach et al. (1970); see also Rokeach (1973).

.93 for the rankings of coders A and B (statistically significant at .001)

In order to generate an estimate of intercoder reliability, five speeches were selected from the 1969 *Daily Reports*. The speeches included: Leoni of Venezuela (January 2, 1969); Pham Von Dong of North Vietnam (January 3, 1969); Svoboda of Czechoslovakia (January 19, 1969); Svoboda of Czechoslovakia (January 21, 1969); and Balaguer of Venezuela (February 28, 1969). When coders A and B were compared, the resulting Spearman's rho was an adequate .83 (significant at the .001 level).

For illustrative purposes, we present some highly aggregated data for 1970 in Table 2.4. Frequencies for the 18 value categories are summed across all 26 states in the 1970 sample for four categories: zero references to the value; one reference; two references; and three or more references. The least frequently appearing values include "happiness," "social recognition," and "wisdom." The values "a world of peace," "freedom," "national security," "progress," and "cooperation" appear most often in this data set. Subsequent analyses, to be presented later in this volume, will focus on the relationship between foreign policy elite values and foreign policy behavior.

THE POLITICAL COMPONENT

Of the five components, the political is undoubtedly the most difficult to conceptualize. Large gaps appear in the existing literature on foreign policy and political phenomena. Of course, past research has never totally ignored the nexus between general domestic conditions and foreign policy behavior (Jensen, 1969; East and Gregg, 1967; Coplin, 1974; K. J. Holsti, 1977). The impact of domestic politics per se has also been chronicled by scholars in this area (Rosenau, 1967; Frankel, 1963; Cohen, 1957; Riggs, 1950). The Watergate affair in American politics and the Iranian revolution are only the most recent in a series of domestic political crises which have exerted an impact on a state's foreign policy behavior (see Papp, 1975; Roberts, 1974).

Beyond a concern with salient and aberrational phenomena such as specific internal political crises, substantive research has

TABLE 2.4
1970: Value Frequencies[a]

Value[b]	0		1		2		3+	
	AF[c]	RF[c]	AF[c]	RF[c]	AF[c]	RF[c]	AF[c]	RF[c]
1. A comfortable life	377	82.9	46	10.1	12	2.6	20	4.4
2. A world of peace	170	37.4	89	19.6	55	12.1	141	40.9
3. Equality	364	89.0	49	10.8	15	3.3	27	5.9
4. Freedom	232	51.0	93	20.4	47	10.3	83	18.3
5. Happiness	396	87.0	40	8.8	12	2.6	7	1.6
6. Governmental security	385	84.6	34	7.5	15	3.3	21	4.6
7. Honor	365	80.2	52	11.4	14	3.1	24	5.3
8. Justice	336	73.8	75	16.5	18	4.0	26	5.7
9. National security	162	35.6	92	20.2	60	13.2	141	31.0
10. Public security	286	62.9	71	15.6	29	6.4	69	15.1
11. Respect	348	76.5	70	15.4	23	5.1	14	3.0
12. Social recognition	421	92.5	17	3.7	7	1.5	10	2.3
13. Wisdom	417	91.6	27	5.9	8	1.8	3	0.7
14. Progress	132	29.0	74	16.3	55	12.1	194	42.6
15. Unity	265	58.2	72	15.8	37	8.1	81	17.9
16. Ideology	256	56.3	51	11.2	41	9.0	107	23.5
17. Cooperation	147	32.3	56	12.3	39	8.6	213	46.8
18. Support of government	371	81.5	40	8.8	23	5.1	21	4.6

a. Total N = 457 speeches for 26 states.
b. Results have been aggregated into the categories of 0 (no references to the value), 1, 2, and 3 or more.
c. AF = Absolute Frequency; RF = Relative Frequency.

been both sporadic and noncomparable. Disproportionate attention has been accorded to the United States as a case study, although some important work is also available on Japan and Western Europe.[3] Empirical inquiry has often been superseded by a concern with normative issues. Hoffman (1962) considers the potential danger posed by crippling or inhibiting domestic restraints and consequent policy immobility; Laski (1944) and Waltz (1967) attempt to determine the optimal domestic arrangements for foreign policy-making.

A necessary step in the process of specifying the boundaries and contents of the political component is the development of criteria for the inclusion of variables. One criterion concerns the distinction between the political and societal components. The political component encompasses factors which pertain to the political sector of a social system while societal variables, such as culture, economic performance, and stability, operate at the state level of analysis. Public opinion, which can affect elite perceptions and thereby impinge on the foreign policy decision process, exemplifies a typical political variable. Culture and national ideology may also function as sources of foreign policy actions, but they are societal or aggregate phenomena. Snyder et al. (1962) conduct their analysis at the group or political level, while the research of Haas (1968) on internal stresses and strains as sources of national conflict behavior is an example of analysis from the societal perspective.

A second criterion involves the distinction between the political component and the governmental structure portion of the state classificatory scheme (discussed in detail in Chapter 3). At first glance, there is apparent overlap among the factors. Many aspects of governmental structure are obviously potential factors within the political variable domain. But we view governmental structure as a relatively static attribute, whereas phenomena such as political performance have a certain degree of variability across time. Thus, the distinction which will be employed separates stable governmental structural characteristics and places them in the state classificatory scheme, while elements of the political performance of the state will be housed within the political component.

It should be apparent that many factors which are generally viewed as political component variables will be assigned to the state classificatory scheme. The frequently employed size, economic development, and political accountability trilogy will appear in the state classificatory scheme, and not among the source variables. Other factors which will not appear in the political component include degree of political competitiveness, type of government, and military power. A state's ranking on these dimensions is not susceptible to sharp and recurring fluctuations.

A further criterion for inclusion is the need for indicators amenable to measurement on a cross-national basis, and not simply for advanced, Western systems. The variable areas which will be outlined in this section are offered as potentially universal categories, even though they are derived from an empirical base which is primarily Western. In the process, we hope to demonstrate their applicability to such systems as the Soviet Union and developing polities.[4]

Figures 2.2 illustrates the impact of three basic variable areas within the political component. Formal institutional factors, linkage mechanisms or domestic pressures, and political system aggregate descriptor variables all shape action at the political or group level of analysis. We turn now to a consideration of each of these domains.

Formal Institutional Factors

Formal institutional factors refer to the constellation of policy structures which is officially responsible for the promulgation and implementation of foreign policy actions. A comprehensive list would include the head of state; ad hoc small groups; formal small groups; deliberative assemblies and parliaments; military, treasury, economic, and intelligence bureaucracies; and internal affairs units (C. F. Hermann et al., 1973: 95-97; C. F. Hermann, 1978). Subsidiary realms of inquiry concern formal influences (such as a decision unit's constitutional status in the foreign policy system) and informal factors (including bureaucratic politics phenomena and social psychological factors such as group decision-making and risk-taking).

It has been traditionally assumed that foreign policy behavior, in contrast to domestic policy-making, involves fewer actors and tends to be restricted to a small foreign policy elite (or even to heads of state themselves). But such trends as pluralization of the policy process, structural differentiation, and convergence between the domains of foreign and domestic policy all suggest that multiple decision units are often involved in the processes of formulating and implementing foreign policies. It is thus important to determine which internal decisional unit or units generate the behavior, and whether the phenomena of institutional conflict or bureaucratic interaction exert an impact on the substance of policy.

The determination of the relative influence of each unit in the foreign policy system is a crucial initial area of inquiry. A unit's

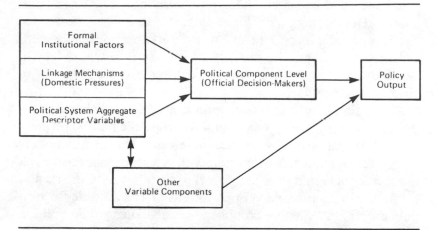

Figure 2.2: The Political Component: Variable Areas
NOTE: The conduct of process analysis would require that the above sequence be reversed.

relative impact will undoubtedly vary by type of foreign policy and type of state. Crises tend to create ad hoc units (Paige, 1968; C. F. Hermann, 1969; Brecher 1977, 1979) or are restricted to elite "senior players" (Brady, 1974: 24). Other types of foreign policies would involve different decision units. In closed and developing systems, the obvious expectation is that fewer units would be participants in the policy process.

Linkage Mechanisms

While in the previous section we highlighted the formal machinery at the state's disposal for generating actions in the foreign policy realm, a second variable area concerns unofficial or "extrasystemic" factors which can affect foreign policy behavior. Public opinion—ranging from mass moods and attitudes to media influences on foreign policy elites—may be viewed as a cluster of inputs which can influence policy outputs (Luttbeg, 1974: 1-10). Figure 2.3 presents a framework for the analysis of these input structures or linkage mechanisms.

Extensive empirical data on public opinion and foreign policy have been amassed (Merritt, 1972). Such data are virtually restricted to the United States, Western Europe, Israel, and Japan. Developing and closed systems have been neglected. While domestic pressures are not without influence in non-polyarchic regimes, the absense of opinion polling and competitive elections poses seemingly insurmountable obstacles to empirical research.

While simplistic stimulus-response models have been abandoned in the study of public opinion and public policy, perplexing theoretical issues await definitive resolution. Most researchers present evidence which simply fails to confront the critical questions concerning the actual influence of opinion inputs and the nature of decision-maker perceptions of and attitudes toward public opinion.[5] Further complicating the issue, public opinion is assumed to be an independent variable but is often a response to elite cues and actions and events in the real world (Abravanel and Hughes, 1973; Campbell and Cain, 1965; Epstein, 1965; Katz and Piret, 1964; Peterson, 1971; Rosi, 1965).

Political System Aggregate Descriptor Variables

A third and final cluster within the political component consists of political system aggregate descriptor variables. These aggregate variables refer to phenomena which characterize the political system as a unit, but tend nevertheless to vary over time. One specific example is the elite profile variable. Changes in elite attributes, bases of recruitment, and prior experiences may be associated with variations in foreign policy outputs.

This variable area has not elicited systematic attention from researchers in the past. Aggregate political variables have often been conceptualized as static forces and would therefore be housed within a classificatory scheme of states. In the present conceptualization, the policy-making institutional complex of a foreign policy system is a static structural factor, whereas policy-making performance is a political system aggregate descriptor variable. Potential rate of change distinguishes classificatory dimensions from political component variables.[6]

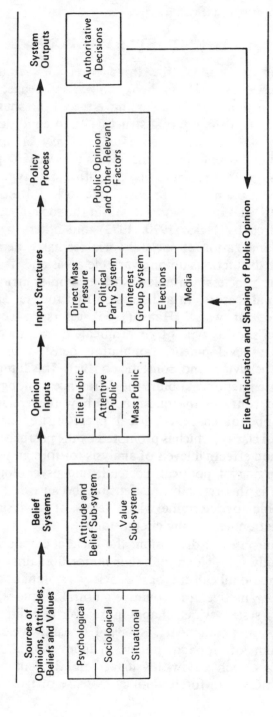

Figure 2.3: Public Opinion and the Foreign Policy Process: An Integrative Framework

THE SOCIETAL COMPONENT

In his analysis of the three levels or "images" which characterize research and theory on war and peace, Waltz (1959) points out that many scholars have traced the sources of external conflict to the internal structures and conditions of states. Some of these factors, such as relatively enduring internal political and economic arrangements and varying political processes and performance levels, constitute state type and political component phenomena in our framework. But other "internal variables" can be categorized within the societal component.

Research by Haas (1970, 1973) and others concerning the dimensionalization of societal variables has generally failed to consider distinctions among variable areas and has thus tended to equate "societal variables" with a complex array of domestic or internal factors. In a discussion of "societal approaches to the study of war," Haas (1965) refers to such domestic characteristics as type of government, degree of urbanization, economic development, population density, unemployment, deviant behavior, and domestic conflict. This lumping together of diverse phenomena blurs the differences among internal factors and confuses the question of how they relate to foreign policy phenomena. A critical prerequisite for progress is analytical clarity, which is promoted by the postulation of distinct causal and effectual levels of analysis for foreign policy inquiry. The merging of political, societal, and psychological variable clusters is theoretically indefensible because it then becomes impossible to determine which levels of analysis tend to be dominant under varying circumstances.

For purposes of discussion, the societal component area can be usefully subdivided into four major domains. The first domain is national culture, or the society's system of cognitive, affective, evaluative, and conative cultural attitudes, beliefs, and values, a system which shapes more overtly political responses, opinions, and judgments. Relevant research which focuses on the realm of foreign policy includes Merkl (1971), who scrutinizes such below-the-surface politico-cultural restraints on West German foreign policy as sense of trust and identity.

Feierabend and Feierabend (1969) consider the relationship between the level of need achievement and foreign conflict. Subsumed here also is research on religion and other aspects of culture which contribute to the politico-cultural climate or subculture. National culture can be tapped operationally by measuring three basic types of variables: basic cultural beliefs about such subjects as political and interpersonal trust; basic values; and need hierarchy rankings.

Societal aggregate descriptor variables constitute the second variable area within the societal component. In contrast to static structural characteristics—to be incorporated into the state classificatory scheme—we refer here to those social and economic factors which fluctuate more rapidly over time. One example is rate of change in national size and capabilities, which Choucri and North (1969) view as independent variables that can generate expansion and changes in military spending and alliance commitments. These intervening phenomena are then related to war involvement. Singer (1972), on the other hand, reports that higher growth rates in population or density do not predict to war proneness.

Economic rates may be especially significant as determinants of national actions or reactions. Trend data on inflation, unemployment, balance of payments fluctuations, economic growth, and other economic indicators may exhibit strong relationships with certain types of foreign policy decisions. Marxist and neo-Marxist interpretations of the significance of private economic interests as causal forces in American foreign policy have frequently been offered (Eley and Petersen, 1973). It is also important to consider aggregate economic trend data as possible influences on foreign policy outputs.

The third variable area in the societal component is social structure. Social structural positions can be expected to influence an individual's foreign policy beliefs, attitudes, and opinions and are thus indirect or remote influences at the political component level. But social structure—including position in society and population characteristics—is conceived here as an aggregate or societal characteristic.

Halle (1966) examines the relationship between social position and foreign policy attitudes. From the societal perspective, variations in overall social structural patterns may be significantly related to foreign policy positions and actions. While East and Gregg (1967) discover that level of ethnic heterogeneity is not related to foreign conflict or cooperation, Mayer (1967) maintains that internal tensions between ethnic and cultural subgroups in Switzerland can be relevant to foreign affairs.

Galtung (1969, 1967) offers a center-periphery theory of attitude propagation and change which is based on the social structural variable. He hypothesizes that position in society will predict to differing opinion structures and reactions. The general direction of influence will be from the center to the periphery (or from elite and attentive to mass strata). Census and other aggregate data on status rank dimensions can be combined to yield national social position profiles which can then be related to foreign policy behavior.

Domestic conflict is the final variable area in the societal component. A variety of factors, ranging from rates of modernization and urbanization to external stresses and fiascoes, may be sources of societal unrest and conflict; static social structural differentiations are by no means the only sources of internal conflict. Internal tension may "spill over" into the sphere of foreign policy, especially if leaders intentionally externalize hostility as a response to internal solidarity problems (Good, 1962; Hazlewood, 1973).

The proposition that internal problems can be solved by externalizing conflicts has solid grounding in sociological conflict theory (Simmel, 1955; Coser, 1956) and in anecdotal accounts of the foreign policy process. Recently, quantitative studies have been undertaken in an effort to ascertain the nature and magnitude of the linkage between domestic and foreign conflict behavior (Rummel, 1968; Wilkenfeld, 1973).

In the course of actually specifying societal variables for data collection and analysis, again it was necessary to make compromises between the ideal of conceptual comprehensiveness and the inescapable constraints of operational realities. At this stage in the research, we determined that variables would be specified in three general societal areas: population characteristics, economic data, and conflict data.

Population Characteristics

Attributes of a state's population may be expected to exert an influence on foreign policy behavior. Realists and national power theorists have asserted that the size and distribution of population are among the determinants of a state's capability to act and influence other actors in the interstate arena. Total population is a relatively stable characteristic and is incorporated into the state classificatory scheme. Rate of population increase, however, is classified within the societal component.

We may hypothesize that the rate of population increase exerts an indirect impact upon foreign policy behavior. A state with a rapidly expanding population may pursue a more active and aggressive foreign policy as a result of internal pressures which accrue and spill over into the realm of interstate relations (see Choucri, 1975; Choucri and North, 1975). Accordingly, *rate of population increase* appears in the societal component.

Economic Data

Whereas static structural attributes appear in the state classificatory scheme, the societal component features factors which are more dynamic in nature and which represent economic trend or rate data. The specific variables are listed below:

(1) percentage of unemployed
(2) average annual rate of growth of gross domestic product (GDP) at constant prices
(3) total annual governmental expenditure
(4) balance of payments
(5) inflation

Data were readily available for the first three economic variables. For the balance of payments factor, it was decided to resort to a multiple indicator approach. There are three major measures of a state's international payments deficit: the trade balance, the balance on current accounts, and the basic balance. There are a number of standard balance of payments deficit measures. No single item can "measure" a state's balance of payments profile. The specific variables for which data have been collected in connection with this research are the following:

(1)   goods and services
(2)   merchandise
(3)   nonmonetary gold
(4)   investment income
(5)   unrequited transfers
(6)   government unrequited transfers
(7)   direct investment
(8)   direct investment by foreigners in the country
(9)   direct investment by nationals abroad
(10) other private long-term capital

An inflation variable is also included. Specifically, data have been assembled from the International Monetary Fund's *International Financial Statistics* publication. For each state for each year, the consumer price index for quarter four of the current year and the previous year was recorded.

Conflict Data

Prior research has probed the nexus between domestic and foreign conflict behavior. A recent example attempts to trace the origins of conflict exchanges in the Middle East to a complex array of determinants, including prior foreign and domestic conflict, conflict interactions, and bureaucratic inertia (Wilkenfeld, 1975). The relationship between domestic turbulence or strife and foreign conflict has been the subject of extensive empirical research (Wilkenfeld, 1968, 1973; Hazlewood, 1973, 1975; Kegley et al., 1978; Zinnes, 1976b; Zinnes and Wilkenfeld, 1971).

Domestic unrest and conflict have also displayed relationships with other forms of foreign policy behavior. The internal conflict-begets-external conflict notion has been shown to be a factor of at least limited significance for explaining conflictual foreign policy outputs. Domestic conflict may also play a role in the generation of other types of foreign policy behavior.

Several sets of domestic conflict time series data are available to researchers. The Banks (1971) domestic conflict data set appeared to be the most appropriate given the temporal and other requirements of the IBA framework. The specific variables appear below:

(1) assassinations
(2) general strikes
(3) guerilla warfare
(4) government crises
(5) purges
(6) riots
(7) revolutions
(8) antigovernment demonstrations
(9) number of coups
(10) number of changes in the executive
(11) number of changes in the cabinet
(12) number of changes in the constitution

In an effort to generate higher-order dimensions of domestic conflict behavior, general factor analyses of the twelve indicators were performed. The correlation matrices contained very weak bivariate Pearsonian correlations, a result which revealed the general absence of a factor structure. The six analyses—one for each year from 1966-1970 and one for the entire period—yielded very unstable results.

The low correlations and their wide fluctuations over time were determined to be functions of the variable distributions. The events which had been coded were uncommon; most entries were zero—even on an annual basis. With this type of discontinuous data, Pearson's r is not an appropriate measure of association and the factor analyses were meaningless. Therefore, it was decided to further explore the relationships among the variables by examining cross tabulations and accompanying measures of association such as gamma and tau c. The contingency tables uncovered some rather strong bivariate relationships.

In order to avoid the problem of induction from a large number of tabulations to a small number of cells, the search for patterns relied on previous empirical research in this area. Studies by Rummel (1963, 1968), Tanter (1966), Wilkenfeld (1973), Gurr (1970), Feierabend and Feierabend (1969), Nesvold (1971), Banks (1972), and others suggested the particular patterns and groupings that could be expected.

In addition, we produced a summary (1966-1970) cross tabulation for each pair of variables, with gamma as the measure of association. These results are presented in Table 2.5. The first group to be identified in this way isolates coups as the core variable, with changes in the executive, changes in the cabinet, changes in the constitution, revolutions, and purges also "clustered" on this factor. This dimension has been designated *governmental instability*.

A second cluster consists of riots, antigovernment demonstrations, and general strikes. This is obviously a less structured and more spontaneous type of dimension, and it has been designated *societal unrest*. Three variables—assassinations, government crises, and guerilla wars—exhibited no particular patterns and were not included in either of the two dimensions.

Certain transformations were necessary because of serious skewness problems. Revolutions, coups, and constitutional changes were dichotomized, with one or more occurrences coded as 1. Cabinet changes and executive changes were trichotomized. No changes were coded as 0, one change was coded as 1, and two or more changes were coded as 2. Purges, riots, antigovernment demonstrations, and general strikes were transformed by grouping according to geometric progression: 0(0), 1(1), 2-3(2), 4-7(3), 8-15(4), 16-31(5), and 32-64(6).

THE INTERSTATE COMPONENT

As we have just noted, the psychological, political, and societal components are derived from the three levels of analysis which generate the internal determinants of foreign policy behavior. The remaining two components are external in nature and yield variables which are derived from realities which

TABLE 2.5

Domestic Conflict Factors: Intercorrelation of Domestic Variables (gamma coefficients)

GOVERNMENTAL INSTABILITY

	PURGES	REVOLUTIONS	COUPS	CABINET CHANGES	CONSTITUTIONAL CHANGES	EXECUTIVE CHANGES
Purges[c]						
Revolutions[a]	.50					
Coups[a]	.49	.94				
Cabinet changes[b]	.44	.59	.93			
Constitutional changes[a]	.37	.71	.98	.58		
Executive changes[b]	.30	.38	.94	.94	.57	

SOCIETAL UNREST

	RIOTS	ANTI-GOVERNMENT DEMONSTRATIONS	GENERAL STRIKES
Riots[c]			
Anti-government demonstrations[c]	.67		
General strikes[c]	.73	.65	

a. Dichotomized.

b. Trichotomized

c. Transformed by geometric progression method.

exist outside—yet are perceived within—the territorial boundaries of sovereign states. These two external components may be traced to the interstate and global levels of analysis (see Figure 1.1).

Analyses of foreign policy behavior have tended to accord primary significance to three fundamental forms of interstate influences upon state behavior: dependency/interdependency relationships, action-reaction processes, and alliance/coalition formation. In fact, the importance of these external factors has been assumed to be overriding, particularly in the so-called "billiard-ball" theory of international politics wherein state behavior is explained solely by reference to interactions with other states, virtually ignoring internal factors and the influence of type of state.

Within the contemporary context of national and global scarcity, external environmental constraints are receiving a great deal of attention (Brown, 1974; Ehrlich and Ehrlich, 1974). Nevertheless, the exclusive reliance on "external" inputs for explanations of foreign policy has been challenged by those who posit a nexus between domestic and international sources of behavior (Rosenau, 1966, 1969, 1973). The IBA framework requires that interstate variables be specified as determinants of foreign policy, but as one component in a multicausal perspective which also includes "internal" sources of foreign policy.

In the following section, we delineate two major clusters of interstate factors: interstate dependency/interdependency relationships and action-reaction processes.[7] Within each domain, variables will be specified and operationalized, and specific data issues will be discussed.

Interstate Dependency/Interdependency Relationships

International economic theory has played an important role in the explanation of international political events for a number of years. Imperialism and war (Fann and Hodges, 1971; Laski, 1935), integration and cooperation (Nye, 1972; Puchala, 1971), coercion and diplomacy (Bergsten and Krause, 1975; Cooper, 1968), and international political development (Bhagwati, 1967) are among the facets of foreign behavior which seemingly force theorists to consider the relevance of interstate economics in their explanations of foreign policy-making. In fact, tomorrow's international system in its entirety may assume radically different characteristics given the dynamics of the interstate economic relations which currently confront the world (Gilpin, 1975).

The task of identifying a valid set of interstate economic indicators that is relevant to the foreign policy process is an imposing one, given the scope of the domain. Interstate economic relations include: (1) trade, trade barriers, and commodity arrangements; (2) international monetary policies and flows; (3) financial and investment dynamics; (4) foreign aid; and (5) multinational and transnational activities. Each of these affects relationships of interdependency, dependency, domination, and advantage. Further complicating the situation, analysis must deal with multistate arrangements as well as individual state policies, with long- and short-term conditions and cycles, and with the inevitable confusion of political with economic aspects of interstate relationships.

With the exception of questions of ownership (involving the issues of foreign investment and multinational firms), interstate economic *exchange* captures the most central aspects of interaction in the economic sphere. When considering states as entities, we can note that relationships are formed by the absolute and relative importance of various types of exchange; each state has resources of various amounts and kinds, and these are used to obtain other resources from abroad. When we deal with these resources and their flows, we focus upon the state's position in the interstate resource marketplace. Resource production, consumption, and flow define the exchange relationships among states. Exports and imports, then, serve to describe interstate relationships on an economic level.

The use of import and export data should, ideally, be supplemented by information regarding consumption and production of commodities within the state. First, interdependency implies not only an absolute level of exchange between states, but also an assessment of the level relative to each state's needs as a producer or consumer. Second, dependency and domination (or economic advantage) are likewise tied to the relative importance of the exchange to total consumption patterns.

Furthermore, gross data on resource flows are not suitable for analyzing complex relationships, and some degree of specificity and comparison must be achieved in the development of indicators in order to utilize information concerning commodity relationships. Dependency, for example, may exist in a relationship insofar as specific resources are concerned, while domination may describe the same directional relationship in the case of other resources. Moreover, complementary relationships may exist across commodities, indicating another form of dependency. Finally, the extent of dependency or interdependency, when evaluated for an overall relationship, may permeate only small sectors of an economy, or it may dominate most aspects of economic life in a state.

The indicators developed by the IBA Project for the purpose of tapping sources of foreign behavior in the realm of interstate economic relations take into consideration the following items of information: (1) export and import flows; (2) production and consumption within states; and (3) commodity-specific relationships, overall relationships, and combinations wherein overall relationships are assessed through an attempt to link specific commodity exchange relationships. Eight indices were specified: four deal exclusively with one commodity (energy or food), one treats the overall relations of a state, and three attempt to combine commodity-specific information into single scales of overall relationships.

INTERSTATE ENERGY RELATIONSHIPS

A great deal of attention has been paid recently to the ability of the state to acquire the energy necessary to meet its demands. Hence, we will focus much of our emphasis here on the realm of commodity-specific indicator development. Utilizing data on imports, exports, production, and consumption of energy, these separate indices were designed to correspond to the three concepts within the interstate economic realm: interdependence, dependency, and domination or economic advantage.

The first variable, *energy interdependency*, is measured by the following formula:

$$\text{energy interdependency} = \frac{\text{energy imports} + \text{energy exports}}{\text{energy consumption}}$$

This measure assumes that total energy trade is the basis of interdependent relationships in the energy sector, but measures this volume against the needs for energy as a control for the importance of the energy sector to the state. Among large consuming states, interdependence exists when trade is quite high; among states which consume little energy themselves, interdependence becomes high with rather low levels of trade.

The second energy-related measure, *energy dependency*, concerns the importance of imports to energy consumption. An energy-dependent economy is one in which a large portion of the consumed energy is imported as opposed to being domestically produced. Even when certain forms of energy are exported, recourse to foreign sources of energy (e.g., in forms not domestically produced) may result in dependent relationships. Our indicator attempts to discount imports which are reexported rather than consumed, without discounting domestically produced energy which is exported:

$$\text{energy dependency} = \frac{\text{energy imports}}{\text{energy consumption} + \text{exports/production}}$$

The major concept tapped in this measure is the proportion of consumed energy which is imported. In order to capture this idea, it is necessary to go beyond a simple measure which divides import total by consumption total; many imports are reexported, often as reprocessed forms of energy. To compensate for this, the index decreases as exports increase relative to production; no exports would allow us to assume that all imports are consumed, while exportation which exceeds production would constitute a large decrease in dependency (as imports are exported). Very small decrements in the dependency score occur when: (1) production energy is exported; or (2) imported energy is exported, but the exports are small relative to production. In this manner, the indicator attempts to control for reexportation in a somewhat imperfect manner, approximating a true measure of import-dependent consumption.

Energy market strength concerns the ability of a state to supply energy resources to other states. An energy supplier need not necessarily be independent in the consumption area, since states may be in a position to supply energy resources which are not of the type currently needed by the economy. The energy market strength index assesses the proportion of total energy accessed which is exported:

$$\text{energy market strength} = \frac{\text{energy exports}}{\text{energy production} + \text{imports}}$$

GENERAL TRADE RELATIONSHIPS

The overall status of an economic relationship is assessed by reference to a structural arrangement which encompasses entire economies (Santos, 1971). Dependency is the obverse of domination within a reflexive relationship, since a dependent economy develops as a reaction to developments in one or more other dominant economies (Bodenheimer, 1971). Here we have a political definition of an economic relationship which is useful when analysis focuses on the substance of commodity exchange within the overall exchange relationship.

The nature of commodity exchanges is perhaps the most obvious indicator of dependency/domination. Dependent economies tend to export unrefined, natural resources while dominant economies tend to export processed, industrial goods, with each serving as the other's marketplace. The index developed to operationalize this dependency/domination continuum for interstate relations divides eight categories of trade into the categories of "industrial" and "unrefined," and computes a score ranging from − 1 (domination) to + 1 (dependency), according to the following formula:

(industrial imports + unrefined
exports) −

$$\text{neocolonial dependency} = \frac{\text{(unrefined imports + industrial exports)}}{\text{total imports + total exports}}$$

Interdependency must be considered in isolation from this conception of dependency and domination. Interdependency as a general interstate relationship which characterizes several commodity arenas connotes the economic involvement of states in the economies of other states. States are interdependent to the extent that they send exports to, and receive imports from, other states. General interdependency is measured by the following formula:

$$\text{economic involvement} = \text{total exports} + \text{total imports}$$

FOOD DEPENDENCY AND ADVANTAGE

Dependency and domination relationships involving food occupy a special position within an economy. Therefore, we have developed a separate indicator, based on the assumption that a state is dependent on food supplies to the extent that it must import food, and that it is in an advantageous position in the food sector to the extent that it exports food. The index assesses the degree of dependency/strength in terms of total food exchange:

$$\text{food dependency} = \frac{\text{food imports} - \text{food exports}}{\text{food imports} + \text{food exports}}$$

THE GENERALITY OF INTERSTATE ECONOMIC RELATIONS

The set of economic indicators outlined above would be incomplete without introducing the notion of specialization. Specialization involves a type of dependency which is typified by reliance on certain commodity markets for economic health.

Export specialization is the condition in which a state relies upon particular commodities for trade income. A state which exports one type of commodity to the virtual exclusion of other types of exports relies both upon the internal production sector on which income hinges and on the external markets from which income must be derived. Thus, the dependency is dualistic.

Import specialization is a condition in which a state relies on certain commodities which must be obtained from abroad. The import-specialized state depends upon a particular foreign supply and prices for necessary goods and reasonable payments. The internal economy, then, exhibits a specialized set of input requirements.

Generality in imports and exports indicates a degree of autonomy or independence from either foreign market domination of the economy or internal production sectors for income. States which import a variety of goods have economies which are independent of single foreign supply arenas; such states have no particularly important vulnerabilities. Similarly, states which export across several commodity sectors can rely upon several sources of export income rather than one dominant market.

In order to assess the relative dependency upon specialization and the degree of generality of a state's interstate economic relations, two indicators are developed. Employing the "concentration ratio" developed by Singer and Ray (1973), the indicator scores range from zero (when export income or import expenditures are distributed equally across commodity arenas) to one (when export income or import expenditures are entirely concentrated in one commodity arena):

$$\text{import concentration} = \sqrt{\frac{(Si)^2 - 1/10}{1 - 1/10}}$$

$$\text{export concentration} = \sqrt{\frac{(Ti)^2 - 1/10}{1 - 1/10}}$$

In the *import concentration* index, Si refers to the percentage share of import expenditures in commodity class i, where ten categories exist. In the *export concentration* index, Ti refers to export income percentages.

Interstate Action-Reaction Processes

Stimulus-response, or action-reaction, has been a pervasive model of international politics for many years. Based originally on the psychological model, action-reaction theories of international politics have emphasized the importance of interaction rather than action within the interstate system. States do not act in a vacuum, but rather react to external conditions. These conditions include messages and actions directed by other states to the nation and its leaders. When foreign policy behavior is affected by the reception of foreign policy actions initiated elsewhere, we are concerned with reactive foreign policy and action-reaction processes.

In order to discover underlying patterns of variation in foreign policy behavior, a series of factor analytic studies of the 22 WEIS categories of conflict and cooperation was undertaken; these results are reported on extensively in Chapter 4. In connection with the present discussion, it can be concluded that conflictual and cooperative behavior-received patterns are of interest; here we find three identifiable factors: a fairly undifferentiated diplomacy factor, a force factor, and a reward factor.

In summary, the interstate component of the IBA Project framework is operationalized with eleven indicators. Three are derived from the action-reaction realm of interstate behavior and are dimensions of foreign policy inputs to the foreign policy machinery of a state. The other eight indicators assess interstate economic relationships and tap—by various means and with varying definitional and substantive concerns—the concepts of interdependence, dependency, and economic leverage or domination.

THE GLOBAL COMPONENT

The final component among the array of determinants of foreign behavior deals with global factors. These are the attributes of the international system which confront the state and which constitute the context within which its actions must be undertaken. Classical international relations theory (Morgenthau, 1948) imputes particular significance to the global realm; considerable research has been devoted to efforts to identify the factors which determine the makeup of the international system (Kaplan, 1957; Rosecrance, 1966; Russett, 1967; K. J. Holsti,

1977). In general, global systemic variables refer to the aggregate sociopolitical and physical realities which constitute the global milieu (for general discussions of these factors, see McGowan and Shapiro, 1973: 161-179; Jones and Singer, 1972: 27-88; Newcombe and Newcombe, 1972: 24-62).

Several clusters of phenomena have traditionally comprised the global component. The first of these groups those variables which refer to the attributes of the global system, such as power stratification, alliance aggregation, and systemic turbulence. Research on systemic attributes is quite extensive. As a result of such endeavors as the Correlates of War Project (Singer and Small, 1972; Singer, 1979a, 1979b), alliance aggregation has emerged as an increasingly salient global variable. Early findings indicate that during the nineteenth century, alliance aggregation functioned as a stabilizing force within the global system, while the level of alliance aggregation exerts a destabilizing effect in the twentieth century (Singer and Small, 1968; Small and Singer, 1969). The concept of systemic turbulence is also an important aspect of the global context (Rosenau, 1971: 157-159; Munton, 1973).

Power stratification represents yet another global systemic dimension. Unlike alliance aggregation and the level of systemic turbulence, variables associated with the global stratification of power have generated considerable controversy. As such competing conceptualizations as bipolarity, multipolarity, and even bi-multipolarity illustrate, scholars have found it difficult to arrive at a consensus concerning the conceptualization and impact of power stratification (Deutsch and Singer, 1964; Waltz, 1964; Rosecrance, 1966).

The second variable cluster features factors referring to a state's status rank (and rank discrepancy) within the global system. Indeed, status has been conceptualized as an independent systemic variable which produces variations in economic (trade) behavior (Reinton, 1967) and diplomatic interactions (Russett and Lamb, 1969). In addition, the perception of status rank discrepancy has been conceptualized as a determinant of global violence (East, 1972, 1973; Wallace, 1973). An additional line of inquiry has been developed by Galtung (1964) in his theory of aggression at the individual, societal, and interstate levels, based on "topdog" versus "underdog" status discrepancies among states.

Subsystemic phenomena constitute a third global cluster. The research of Russett (1968a, 1968b, 1968c, 1966) is particularly relevant to the specification of this variable domain. To what extent is behavior conditional or affected by regional and other subsystemic attributes? How might regions and subsystems be accurately identified? How do subsystemic organizations and agreements impinge on interactions?

The final variable cluster within the global component is comprised of what Brecher et al. (1969) refer to as "textural" variables. Such variables refer to global culture, "rules," and norms—to the extent that such factors exert any influence at all. The roles of global organizations and international law are thus categorized here.

The nature of the framework which we have developed dictates the exclusion of the vast majority of the factors mentioned above. In virtually all of the cases, the attributes referred to are static in nature and cannot be classified as variables, at least in the short run. Rather, they must be considered as contextual factors, providing a stable and identical systemic milieu in which all of the states in the system must operate at any given point in time. The logical conclusion of the argument being advanced here is that just as we viewed static structural characteristics of states as a set of factors upon which to base a classificatory scheme for states, so too can the global milieu be conceived as a context and a "given" for all states which interact in the international system.[8]

However, we may consider those systemic-level phenomena in which each state occupies a unique role, thereby introducing interstate variation within a global context. Performance or position in the global situation may then be analyzed. The indicators which we actually develop in the global realm fall into two classes: international governmental organization membership and the extent of conflict involving bordering states.

International Governmental Organization Membership

The extent to which a state is involved in the international system can be indirectly assessed on a yearly basis by amassing data on the number of international governmental organizations (IGOs) of which it is a member. It could be argued that we have already measured the extent of international involvement in the measures of trade which are included in the interstate component. However, the type of international involvement that is gauged by IGO memberships attempts to tap a more subtle type of political commitment on the part of the state to participation in a global framework. Furthermore, fluctuations in a state's number of memberships across a period of years register an increase or decrease in the state's commitment to this global perspective.

In this connection, two indicators were developed to assess the state's participation in IGOs:

(1) total IGO memberships per year, 1966-1970
(2) total new IGO memberships per year, 1966-1970

The first indicator deals with the commitment or contribution of a state to the international organizational framework, while new memberships indicate an increased effort in this global arena.

Conflict Involving Bordering States

One of the hypotheses which has received a considerable amount of attention in the realm of international conflict analysis predicts a direct relationship between the number of states which border on a state and the amount of conflict in which that state can be expected to engage. The reasoning here is that states tend to engage in conflict primarily with bordering states. The larger the number of states which border a particular state, the higher the probability that any one of these dyads will develop a conflictual relationship.

We have extended this argument somewhat further. It is our contention that states which border other states which are, in turn, involved in conflict behavior, have a certain probability of becoming involved in these conflicts themselves. That is, conflicts may tend to spill over into initially uninvolved states through a process of diffusion, and the probability is quite high that such a spillover will involve states which share borders with the initial combatants (for related reasoning, see Midlarsky, 1974).

For purposes of the present research, we have identified four classes of borders.[9] These are: (1) direct land borders; (2) colonial land borders; (3) direct sea borders; and (4) colonial sea borders. In addition, we include two indicators of conflict behavior for these bordering states, derived from the World Event/Interaction Survey (WEIS) data. The first, conflict, refers to the WEIS categories which loaded on the nonmilitary conflict sent factor (to be discussed at length in Chapter 4), and includes the behaviors accuse, protest, demand, threaten, demonstrate, expel, and seize. The second indicator, force, includes the single WEIS variable force, and is clearly distinguishable from less serious forms of conflict (Art and Waltz, 1971). For each state, we assess the amount of conflict or force involving states with each designated type of border:

(1) direct land borders: conflict
(2) direct land borders: force
(3) colonial land borders: conflict
(4) colonial land borders: force
(5) direct sea borders: conflict
(6) direct sea borders: force
(7) colonial sea borders: conflict
(8) colonial sea borders: force

Measurement of these variables is quite straightforward. In the case of the IGO variables, the number of memberships and new memberships for each state was recorded from the *Yearbook of International Organizations*. While this source lists both governmental and nongovernmental organization memberships, only the former were included. The two IGO membership variables were found to be relatively uncorrelated ($r = .20$).

TABLE 2.6
The Specification of Source Components for
the Comparative Study of Foreign Policy

I. Psychological Component

Psychodynamic factors
Personality traits
Belief systems

II. Political Component

Formal institutional factors
Linkage mechanisms
Political system aggregate descriptors

III. Societal Component

National culture
Societal aggregate descriptors
Social structure
Domestic conflict

IV. Interstate Component

Action-reaction patterns
Dependency/interdependency relationships

V. Global Component

Global system aggregate descriptors
Status-rank conditions
Subsystemic phenomena
Textural factors

In the case of the borders data, scores for conflict and force were computed by summing all acts sent and received by the states which bordered on the state in question. These two combined scores provide us with an estimate of the magnitude of turbulence within the immediate surroundings of a given state. While the degree of intercorrelation among the border variables was moderate—in the $r = .60$ range—we concluded that this would not preclude subsequent analyses of the borders variables.

SUMMARY

Table 2.6 provides a concise summary by listing the variable groupings which are identified within each of the five components. As we have previously noted in our discussion of clusters, not all of the domains within the five components have been operationalized. Indeed, the political component will not be included in any of the subsequent analyses reported in this volume. However, what we present here in summary form is our conceptualization of a comprehensive, comparative, operationalizable, and policy-relevant set of indicators which serve as the sources of foreign policy behavior. The components, in conjunction with the state and event classificatory schemes to be discussed in detail below, form the major elements of the IBA framework for the comparative analysis of foreign policy behavior.

NOTES

1. Although it may be useful to measure the belief systems of subelites and lower officials (to generate modal belief-value maps for foreign policy bureaucracies), such an effort is beyond the scope of the present project.

2. In addition to the works cited in the text, see the following studies: Rokeach (1969b, 1968-1969); Bishop et al. (1972); Rokeach et al. (1970).

3. On the impact of legislative institutions, public opinion, interest groups, and the mass media in Britain, France, West Germany, the Soviet Union, and Japan, see Macridis (1972). Hellman (1969) offers an analysis of Japanese domestic politics and foreign policy which is patterned after Cohen's (1957) seminal case study of American politics and the Japanese peace treaty.

4. Available evidence does indicate that in relatively closed polities such as the Soviet Union, domestic politics impinges upon and sometimes shapes the contours of the foreign policy-making process (Schwartz, 1975; Dallin, 1969; Armstrong, 1965; Ploss, 1963). Interest group inputs are transmitted to elites in the Soviet system (Stewart, 1969; Schwartz and Keech, 1968), although the nature of the process is more circuitous (see Aspaturian, 1972). Similarly, while many of the Western categories do not apply to developing states (Weinstein, 1972), we are convinced that we will eventually be able to construct foreign policy frameworks relevant to the processes in these states.

5. Excellent critiques of the existing literature can be found in Rosenau (1961) and Cohen (1973).

6. Due to the complexity of the makeup of the political component, we have not as yet undertaken the operationalization of cross-national variables or the collection of data in this realm. Therefore, the political component will not be incorporated in the analyses to be presented below.

7. While we note the alliance/coalition formation factors at this point, they will not be included in subsequent analyses. At the operational stage, we encountered problems of data collection, as well as problems of index development. There is also some difficulty in distinguishing between these and global phenomena. In addition, many of these indicators proved to be too static in nature for inclusion among the independent variables.

8. A somewhat different line of reasoning resulted in the exclusion of the notions of status and rank from the ultimate operationalization of the global component. While one could argue that these characteristics are also relatively stable over time, it is also the case that aspects of status and rank are included within the state classificatory scheme. Thus, the scores which are developed for each state (see Chapter 3) implicitly measure the ranking of states within the international community on such characteristics as military and economic capabilities.

9. Starr and Most (1976) provide an extensive discussion of the issues involved in the identification of borders.

Chapter 3

Classifying States for Foreign Policy Analysis

In this chapter we present both conceptual and empirical work pertaining to the development of a classification scheme for foreign policy actors. As we have already noted, this scheme constitutes the intervening variable cluster within a general framework for the comparative analysis of foreign policy behavior. This chapter will deal with the specification of the classificatory scheme, the operationalization of the variables which are used to measure its characteristics, the specification of the data to be analyzed, and some empirical results from analyses of these data.

The careful construction of classificatory schemes is an important stage in the development of knowledge, whether this be in the physical, biological, or social sciences. The act of classification is obviously a precondition for differentiating among the conditions which give rise to phenomena in all disciplines. Without an ability to type phenomena, we confront the impossible task of attempting to explain the behavior of individual units of analysis. As Rummel has pointed out:

AUTHORS' NOTE: *Some of the sections of this chapter constitute expanded versions of material which originally appeared in Wilkenfeld et al. (1978).*

The virtue of typing is that it enables parsimonious description of objects and facilitates reliable predictions about them based upon their tendency to group. Classification is a process of ordering cases into groups that best represent certain empirically measured relations of contiguity, similarity, or both [Quoted in Phillips and Hall, 1970:65].

Lijphart (1968) notes that a classificatory scheme must exhibit categories which are jointly exhaustive and mutually exclusive. In this sense, classification is the step which logically precedes the formulation of general propositions. The classification scheme should perform two functions:

(1) It should facilitate comparison among different types and aid in the discovery of significant characteristics that are logically independent of the criteria defining the types but empirically associated with the different types.
(2) It should also facilitate comparisons within each type, with the attributes held in common by all of the systems within the type serving as the control variables, or parameters (Lijphart, 1968:7).

While work on classification has been central in the biological sciences, scholars in international politics and foreign policy have only recently begun to recognize that classification which leads to explanation is essential for developing empirical theory (Kean and McGowan, 1973: 223). The usefulness of the classificatory scheme lies in its ability to facilitate the prediction of distinctions in the internal and external behavior of the polities which are classified (Phillips and Hall, 1970:67).

Most classification work in political science has focused upon the type of political structure (see, for example, Blondel, 1972; Almond and Powell, 1966; Lijphart, 1968; Dahl, 1970; Cutright, 1963). The degree of stability of the political system has also been a major concern (Lipset, 1959; Gurr, 1970; Eckstein, 1962). The level of military capability, and the extent to which it strengthens a regime and affects decision-making, has also been viewed as an important classificatory consideration (Blondel, 1972).

Paralleling these efforts has been extensive research in international politics which has focused on the development of empirically based classificatory schemes. These efforts, relying heavily upon factor analytic studies of large sets of cross-national aggregate data, have revealed the centrality of such factors as size, economic development, and political structure as overarching classificatory clusters (Rummel, 1969, 1972; Russett, 1967; Russett et al., 1964; Sawyer, 1967; Banks and Gregg, 1965).

It is only recently that students of foreign policy have recognized the importance of classification. Indeed, Rosenau's (1966) pre-theoretical scheme represents one of the few which explicitly deals with foreign policy concerns. Reliance on Rosenau's classificatory variables of size, economic development, and political accountability has been quite extensive (see, for example, Rosenau and Hoggard, 1974; Rosenau and Ramsey, 1975; Salmore and Hermann, 1969; Moore, 1974; Salmore, 1972; East and Hermann, 1974). While theoretically rather than empirically derived, the Rosenau classificatory categories closely parallel those derived by Rummel, Sawyer, and Russett.

In our initial work on the Interstate Behavior Analysis Project classificatory scheme, it was necessary to resolve three methodological issues. First, we perceived a need to distinguish between those attributes which are relatively stable over time, and which constitute the basic structural characteristics of states, and those factors which are more dynamic in nature and are subject to short-term fluctuations. These short-term factors, hereafter referred to as performance characteristics, will have direct impact on the formulation of foreign policy within states. The more stable attributes, to be subsequently referred to as structural characteristics, may be viewed as providing the static context within which foreign policy decisions are made.

The structure/performance distinction as defined above constitutes a major innovative characteristic of the present classificatory scheme. Excessive confusion concerning this important distinction has permeated the treatment of these concepts in the literature on the comparative study of foreign policy behavior. While we concede that it will not always be possible to maintain a rigid distinction between structure and performance, we will attempt to be as clear as possible on this point.

A second methodological issue pertains to the type of index which will be generated by the classificatory scheme. Prior foreign policy research has failed to incorporate a sufficiently large sample of relevant variables. In fact, empirical work has traditionally involved the use of only one variable for each classificatory dimension. Thus, the political dimension is frequently reduced to an accountability measure which is indexed by freedom of the press. Total gross national product is used to represent the size factor. The economic factor is often equated with economic development; gross national product per capita is then employed to operationalize development. We contend that a multiple-indicator strategy is empirically more realistic and theoretically more productive.

A third issue concerns the level of measurement appropriate for the index under construction. This issue revolves around the relative utility of nominal versus interval coding, and the question of whether we will then obtain discrete as opposed to continuous measures. Implicit in the work of Rosenau and others who have utilized his eightfold scheme is the notion that the dichotomization of classificatory factors is the most efficient way to deal with this problem. The argument against this approach is that the dichotomous distinction is too gross and that much useful information is consequently lost. Therefore, the IBA Project has opted for the development of continuous indicators, based on a multiple-indicator approach.

The classificatory scheme developed below is based on the premise that the structural attributes of states which provide the context in which foreign policy actions are taken may be derived from three general areas: economic structure; capability (size, military power, resource base); and governmental structure (political development, structure, stability). In contrast to the single-indicator approach, we operationalize the structural attribute domain with 23 specific variables. Below we discuss each of the structural domains.

ECONOMIC STRUCTURE DIMENSION

Both the theoretical and empirical work in foreign policy analysis have identified economic structure—usually as represented by economic development—as a key factor in both source and process analysis. Studies by Rosenau (1966, 1967), Casanova (1966), O'Leary (1969), and Butwell (1969) all attest to the presumed impact of economic variables on foreign policy behavior. In addition, empirical work by East (1973), Kean and McGowan (1973), East and Hermann (1974), Salmore and Hermann (1969), and Salmore (1972) all identify economic development as one of several structural factors which play a critical role in determining differences in the foreign policy behavior of states.

It should be pointed out that the literature just cited has often failed to distinguish carefully between the structural and performance aspects of the economic factor. There has also been some confusion about the concepts of economic development, modernization, and national development in general. Furthermore, much of the literature ignores the distinction between level of economic development and type of economic system, a more politically related concept. Finally, there is a lack of consensus about the general question of what constitutes the most useful indicators of level of economic development.

Underlying all work involving economic structure and its relation to foreign policy behavior is the notion that the basic economic structure imposes certain constraints—and creates certain opportunities—in the foreign policy realm. The interaction between the agricultural and the industrial nature of a society, coupled with its level of economic development (regrettably, a rather stable characteristic), produce for the state a rather narrow set of options in interstate behavior. As we have noted, these contextual characteristics are quite different from a second class of economic indicators, such as crop failures, inflation and recession, and unemployment levels, which may have short-term and fluctuating impacts on foreign policy behavior.

Six variables representing economic structural characteristics were identified as potentially relevant intervening variables in the foreign policy process:

(1) gross national product per capita
(2) percentage of gross domestic product originating in agriculture
(3) percentage of gross domestic product originating in industry
(4) energy consumption per capita
(5) percentage of total economically active male population engaged in agricultural occupations
(6) percentage of total economically active male population engaged in professional and technical occupations.

CAPABILITY DIMENSION

Within the capability dimension we incorporate a mix of structural attributes loosely referred to in the literature as representing "power." Three distinct groupings of attributes can be identified: size, military power, and resource base.

While each of these groupings concerns a different aspect of capability and power potential, there has been a general lack of clarity in the literature concerning the role which each plays in the foreign policy process. Much of the literature simply zeroes in on one of these factors. For example, the Rosenau (1966) scheme utilizes size, usually operationalized as population, in order to classify foreign policy actors. Similarly, the importance of resource base as a factor in foreign policy behavior has been emphasized (Sprout and Sprout, 1971). The evolution of the recent rounds of the energy crisis in 1973, 1978, and 1979 highlights the fact that those states which are relatively weak in terms of size and military capability, but which possess a vital natural resource such as petroleum, can play a profound role in the international arena.

Once again, the reasoning which justifies the inclusion of such a grouping of structural characteristics as contextual variables involves the restrictions and opportunities which they provide to a state in the pursuit of its foreign policy. Unlike the economic realm, it is difficult to conceive of parallel short-term performance factors, since almost any change in the capability characteristics of a state will become a permanent factor in the size, military power, or resource realms. While a few states have dramatically altered their rankings on the capability dimension, this remains a relatively stable characteristic of states.

The variables which will be utilized to index the capability dimension are subdivided into three groups:

Size
(7)   total area
(8)   total population
(9)   gross national product

Military Power
(10)   total military manpower
(11)   total defense expenditure
(12)   defense expenditures per capita

Resource Base
(13)   percentage of energy consumed domestically produced

GOVERNMENTAL STRUCTURE DIMENSION

Scholars of comparative and interstate politics agree that type of political structure represents a critical factor in the classification of states. In fact, it is perhaps the only dimension which is emphasized both by those concerned with classifying domestic systems and by those concerned with foreign policy analysis.

The most widely used distinction with regard to governmental structure is the extent to which the political system is open or closed (Farrell, 1966). Important distinctions should also be made among the concepts of democratization, political development, and political stability (Gillespie, 1971: 376-377). Empirical research has clearly established the importance of governmental structure as a factor in explaining foreign policy behavior. Studies by Salmore (1972), Salmore and Hermann (1969), East and Hermann (1974), Moore (1974), Rosenau and Hoggard (1974), Rosenau and Ramsey (1975), Feierabend and Feierabend (1969), and Phillips and Hall (1970) have all attempted to assess the potency of political structure relative to other societal variables in explaining foreign policy behavior. We intend to continue these efforts by supplementing the open versus closed categories with a wide range of governmental structure variables.

The measures for the governmental structure dimension are considerably more elusive than those for the economic and capability dimensions. We were aided by considering the distinctions among political development, political structure, and political stability. Data on the stability indices were collected for the period 1946-1965, with an expected value calculated based on the predictability of an event of a certain type occurring during the period in question. Here we assume that the immediately preceding period provides the context in which other short-term instability events may occur. Once again, then, we highlight the distinction between structure and performance.

The following variables were incorporated into the classificatory scheme:[1]

Political Development
(14) number of political parties
(15) horizontal power distribution
(16) local government autonomy

Political Structure
(17) selection of effective executive
(18) legislative effectiveness
(19) legislative selection

Political Stability
(20) average number of coups per year, 1946-1965
(21) average number of constitutional changes per year, 1946-1965
(22) average number of major cabinet changes per year, 1946-1965
(23) average number of changes in effective executive per year, 1946-1965

DATA

Data were collected on variables 1-19 for the five-year period 1966-1970. Data on variables 20-23 were collected for the period

1946-1965. The 56-state sample discussed in Chapter 1 was the basis for data collection. The following is a brief description of the distribution characteristics of the data set. Missing data problems were evident for several of the variables. These were generally handled with the aid of estimation techniques for variables 2, 3, and 5, while the mean was generally substituted in the case of variable 6. Variables 7-13 were particularly affected by skewness and kurtosis problems, and were transformed utilizing the logarithm to the base 10 transformation.[2] Variable 14, pertaining to the number of political parties, was dichotomized into the categories of one party and more than one party.

FACTOR ANALYTIC RESULTS

Given the nature of the multiple-indicator approach adopted here, it was necessary to utilize a technique for consolidating the variables into indices. Factor analysis was identified as a suitable technique for this task, since it not only facilitates the identification of clusters of variables, but also indicates the relative weightings to be assigned to the variables within each cluster. In addition, through the computation of factor scores, precise interval scale values for each state on each of the factors generated can be calculated. While we recognize that the use of factor analytic techniques is fraught with statistical hazards, it was our judgment that it was an appropriate technique in this case, given the nature of the data and the ways in which the results were to be used.

Principal component analysis was utilized; a separate solution was computed for each of the five years for which data were collected, 1966-1970.[3] For purposes of brevity, only the solutions for 1966 and 1970 will be presented here. Tables 3.1 and 3.2 present the orthogonal rotations, with unities inserted as the diagonal elements. While the original variables were conceptualized into three categories, these results clearly indicate a four-factor solution, accounting for 72 to 74 percent of the total variance, with the governmental variables split into two distinct factors.

Factor I, which has been labeled "economic," accounts for about 35 percent of the common variance and is clearly the dominant factor in this solution. All six economic variables have high and exclusive loadings on this factor. In addition, defense expenditures per capita, originally conceptualized as a capability variable, also loads exclusively on this factor. Two other capability variables, GNP and total defense expenditures, have moderately high loadings on the economic factor, although their loadings are much stronger on the capability factor (Factor III).

Factor II, labeled "governmental," is composed solely of the variables which were intended to index political development and political structure. This factor explains about 26 percent of the common variance. Excluded from this factor are all four variables pertaining to political stability. This factor is quite homogeneous and exhibits no overlap with any of the other domains.

Factor III, which is comprised of the capability variables, explains about 22 percent of the common variance. It should be noted that this "capability" factor incorporates variables from all three of the capability subsets of size, resources, and military power. As we noted in connection with our discussion of Factor I, there is apparently a certain amount of conceptual as well as empirical overlap between the economic and capability dimensions.

Finally, Factor IV is obviously an "instability" indicator; the four variables which comprise it measure the extent of instability during the period 1946-1965. This factor, a subset of the originally conceptualized governmental cluster, accounts for 16 percent of the common variance.

Perhaps the most unique feature of the factor analytic solution discussed above is the identification of a four-factor structure. Much of the theoretical and empirical literature on the comparative study of foreign policy behavior classifies states into three broad categories: type of political system, level of economic development, and size (Rosenau, 1966; Sawyer, 1967; Rummel, 1969, 1972; Russett 1967; Russett et al., 1964). Here we

TABLE 3.1
Factor Analysis of Structural Attribute Data,
Orthogonal Rotation (1966)

	FACTOR I Economic	FACTOR II Governmental	FACTOR III Capability	FACTOR IV Instability	Communality
VAR. 1	(.81)	.38	.13	−.17	.85
VAR. 2	(−.82)	−.29	.11	−.08	.78
VAR. 3	(.72)	−.30	.26	−.16	.70
VAR. 4	(.80)	.27	.22	−.20	.81
VAR. 5	(−.84)	−.34	−.04	.16	.84
VAR. 6	(.88)	.30	−.10	−.15	.89
VAR. 7	−.14	.02	(.76)	.12	.62
VAR. 8	−.18	.19	(.93)	−.09	.95
VAR. 9	(.51)	.32	(.72)	−.23	.94
VAR. 10	.19	.07	(.82)	−.08	.72
VAR. 11	(.63)	.17	(.71)	−.17	.96
VAR. 12	(.93)	.04	.09	−.15	.91
VAR. 13	.17	−.18	(.61)	−.11	.44
VAR. 14	.15	(.82)	.12	−.01	.71
VAR. 15	.20	(.80)	.04	−.02	.69
VAR. 16	.24	(.64)	.02	−.06	.47
VAR. 17	.02	(.84)	−.06	.04	.71
VAR. 18	.30	(.82)	.11	−.27	.86
VAR. 19	.20	(.58)	.16	−.47	.62
VAR. 20	−.10	−.32	−.03	(.76)	.69
VAR. 21	−.37	−.08	.00	(.74)	.69
VAR. 22	−.04	−.11	−.16	(.71)	.55
VAR. 23	−.08	.21	−.01	(.77)	.64
% Total Variance	26.22%	19.13%	16.30%	12.22%	73.88%
% Common Variance	35.49%	25.89%	22.06%	16.54%	100.00%

NOTE: Principal component analysis, communalities of 1.0 inserted as diagonal elements. Parentheses indicate loadings $\geqslant \pm$ .50.

clearly unearth two distinct subsets of a political or governmental dimension. First, we have a factor which is roughly equivalent to the political accountability, open-closed, political development notions. We also encounter an additional factor, one which indicates degree of instability. In contrast to prior work in this area (Wilkenfeld, 1968, 1972; Zinnes and Wilkenfeld, 1971; Hazlewood, 1975), where short-term instabilty was treated exclusively as an independent variable in analyzing foreign policy behavior, long-term instability will now be incorporated as a contextual or mediating factor.

TABLE 3.2
Factor Analysis of Structural Attribute Data,
Orthogonal Rotation (1970)

	FACTOR I Economic	FACTOR II Governmental	FACTOR III Capability	FACTOR IV Instability	Communality
VAR. 1	(.81)	.40	.11	−.20	.87
VAR. 2	(−.86)	−.20	.10	−.12	.80
VAR. 3	(.66)	−.37	.24	−.01	.63
VAR. 4	(.79)	.30	.19	−.24	.81
VAR. 5	(−.84)	−.34	−.05	.17	.85
VAR. 6	(.86)	.26	−.20	−.23	.89
VAR. 7	−.14	.04	(.76)	.08	.61
VAR. 8	−.19	.19	(.93)	−.11	.95
VAR. 9	(.53)	.30	(.72)	−.24	.94
VAR. 10	.12	.02	(.85)	−.15	.76
VAR. 11	(.60)	.12	(.74)	−.19	.95
VAR. 12	(.92)	−.02	.11	−.15	.88
VAR. 13	.20	−.32	(.59)	.12	.50
VAR. 14	.04	(.78)	.15	.03	.63
VAR. 15	.16	(.84)	.04	−.01	.73
VAR. 16	.22	(.71)	.01	−.11	.57
VAR. 17	−.04	(.79)	−.06	.09	.63
VAR. 18	.34	(.81)	.05	−.14	.79
VAR. 19	.18	.48	.04	−.18	.30
VAR. 20	−.17	−.17	−.01	(.73)	.60
VAR. 21	−.35	−.03	.01	(.77)	.72
VAR. 22	.00	−.15	−.15	(.72)	.56
VAR. 23	−.04	.14	−.03	(.78)	.63
% Total Variance	25.60%	18.48%	16.48%	11.61%	72.17%
% Common Variance	35.47%	25.61%	22.83%	16.09%	100.00%

NOTE: Principal component analysis, communalities of 1.0 inserted as diagonal elements. Parentheses indicate loadings $\geq \pm$ .50.

Since the classificatory scheme which we are developing is based on the assumption that the structural characteristics of states are relatively stable over the short run, we must demonstrate that this is in fact the case with the particular data set at hand. Table 3.3 presents a summary of the yearly results in terms of the variance explained by each of the four factors generated for each year. It will be noted that there is remarkable stability across all five years, with the percentage of total variance explained varying between 72 and 74 percent.[4] Furthermore, the individual factors remain quite stable in terms of the percentage of common variance which each explains. Examination of the tables for each year reveals that the weightings of the variables within each factor across all five years remain stable. Thus, we have overwhelming evidence that the factors which we have identified constitute basic structural characteristics of states, which should be clearly differentiated from the more widely fluctuating performance variables incorporated in the independent variable clusters.

After generating these factor analytic results, two distinct strategies were pursued to produce a classificatory scheme. The first was the calculation of the factor scores for each state on the four structural dimensions for each of the five years in question. The second approach entailed the generation of a Q-factor analysis, resulting in the grouping of the 56 states into distinct typological categories based on the original 23 structural characteristic variables. Since each of these strategies yields results with utility for different types of analyses, both will be presented below.

Ranking of States on Structural Dimensions Based on Factor Scores

The calculation of factor scores for each state on each structural dimension enables us to generate a unique description for each state. These interval-level scores offer a very precise descriptive device; furthermore, states can be easily compared to each other in terms of their rankings on the structural dimension.

A straightforward calculation of factor scores, in which all 23 variables contributed to the calculation of each score for each state on each of the four dimensions, resulted in certain peculiarities on the economic and government factors. This was largely the result of "noise" from variables with loadings which approached but did not exceed .50 on a given factor. The use of oblique rotations did not improve the situation; in order to overcome the original problem, rotations of extreme degrees were required, resulting in too much conceptual clarity being

TABLE 3.3
Summary of Yearly Factor Analyses (1966-1970)

	1966	1967	1968	1969	1970
FACTOR I					
% Total Variance	26.22	26.70	25.78	26.00	25.60
% Common Variance	35.49	36.08	35.21	35.66	35.47
FACTOR II					
% Total Variance	19.13	18.83	17.78	18.26	18.48
% Common Variance	25.89	25.41	24.29	25.04	25.61
FACTOR III					
% Total Variance	16.30	16.39	16.35	16.17	16.48
% Common Variance	22.06	22.12	22.33	22.18	22.83
FACTOR IV					
% Total Variance	12.22	12.09	13.30	12.48	11.61
% Common Variance	16.54	16.34	18.17	17.12	16.09
SUMMARY					
Total Variance	73.88	74.01	73.21	72.91	72.17
Common Variance	100.00	100.00	100.00	100.00	100.00

sacrificed. The emerging factors were so highly correlated that there was a risk of encountering serious statistical problems in subsequent analyses.

A second strategy ultimately produced a set of factor scores[5] which apparently met our dual requirements of conceptual clarity and methodological simplicity. While the normal factor score calculations utilize factor-score coefficients for each variable on each factor, only those coefficients representing variables with loadings greater than or equal to .50 were utilized in the calculation of the present factor score. Although we thereby sacrificed the true orthogonality of the factors, and in fact would up with some moderately correlated factor score series, the level of correlation was far below the multicollinearity danger point. This solution, referred to as the "selectively generated factor scores," is presented in Table 3.4 for 1966 and Table 3.5 for 1970.[6]

In examining the ranking of states on the four structural dimensions, it should be reemphasized that the classificatory scheme has been generated for foreign policy analysis and therefore is based on those structural characteristics which are deemed to be critical in that policy area. Hence, the usefulness of this scheme for studies which focus on phenomena other than foreign policy processes is limited. Furthermore, the classificatory scheme is unique to the 56 states comprising our sample, i.e., those which were most active in the interstate realm during the period 1966-1970. It has been our contention all along that the level of interstate interaction exhibited by states occurs within the context of their structural characteristics, and consequently we would expect the structural characteristic scores for the less active 90 or so states to be considerably different from those which are presented here.

Grouping States by Q-Factor Analysis

A second analytic strategy adopted was that of Q-factor analysis. This classificatory technique is relevant to the present endeavor for several reasons. First, a classificatory scheme has traditionally been sought in order to parsimoniously categorize states into meaningful (i.e., theoretically effective) types distinguished by empirically unique combinations of values on several variables. These combinations, according to the framework, will affect the relative influence of variables upon foreign policy behavior.

Second, a discrete empirical typology of states simultaneously accepts the nomothetic model of research and permits "most similar systems" designs of comparison (Przeworski and Teune, 1972). Grouping states and analyzing within-group behavior allows hypothesis-testing under established parameters which cannot *account for* behavior but may, when varied, *discriminate* between group differences in behavior patterns (Lijphart, 1968).

Finally, such a classification scheme adds flexibility to research. It serves as an alternative method of parameter control to dimensions which, as continuous variables, may be controlled through statistical means only. Thus, the investigator may be

TABLE 3.4
Rank Ordering of States for Selectively Generated
Factor Scores (1966)

RANK	FACTOR I Economic	FACTOR II Governmental	FACTOR III Capability	FACTOR IV Instability
01	USA 2.375942	USA 1.639844	USR 2.491091	SYR 3.711786
02	SWD 1.738747	CHL 1.391912	USA 2.450612	COP 2.558101
03	CAN 1.668978	SWD 1.304250	CHN 2.296216	KEN 2.036827
04	GMW 1.610974	JAP 1.304250	IND 1.685975	ALG 1.785237
05	UNK 1.473933	PHI 1.124901	BRA 1.057577	LAO 1.518303
06	FRN 1.375375	GMW 1.056318	FRN 1.031772	IRQ 1.510479
07	CZE 1.351688	ITA 1.056318	GMW .995042	VTS 1.243833
08	GME 1.235346	DEN 1.056318	UNK .902993	FRN 1.113096
09	BEL 1.175229	TUR 1.056318	CAN .870481	UAR 1.056624
10	AUL 1.162059	IND 1.056318	JAP .849591	IRN .897628
11	USR 1.111959	AUL 1.056318	INS .762620	TAI .620232
12	DEN 1.110420	CAN 1.037239	ITA .734653	GRC .394794
13	NTH .987174	KEN .962891	PAK .664565	KOS .315504
14	ISR .889940	FRN .876972	IRN .610289	BRA .272735
15	HUN .789122	UNK .789307	POL .610285	JAP .271080
16	POL .756749	NTH .789307	SPN .553509	HUN .236951
17	ITA .575882	BEL .789307	TUR .516515	CAM .112169
18	RUM .402478	ISR .789307	AUL .447042	YEM .101444
19	JAP .402250	LEB .646379	RUM .359869	TUR −.065583
20	BUL .313856	MAL .627298	UAR .347537	GHA −.069088
21	CHL .232232	KOS .552952	YUG .244980	PAK −.073348
22	SAF .228992	SAF .541378	CZE .244582	CHL −.188479
23	SAU .143847	CYP .533869	GME .195233	JOR −.215349
24	CUB .046540	BRA .465288	ALG .150378	ITA −.232563
25	SPN .021495	PAK .379368	NIG .134221	CUB −.243246
26	IRQ .005920	GRC .274365	KOS .111536	NIG −.275038
27	YUG −.021870	UAR .254011	SAF .089106	LEB −.313835
28	PRO −.054022	YUG .061343	SAU .019302	BEL −.320163
29	CHN −.173604	IRN −.223239	IRQ −.039035	INS −.348373
30	JOR −.292909	POR −.348596	SWD −.095043	ISR −.347280
31	ALB −.298020	BUL −.348596	HUN −.114750	PHI −.383591
32	BRA −.325292	HUN −.417177	BUL −.170998	CZE −.393301
33	LEB −.378358	CZE −.436260	NTH −.197173	DEN −.454269
34	GRC −.383378	GME −.522180	TAI −.199571	BUL −.504111
35	IRN −.403022	COP −.535525	CHL −.253493	GMW −.534534
36	UAR −.407349	VTS −.591261	VTS −.276788	CHN −.544329
37	CYP −.430721	POL −.684190	GRC −.329028	GME −.550559
38	ALG −.592300	ALB −.684190	BEL −.335596	NTH −.551537
39	COP −.651511	RUM −.684190	COP −.353189	YUG −.581118
40	MAL −.661900	USR −.684190	POR −.364821	POL −.593207
41	TUR −.673512	CHN −.684190	PHI −.430763	SAF −.605293
42	SYR −.702350	CAM −.684190	ETH −.534725	ALB −.620546
43	VTS −.753070	SPN −.830155	CUB −.728168	POR −.624534
44	LAO −.787866	INS −.839190	MAL −.750682	CYP −.644541
45	KOS −.852716	TAI −.881169	DEN −.877409	IND −.647574
46	PHI −.969091	ETH −.983134	GHA −.972578	UNK −.657555
47	YEM −.973201	CUB −1.138132	SYR −1.035411	SAU −.720980
48	GHA −1.119487	ALG −1.138132	ISR −1.103774	RUM −.725816
49	IND −1.186360	IRQ −1.138132	KEN −1.133383	CAN −.733066
50	CAM −1.218724	SYR −1.138132	CAM −1.161989	ETH −.765998
51	TAI −1.264239	JOR −1.170062	ALB −1.218215	USR −.768407
52	PAK −1.256483	NIG −1.189145	LAO −1.440949	SWD −.787748
53	KEN −1.446887	LAO −1.189145	JOR −1.467068	USA −.808580
54	ETH −1.574867	GHA −1.437075	YEM −1.628046	AUL −.853590
55	NIG −1.591844	SAU −1.437075	LEB −1.757568	SPN −.929103
56	INS −1.642182	YEM −1.437075	CYP −2.457362	MAL −1.070456

TABLE 3.5
Rank Ordering of States for Selectively Generated
Factor Scores (1970)

RANK	FACTOR I Economic	FACTOR II Governmental	FACTOR III Capability	FACTOR IV Instability
01	USA 2.113028	USA 1.559754	USR 2.491738	SYR 3.772187
02	SWD 1.679824	CHL 1.283823	USA 2.383332	COP 2.639414
03	CAN 1.480558	SWD 1.255061	CHN 2.280417	KEN 2.109843
04	GMW 1.475811	JAP 1.255061	IND 1.655759	ALG 1.828538
05	UNK 1.261261	PHI 1.007747	BRA 1.082355	IRQ 1.543293
06	CZE 1.244414	GMW .979129	FRN .937995	LAO 1.524397
07	FRN 1.232169	ITA .979129	GMW .922234	VTS 1.237957
08	BEL 1.213791	DEN .979129	CAN .809321	FRN 1.145948
09	GME 1.189147	TUR .979129	INS .804086	UAR 1.083441
10	AUL 1.073924	IND .979129	UNK .789040	IRN .916072
11	USR 1.063352	AUL .979129	JAP .741313	TAI .620784
12	ISR 1.057062	CAN .978986	IRN .738782	GRC .404136
13	DEN 1.005672	KEN .832682	PAK .683139	KOS .319586
14	NTH .976766	FRN .731818	NIG .672194	JAP .285150
15	POL .727335	UNK .703054	ITA .659519	BRA .279243
16	HUN .666379	NTH .703054	POL .563649	HUN .224145
17	JAP .629544	BEL .703054	AUL .495980	CAM .127363
18	ITA .538359	ISR .703054	TUR .487547	YEM .106775
19	RUM 534514	VTS .657616	SPN .480795	PAK −.065969
20	BUL .415967	LEB .528134	UAR .465410	TUR −.067760
21	SAU .184051	SAF .427124	RUM .297867	GHA −.073853
22	SPN .164054	KOS .381686	GME .152435	CHL −.191400
23	CHL .151058	CYP .381539	YUG .151021	JOR −.212020
24	SAF .104082	BRA .352923	CZE .149469	ITA −.235779
25	YUG .033293	MAL .177855	ALG .127703	CUB −.257949
26	CUB −.023504	UAR .088275	SAU .056012	NIG −.271359
27	POR −.025508	TAI .048232	SAF .005339	LEB −.318123
28	IRQ −.048452	GHA −.024019	KOS −.022302	BEL −.329331
29	GRC −.155660	YUG −.043500	IRQ −.044179	INS −.347648
30	CHN −.166539	INS −.199084	TAI −.130915	ISR −.361957
31	IRN −.213636	COP −.218418	NTH −.145234	PHI −.390641
32	COP −.287697	IRN −.328710	SWD −.166331	CZE −.405612
33	ALB −.298978	POR −.494495	HUN −.178871	DEN −.463839
34	BRA −.340189	BUL −.494495	VTS −.228612	BUL −.513131
35	JOR −.354214	PAK −.503775	BUL −.236259	GMW −.543826
36	UAR −.359880	HUN −.523256	CHL −.293997	GME −.557956
37	LEB −.429490	GME −.624120	COP −.305225	CHN −.560473
38	CYP −.465597	JOR −.643456	GRC −.325243	NTH −.565852
39	SYR −.540919	IRQ −.678843	POR −.399126	YUG −.586452
40	ALG −.637829	SPN −.799186	PHI −.413104	POL −.602576
41	KOS −.742087	POL −.799186	BEL −.443680	SAF −.618697
42	TUR −.750727	CZE −.799186	MAL −.556144	ALB −.629338
43	MAL −.805762	ALB −.799186	ETH −.590104	POR −.635624
44	LAO −.836249	RUM −.799186	SYR −.604764	CYP −.651451
45	VTS −.937104	USR −.799186	CUB −.639416	IND −.657930
46	PHI −.955226	SYR −.799186	ISR −.736898	UNK −.675651
47	CAM −1.022764	CHN −.799186	GHA −.899524	SAU −.736957
48	YEM −1.083095	CAM −.799186	DEN −1.038458	RUM −.741190
49	NIG −1.087534	LAO −.818669	CAM −1.138265	CAN −.753078
50	TAI −1.102948	CUB −.974254	ALB −1.244316	ETH −.782020
51	IND −1.247037	ALG −.974254	KEN −1.309865	USR −.789679
52	GHA −1.338779	NIG −.993737	JOR −1.424354	SWD −.806606
53	PAK −1.424004	ETH −1.094599	LAO −1.550109	USA −.830509
54	KEN −1.424774	GRC −1.269666	YEM −1.683547	AUL −.875571
55	INS −1.472481	SAU −1.269666	LEB −1.788673	SPN −.958002
56	ETH −1.645551	YEM −1.269666	CYP −2.551937	MAL −1.099395

freed from the theoretically premature assumptions which particular statistical testing procedures require.

The use of Q-factor analysis in international politics has been relatively limited. Russett (1967) and Banks and Gregg (1965) have utilized the technique to group states according to their attributes, while Young (1975) has employed Q-analysis to group states according to behavioral characteristics.

Concerning the technique, Q-factor analysis quite simply reverses the variables and cases of a conventional R-factor analysis. Thus, for Q-factor analysis, the variables become the cases and the states become the variables. This results in factors which, in the present analysis, are composed of groupings of states, and the loadings indicate the extent to which a particular state is associated with a particular grouping of states.

The Q-factor analysis was performed on a 56×56 correlation matrix,[7] with five factors extracted on an orthogonal rotation (equimax). The results of this analysis are presented in Table 3.6 and in summary form in Figure 3.1. The major distinction identified by the analysis was that between the states of the "North" and the "South." Generally, all states which might be considered "developed" load on the first two factors, while the "less-developed" states load on factors three, four, and five. This might have been anticipated given the relative pervasiveness of economic variables in the data set, and lends support to perhaps the most widely discussed distinction underlying internation differences.

Perhaps more significantly, the pattern of state magnitude similarities on the stability and governmental variables delineated five rather than two types of states. Factors one and two, representing developed types, appear to support the familiar East-West distinction. The three less-developed groups apparently distinguish among *large developing* states, i.e., those with a growing measure of power in the international system; *unstable* states, with a moderately enriching economy; and *poor* states, those which constitute the "fourth world" of the globe. Six states—Thailand, Ghana, Kenya, Greece, Saudi Arabia, and Nigeria—could not be classified on any of the factors extracted.[8]

TABLE 3.6
Q-Factor Analysis of States on Structural Attribute Data
(1966-1970)

	West	Closed	Large Developing	Unstable	Poor	Communalities
UNITED STATES	(.61)	.37	.30	.15	.09	.63
CANADA	(.76)	.36	.23	.10	.17	.80
CUBA	.22	.44	.11	(.59)	.36	.73
BRAZIL	.28	.17	(.67)	.43	.13	.76
CHILE	(.64)	.00	.37	.27	.40	.78
UNITED KINGDOM	(.73)	.36	.30	.12	.11	.77
NETHERLANDS	(.77)	.36	.13	.15	.33	.87
BELGIUM	(.83)	.32	.04	.20	.29	.91
FRANCE	(.68)	.28	.22	.34	.08	.71
SPAIN	.25	(.67)	.36	.29	.13	.74
PORTUGAL	.22	(.55)	.21	.27	.46	.67
WEST GERMANY	(.77)	.37	.29	.15	.08	.84
EAST GERMANY	.50	(.60)	.07	.29	.11	.70
POLAND	.30	(.84)	.21	.21	.15	.89
HUNGARY	.36	(.62)	.01	.39	.30	.75
CZECHOSLOVAKIA	.48	(.71)	.06	.26	.21	.84
ITALY	(.74)	.20	.46	.11	.15	.83
ALBANIA	.17	.49	.12	.26	(.61)	.72
YUGOSLAVIA	.29	(.51)	.42	.04	.44	.71
GREECE	.19	.41	.24	.42	.42	.63
CYPRUS	.36	.11	.12	.28	(.77)	.82
BULGARIA	.26	(.69)	.11	.29	.39	.79
RUMANIA	.21	(.81)	.22	.23	.27	.87
USSR	.38	(.66)	.42	.20	.00	.79
SWEDEN	(.80)	.29	.16	.05	.33	.85
DENMARK	(.79)	.20	.09	.15	.46	.90
GHANA	.05	.23	.36	.51	.51	.70
NIGERIA	.00	.41	.48	.53	.27	.75
ZAIRE	.14	.14	.31	(.75)	.34	.81
KENYA	.77	.06	.41	.48	.50	.72
ETHIOPIA	-.06	.35	.49	.32	(.55)	.76
SOUTH AFRICA	(.52)	.30	.43	.14	.32	.66
ALGERIA	.09	.32	.33	(.75)	.24	.84
IRAN	.18	.38	.44	(.59)	.11	.72
TURKEY	.36	.03	(.72)	.23	.34	.81
IRAQ	.16	.38	.19	(.76)	.20	.86
UNITED ARAB REPUBLIC	.16	.23	.45	(.60)	.28	.71
SYRIA	.16	.20	.21	(.76)	.38	.82
LEBANON	.43	.03	.21	.30	(.69)	.79
JORDAN	.27	.22	.14	.35	(.63)	.66
ISRAEL	(.72)	.23	.02	.26	.45	.84
SAUDI ARABIA	.20	.54	.21	.56	.20	.72
YEMEN	.04	.25	.23	.53	(.58)	.73
CHINA	.19	.58	(.65)	.27	.04	.87
SOUTH KOREA	.19	.16	(.57)	.42	.38	.70
JAPAN	(.70)	.15	.44	.17	.16	.75
INDIA	.30	.21	(.83)	.16	.21	.88
PAKISTAN	.05	.26	(.75)	.40	.27	.86
THAILAND	.06	.21	.51	.50	.41	.72
CAMBODIA	.00	.26	.38	.38	(.65)	.77
LAOS	.08	.20	.26	.44	(.60)	.67
SOUTH VIETNAM	.20	.12	.40	(.53)	.40	.65
MALAYSIA	.27	.23	.53	.10	(.59)	.76
PHILIPPINES	.38	-.02	(.62)	.21	.52	.83
INDONESIA	.03	.33	(.69)	.47	.20	.85
AUSTRALIA	(.75)	.29	.26	.09	.24	.78
% TOTAL VARIANCE	18.53%	14.25%	14.73%	14.66%	14.36%	75.53%
% COMMON VARIANCE	24.53%	18.67%	19.50%	19.40%	19.01%	100.00%

NOTE: The scores reported here are average loadings, communalities, and percentages of variance explained over the five-year period 1966-1970. Parentheses indicate loadings $\geq$ .50, and into which factor a state will be classified.

West		
Belgium	.83	United Kingdom .73
Sweden	.80	Israel .72
Denmark	.79	Japan .70
West Germany	.77	France .68
Netherlands	.77	Chile .64
Canada	.76	USA .61
Australia	.75	South Africa .52
Italy	.74	

Large Developing

India	.83	Brazil .67
Pakistan	.75	China .65
Turkey	.72	Philippines .62
Indonesia	.69	South Korea .57

Poor

Cyprus	.77	Laos .60
Lebanon	.69	Malaysia .59
Cambodia	.65	Yemen .58
Jordan	.63	Ethiopia .55
Albania	.61	

Closed

Poland	.84	USSR .66
Rumania	.81	Hungary .62
Czechoslovakia	.71	East Germany .60
Bulgaria	.69	Portugal .55
Spain	.67	Yugoslavia .51

Unstable

Syria	.76	Egypt .60
Iraq	.76	Iran .59
Algeria	.75	Cuba .59
Zaire	.75	South Vietnam .53

Figure 3.1: Groupings of States

Table 3.7 presents a convenient way to acquire insight into the nature of the five factors extracted. Here we have computed the mean factor scores for each of the state groups on each of the factors extracted in the earlier R-factor analysis. Thus, we can see that the *Western* group has very high average scores on the economic and governmental dimensions, but is not nearly as strong on the capability dimension. Its level of instability is low and relatively indistinguishable from all but the *unstable* group.

The *closed* group ranks second behind the *Western* group in terms of its mean score on the economic dimension. Its governmental structure score is clearly distinguishable from the *Western* and *large developing* groups, but is similar to the *unstable* and *poor* states. As noted above, the score for this group on the capability dimension is similar to that of the *Western* and *unstable* states. In fact, it is only clearly distinguishable in this respect from the *poor* states. Finally, this group shows the most negative scores of all the groups on the instability dimension (i.e., it is the most stable group).

The *large developing* group ranks lowest in terms of the economic dimension, closely resembling the *poor* group in this respect. These states are most similar to the *Western* group in terms of governmental structure. The *large developing* group possesses the highest score on the capability dimension, although this score may not be significantly different from the *Western* and *closed* groups. In terms of instability, it is basically indistinguishable from all but the *unstable* group.

The *unstable* group ranks among the lowest in terms of economic power, and is similar to the *closed* and *poor* groups on the dimension of governmental structure. The capability score for the group is quite low, while it is the most unstable of all groups by a considerable margin.

Finally, the *poor* states exhibit a low mean score on the economic dimension and a score similar to the *closed* and *unstable* groups on the governmental dimension. This is clearly the weakest group in terms of capabilities. Concerning instability, this group is clearly distinguishable only from the *unstable* group.

TABLE 3.7

Group Means on Structural Dimensions (1966-1970)[a]

	Economic	Governmental	Capability	Instability
West	1.09(±.29)[b]	.99(±.16)	.35(±.45)	−.37(±.25)
Closed	.59(±.31)	−.57(±.16)	.37(±.51)	−.54(±.20)
Large Developing	−.90(±.33)	.34(±.51)	.84(±.61)	−.18(±.23)
Unstable	−.41(±.21)	−.52(±.43)	−.12(±.35)	1.53(±.80)
Poor	−.76(±.29)	−.45(±.49)	−1.40(±.39)	−.21(±.49)

a. These means were calculated yearly for 1966-1970. The means reported here are averaged over the five years.
b. From these scores, a 95% confidence interval can be calculated. Thus, we can tell the extent to which these means are significantly different from each other within a single structural dimension.

There are several additional ways in which we can profile the distinctions among the five groups of states identified here. Quite obviously, the East-West, North-South classifications which have been dealt with so extensively in prior research are present in this scheme. Furthermore, the notion of sociocultural regions is also pertinent here. Finally, an examination of the groups in terms of conventional geographic regions reveals close similarities. It should be pointed out that although East-West, sociocultural, and geographic factors were not explicitly included in the 23-variable structural scheme, the Q-factor solution discussed above clearly identifies groupings which relate to these well-known factors. The intermix of these three factors argues strongly for the reliability of this approach to classificatory scheme construction. The fact that patterns resemble these important distinctions, and yet exhibit at the same time significant deviations, generally supports the multivariate, structural approach adopted here.

These patterns, however, should not detract from the uniqueness of the present solution. To the extent that we have carefully specified those structural characteristics of states which are most relevant as a context for foreign policy behavior, this classificatory scheme should provide more reliable descriptions of foreign policy behavior than we have had in the past.

CONCLUSION

It might be worthwhile to return briefly to a question which we posed earlier in this chapter: Why classify? The answer clearly lies in our increased ability to describe, explain, and predict foreign policy phenomena. We are not implying that there is complete uniformity among the states which comprise a particular typological group. As we have noted, if the researcher is interested in a unique description of the structural characteristics of a particular state, the selectively generated factor scores of that state derived from the R-factor analyses, which designate four structural dimensions, would be the most helpful. Here we refer to the individual scores on the four dimensions of economic structure, governmental structure, capability, and instability.

However, the Q-factor analytic groupings of *Western*, *closed*, *large developing*, *unstable*, and *poor* allow for the generation and testing of propositions concerning the differences among these groups, and in that sense make a contribution to the scientific study of foreign policy behavior. If a reliable, valid classificatory scheme is a precondition for producing viable generalizations, as we have posited from the beginning, then noteworthy findings should emerge in subsequent empirical research.

As we noted at the outset, while foreign policy analysis has elicited an increasing amount of attention in the past decade and a half, the research product, in terms of its reliability and usefulness, has not been commensurate with the volume. One egregious manifestation of this gap between quality and quantity is the continued reliance on classificatory schemes which fail to incorporate a representative or comprehensive sample of critical state attributes. The classificatory scheme which we have outlined here both conceptually and empirically is an integral feature of an analytical framework for analyzing foreign policy behavior. In subsequent chapters we will begin to test the utility of this scheme for describing, explaining, and predicting foreign policy behavior.

NOTES

1. Data for several of the variables in this section were taken from Banks (1971). In the cases of variables 20-23, the data were appropriately standardized for new states with less than twenty years of data.

2. The proper transformation was determined by comparing the shape of the distributions of the IBA variables to skewed distributions presented by Rummel (1970). All the skewed cases exhibited a right skew, and consequently the logarithm to the base 10 transformation was deemed the most appropriate. In fact, it solved virtually all of the skewness problem.

3. At this point two analytic strategies were possible. On the one hand, we could have combined all five years of data, producing 5×56 cases, and performed a single-factor

analysis on this data set. On the other hand, we could have factor analyzed the data set for each year separately, thus producing five distinct solutions. The latter strategy was ultimately chosen, since we wished to demonstrate the stability of the structural indicators over time.

4. It should be noted that for each of the five yearly factor analyses, the same instability data pertaining to the period 1946-1965 were used. Thus, the stability of this factor across the five years should not be at all surprising.

5. We use the term "factor score" loosely since, strictly speaking, the score we calculate here does not meet the normal definition of a factor score.

6. As was the case with the factors themselves (see Table 3.3), the rankings of states on the factor scores reveal remarkable stability over the five-year period. Correlations of factor scores over the five years reveal values around .99 for the most part.

7. The Q-factor analysis was performed on a matrix of eta coefficients, where each eta represented a pattern-magnitude measure of similarity (Rummel, 1970:301) between two states for 23 variables. The statistic was computed according to the ANOVA formula (Blalock, 1972) after modifications to the multivariate, two-case situation were made. Estimates of within- and between-class variances were made according to formulae supplied by Kendall and Stuart (1958). See also Rummel (1970: 301-302). This method was judged superior but complementary to the Kendall and Stuart r_i.

8. A state was categorized in the factor-type for which it had the highest mean loading, if this loading was greater than .50 and exceeded the second highest mean loading by .05. The first criterion assured a minimum level of similarity between the state and a factor-type. The second criterion sought to eliminate states which were similar to more than one factor-type and thereby made categorization difficult.

Chapter 4

Classification of Foreign Policy

As we noted in the previous chapter, the careful construction of classificatory schemes is essential to the production of reliable and useful knowledge in the realm of foreign policy analysis. We postulated at the outset that an adequate foreign policy framework should include two classificatory devices. The first, dealt with in Chapter 3, concerns the typing of foreign policy actors on the basis of their stable structural characteristics. The second, outlined in the current chapter, focuses upon the conceptualization of typological dimensions which describe foreign policy action.

To a great extent, the lack of systematic progress in scientific foreign policy analysis is directly attributable to the collective failure of researchers to define, depict, and observe with consistency the basic unit of analysis—foreign policy (Meehan, 1971; Morse, 1971). As Rosenau et al. (1973: 12) concluded in their evaluation of the Inter-University Comparative Foreign Policy Project (ICFP):

> The issue most constraining to subsequent research proved to be our inability to make progress in solving the problem of identifying, classifying, and operationalizing types of foreign policy behavior.

If the subfield of foreign policy is to experience progress, the perplexing problems which pervade efforts to conceptualize, classify, and operationalize foreign policy must be solved.

While definitions of foreign policy abound, they have rarely shared common analytical assumptions. All too often, researchers have attempted to define foreign policy on the basis of "mental model(s) of the distinguishing features of state behavior... on the assumption that the classes defined represent characteristics which cluster empirically" (Kegley, 1973: 8). Accordingly, foreign policies have been defined on the basis of regional identifications, goals, orientations, and inferred motivations, to cite a few examples (see the summaries in C. F. Hermann, 1972; Salmore and Munton, 1974; Kegley, 1973).

Scholars who are social scientific in orientation have defined foreign policy as a behavioral concept and as a phenomenon which is based solely upon "action properties" (C. F. Hermann, 1972: 61). These "behavioralists" have directed foreign policy analysis to the study of interstate activities. In the process, they have moved away from simple intuitive labeling and toward definitions of foreign policy which reflect systematic observations.

Our intention has been to develop a definition of foreign policy which is based on action properties. While strategies, goals, and other attitudinal factors are important components in the study of foreign policy, we will assume that behavioral output is the major concern of foreign policy analysis. For our purposes, foreign policy may thus be viewed as *consisting of those official actions (and reactions) which sovereign states initiate (or receive and subsequently react to) for the purpose of altering or creating a condition (or problem) outside their territorial-sovereign boundaries.*

CONCEPTUALIZING FOREIGN POLICY

The above definition of foreign policy is clearly based on action properties; hence, the concept of "action" should be briefly examined. In the present conceptualization, the term "event" may be posited to be a conceptual equivalent of the term "action." As an abstract concept, events have been portrayed as subjectively differentiated portions of reality (Riker, 1957: 58-59):

> Although reality is continuous, human perception is not. For a variety of reasons we are unable to comprehend the whole of this continuous reality. For one reason, we are temporally and spatially inside it...and thus lack an external perspective. For another, more immediate reason, we cannot comprehend because of the complexity of detail that confronts us.
>
> Faced with the complexity of continuous reality, humans understand it by breaking it up into pieces. Although a continuous reality cannot, by definition, consist of discrete motions and actions, we imagine starts and stops. What lies between the starts and stops we call events. Events are motion and action separated out of the continuous reality by the verbal imposition of boundaries.

Foreign policy analysts, "faced with the complexity of continuous reality," must break it up into pieces—or events—which can be more easily scrutinized. As the only available units of observation, events serve as the empirical referent for the definition and description of foreign policies, and therefore as the standard unit of comparison among foreign policies (C. F. Hermann, 1971).

In order to utilize the event concept in portraying and comparing foreign policies, we must assume that all events are comprised of a number of common attributes; the latter collectively determine the overall nature of events. Such attributes cluster around the following six abstract dimensions: (1) spatial; (2) temporal; (3) relational; (4) situational; (5) substantial; and (6) behavioral.

The *spatial* dimension refers to the particular area in which the event is occurring. In foreign policy analysis, this consists of the particular geographic positions occupied by the states which act and interact.

The *temporal* dimension refers to the time period in which an event is occurring or has occurred.

The *relational* dimension yields attributes which concern the event's participants. Here we focus on the number of parties involved in the event, as well as on their hierarchical order. In foreign policy analysis, relational attributes can refer to geographic proximity, to the actual number of actors involved in an event, and to the states' relationships to the initiation and reception components of action.

Subsumed under the rubric of *situational* attributes is the operational context within which a decision must be made. This dimension features the answers to such decision-maker questions as: "How much time have I got?"; "How serious is that?"; "Were we prepared for this (event), or did it take us by surprise?" Furthermore, situational attributes refer to the context of other events.

The *substantial* dimension specifies the issue-specific context of the event. Is the event, by nature, economic, political, military, or diplomatic?

The *behavioral* dimension generates attributes which relate to behavioral characteristics; this may be conceptualized in terms of a cooperative-conflictual continuum along which behavioral attributes might be identified.

From an analytical perspective, the identification of six‧ distinct dimensions assures the delineation of virtually all of the major attributes of an event.[1] While many analysts have found it convenient to operationalize their conceptualizations of foreign policy events on the basis of "*who* does *what* to *whom*?" (Shapiro and O'Leary, 1974: 2), we are now in a position to ask "*who* does *what to whom*, *where*, *when*, *over what*, and in what immediate *context*?"

CLASSIFYING FOREIGN POLICY

Foreign policy events thus consist of six abstract, universal dimensions upon which more concrete attributes may be located. We should note that several foreign policy analysts have at least implicitly employed some of the six dimensions to "code" foreign policy events. Analysts such as McClelland and Young (1969), Azar (1971), Rummel (1972), and C. F. Hermann et al. (1973) have attempted to construct definitional and ad hoc classificatory schemes (Burgess and Lawton, 1972). For purposes of conceptual comprehensiveness, we have identified a relatively large number of dimensional attributes.

Spatial dimensional attributes include: (1) Africa; (2) East Mediterranean; (3) Eastern Europe; (4) Western Europe; (5) North-Central Asia; (6) East Asia; (7) South Asia; (8) North America; (9) Central America; and (10) South America.

The relational dimension is comprised of attributes which refer to the relative position, identity, and "nature" of the entities in action or interaction. The distinction between the arena in which action takes place and the nature of that arena is a logical one from the perspective of the policy maker. That is, foreign policy behavior is affected by the relative positions of the involved parties and by the issue of where the parties are situated in relation to other parties.

The situational dimension has recently elicited considerable attention (Paige, 1968; C. F. Hermann, 1969; C. F. Hermann et al., 1973; Brady, 1974, 1978). C. F. Hermann (1969) suggests that foreign policy events may be categorized along three situational—or contextual—continua: (1) decision time; (2) awareness; and (3) threat. Along the individual continuum, Hermann juxtaposes short and extended decision time, anticipation and surprise with regard to awareness, and high and low threat.

The substantial dimension has also received extensive prior scrutiny (Rosenau, 1966; Brecher et al., 1969; Leutner, 1974; Shapiro and O'Leary, 1974). The present scheme accords significance to the following issue areas (attributes) from both the policy maker's and the analyst's points of view: (1) military; (2) economic; (3) territorial; (4) scientific; (5) cultural; (6) organizational; and (7) legal.

The behavioral dimension features attributes which describe the level of cooperation or conflict which characterizes the event. Events may be categorized according to forms and intensities of cooperation or conflict.

Figure 4.1 summarizes this classificatory scheme of foreign policy events. The events are related to foreign policy actions when, within the relational dimension, states which initiate the event can be identified. Those events initiated by a state comprise that state's foreign policy acts.

OPERATIONALIZING FOREIGN POLICY BEHAVIOR: INDEPENDENT AND DEPENDENT VARIABLES

The above definition and conceptualization of foreign policy behavior raises three issues for the operationalization stage. First, foreign policy indicators should rely upon structured observations and codifications of interstate events. Second, the individual foreign policy actions of a state, described as events, should relate to a portrayal of foreign policy activity. Third, the foreign policy events should provide information pertaining both to state behavior and to actions which are initiated by other states and may affect foreign policy (as a part of the interstate component).

The observation and description of international events pose several problems for the empirical researcher. As Burgess and Lawton (1972: 59-68) have noted, the process of identifying and categorizing events is subject to massive reliability and validity difficulties. Especially troublesome is the effect upon validity of the chosen source of information; questions of source coverage, combined with the tendencies of newspapers to idiosyncratically underreport and overreport various event sequences, lead to errors in the data-definition stage. Conversely, a truly ambitious data-collection effort, perhaps one which utilized non-public sources, could result in the identification of so many events that data management would become difficult and events would become similar to transactions (Burgess and Lawton, 1972: 66).

The IBA Project chose to rely upon the most complete, current, and frequently used set of events data which is available: the World Event Interaction Survey (WEIS) data set (see McClelland, 1968; McClelland and Hoggard, 1969; McClelland and Young, 1969). The WEIS events cover all members of the

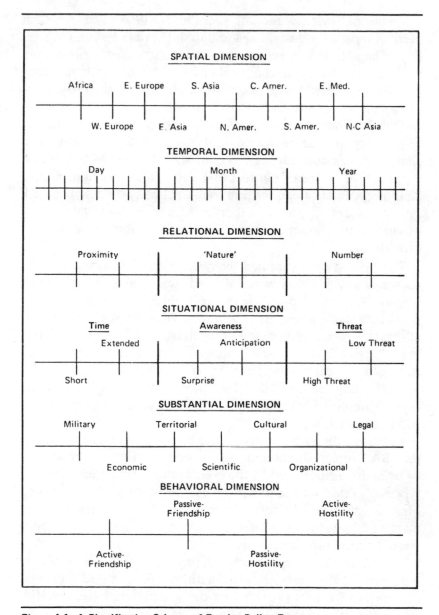

Figure 4.1: A Classification Scheme of Foreign Policy Events

international system and all years since 1966. Because each event is separately described and dated, the data set is most flexible. The sole-source reliance upon the *New York Times* may lead to some biased overreporting of events of particular concern to the United States, but this publication is the most commonly utilized events-data source.[2]

The WEIS data set supplies information on each event corresponding to the temporal dimension (date of event) and spatial dimension (arena). Table 4.1 depicts a behavioral typology; 63 forms of conflict and cooperation, organized into 22 more general categories, are used to classify events. The data set also codes the relational roles of the initiator and target of each event. Situational and substantial information are not provided.

The information supplied by WEIS allows us to specify, for each state, which acts were initiated, when, and toward which targets. We may also denote the acts which were directed at the particular state, when, and by whom. Thus the WEIS data base allows the operationalization of foreign policy behavior sent (initiated) by each state and of foreign policy behavior received by (targeted to) each state. The latter concern refers to the interstate component of the IBA framework, which includes actions (stimuli) of other states as explanations of foreign policy behavior (see Chapter 1).

Given an ability to describe foreign policy events or actions, the IBA Project sought a means to depict foreign policy activity or behavior as indicated by the events data. Knowledge of which types of events were initiated by (or directed at) the state is of limited value in comparative research. The classified events must yield a set of measures which can be compared and contrasted across time and across states.

The most basic comparative measure of foreign policy behavior is the frequency of action. Using the 22 general categories of events provided by the WEIS data base, the IBA Project computed the number of events of each type which were initiated by the state during a given year. Similarly, the number of events of each type which were directed to the state defined 22 indicators of foreign policy behavior stimuli received by the state.

TABLE 4.1
The Weis Events Coding Scheme

1. YIELD

011	Surrender, yield to order, submit to arrest, etc.
012	Yield position; retreat; evacuate
013	Admit wrongdoing; retract statement

2. COMMENT

021	Explicit decline to comment
022	Comment on situation-pessimistic
023	Comment on situation-neutral
024	Comment on situation-optimistic
025	Explain policy or future position

3. CONSULT

031	Meet with; at a neutral site; or send note
032	Visit; go to
033	Receive visit; host

4. APPROVE

041	Praise, hail, applaud, condolences
042	Endorse other policy or position; give verbal support

5. PROMISE

051	Promise own policy support
052	Promise material support
053	Promise other future support
054	Assure; reassure

6. GRANT

061	Express regret; apologize
062	Give state invitation
063	Grant asylum
064	Grant privilege, diplomatic recognition de facto relations, etc.
065	Suspend negative sanctions; truce
066	Release and/or return persons or property

7. REWARD

071	Extend economic aid
072	Extend military assistance
973	Give other assistance

8. AGREE

081	Make substantive agreement
082	Agree to future action or procedure; agree to meet, to negotiate

9. REQUEST

091	Ask for information
092	Ask for policy assistance
093	Ask for material assistance
094	Request action; call for
095	Entreat; plead; appeal to

10. PROPOSE

101	Offer proposal
102	Urge or suggest action or policy

11. REJECT

111	Turn down proposal; reject protest demand, threat, etc.
112	Refuse; oppose, refuse to allow

12. ACCUSE

121	Charge; criticize; blame; disapprove
122	Denounce; denigrate; abuse

13. PROTEST

131	Make complaint (not formal)
132	Formal complaint or protest

14. DENY

141	Deny an accusation
142	Deny an attributed policy, action, role or position

15. DEMAND

150	Issue order or command, insist; demand compliance, etc.

16. WARN

160	Give warning

17. THREATEN

171	Threat without specific negative sanctions
172	Threat with specific negative sanctions
173	Threat with force specified
174	Ultimatum; threat with time limit and negative sanctions specified

18. DEMONSTRATE

181	Nonmilitary demonstration; walk-out on
182	Armed force mobilization, exercise and/or display

19. REDUCE RELATIONSHIP

191	Cancel or postpone event
192	Reduce routine international activity; recall officials, etc.
194	Halt negotiations
195	Break diplomatic relations

20. EXPEL

201	Order personnel out of country
202	Expel organization or group

21. SEIZE

211	Seize position or possessions
212	Detain or arrest person(s)

22. FORCE

221	Non-injury destructive act
222	Nonmilitary injury/descruction
223	Military engagement

These variables, then, were analyzed for the purpose of delineating a more concise set of indicators of foreign behavior. It was felt that underlying dimensions of foreign policy activity or behavior account for the frequencies of action-types observed across states. In order to identify these dimensions, we consulted previous analytical work in the foreign policy events sub-field (e.g., Young, 1975; Rummel, 1963; Tanter, 1966). Initial-ly, we accepted the operationalization which was suggested in Young's (1975) analysis. Using WEIS data from 1966 through 1969, Young found that three aspects of foreign policy behavior underlie event frequencies: diplomatic exchange activity, non-military conflict activity, and military conflict behavior. Employing a weighted summation of event frequencies, scores could be attributed to each state for each dimension of foreign policy behavior. Moreover, scores could be computed on these dimensions for behavior received by (targeted to) the state.

Further consideration of these results led the IBA Project to analyze the WEIS data more thoroughly and reject the assumption that dimensions of foreign policy behavior are consistent for actions sent and actions received. Phillips (1973) discovered that conflict initiation dimensionalizes differently from conflict reception. For our wider range of foreign policy events, a similar situation seems plausible. In the absence of an over-whelming stimulus-response mechanism wherein a received event always results in a particular action-type, the structure of decision makers' behavior is likely to differ from the structure of stimuli which enters the state's perceptual apparatus.[3]

Tables 4.2 and 4.3 present the factor analytic results for behavior sent and behavior received for the sample of 56 states for the 1966-1970 period. These analyses can be viewed as over-time factor analyses in the sense that each country-year con-stitutes a separate case, yielding 56×5 or 280 cases. A principal component solution was chosen with communality estimates replacing the main diagonal elements in the correlation matrices, and a varimax rotation.

A comparison of the factor analytic results for behavior sent and behavior received is quite revealing. The analysis of the behavior-sent data is virtually identical to the Young (1975) analysis, despite the fact that less than half of the states which were examined in that earlier analysis were analyzed here. Fur-thermore, an additional year (1970) of data has been added to the current analysis.

The first factor, designated as "constructive diplomatic behavior," explained 49 percent of the total variance and large-

TABLE 4.2
Factor Analysis of Weis Behavior-Sent Data,
Varimax Rotation (1966-1970)

	I	II	III	h^2
Yield	(.77)	.17	.21	.67
Comment	(.88)	.20	.34	.92
Consult	(.87)	.37	.19	.93
Approve	(.87)	.34	.14	.90
Promise	(.89)	.35	.08	.92
Grant	(.81)	.38	.04	.80
Reward	(.91)	.21	.03	.88
Agree	(.78)	.43	.05	.80
Request	(.82)	.24	.36	.87
Propose	(.91)	.31	.10	.93
Reject	(.68)	.48	.29	.78
Accuse	.37	(.74)	.32	.80
Protest	(.50)	(.74)	.09	.81
Deny	(.80)	.26	.36	.84
Demand	.25	(.84)	.14	.79
Warn	(.67)	(.56)	.37	.90
Threaten	.46	(.51)	.41	.63
Demonstrate	.26	(.70)	.01	.56
Negative Sanction	(.64)	.36	−.05	.54
Expel	.19	(.70)	−.05	.53
Seize	.14	(.63)	.30	.51
Force	.17	.14	(.87)	81
% Total Variance	49.23%	23.50%	8.50%	81.23%
% Common Variance	60.60%	28.93%	10.46%	100.00%

NOTE: Parentheses indicate loadings $\geq \pm$ .50.

ly underlies the following 14 foreign policy event categories:
yield, comment, consult, approve, promise, grant, reward,
agree, request, propose, reject, deny, warn, and negative sanc-
tions. The dimension includes actions of a cooperative nature.
The four conflictual actions included in the diplomatic dimension should be interpreted as manipulative tools for constructive, as opposed to destructive, diplomatic relationships. The second factor, labeled "nonmilitary conflict," accounted for 23
percent of the total variance, and included actions of a decidedly negative orientation: accuse, protest, demand, threaten,
demonstrate, expel, and seize. Finally, a third factor emerged
which explained only 9 percent of the total variance; only the
force category loaded here and this dimension was appropriately labeled "force." Overall, these three factors explained 81 percent of the variance.

TABLE 4.3
Factor Analysis of Weis Behavior-Received Data,
Varimax Rotation (1966-1970)

	I	II	III	h^2
Yield	.23	.13	(.74)	.61
Comment	(.90)	.18	.21	.88
Consult	(.90)	.28	.18	.92
Approve	(.90)	.18	.16	.87
Promise	(.52)	.35	.41	.56
Grant	(.92)	.14	.19	.91
Reward	.03	.14	(.79)	.64
Agree	(.88)	.08	.21	.83
Request	(.89)	.31	.14	.91
Propose	(.87)	.32	.18	.90
Reject	(.93)	.17	.17	.92
Accuse	(.88)	.41	.03	.95
Protest	(.76)	.22	.10	.64
Deny	(.56)	(.56)	.12	.65
Demand	(.78)	.39	.14	.79
Warn	(.83)	.43	.10	.88
Threaten	(.62)	(.57)	.09	.72
Demonstrate	(.91)	.11	.10	.85
Negative Sanction	(.64)	.24	.25	.53
Expel	(.87)	.11	.02	.77
Seize	(.83)	.30	.18	.81
Force	.08	(.78)	.40	.77
% Total Variance	58.32%	11.50%	8.82%	78.64%
% Common Variance	74.16%	14.62%	11.21%	100.00%

NOTE: Parentheses indicate loadings $\geqslant \pm$ .50.

The analysis of the behavior-received data revealed significantly different patterns. A single dominant foreign behavior factor was extracted; this factor explained 58 percent of the total variance and incorporated 19 of the 22 variables. The factor contained a mix of both conflict and cooperation indicators, although it is a somewhat different combination of indicators than that observed in the constructive diplomatic behavior factor above. We designated the factor "diplomatic behavior." The second factor, "force," reflected force acts and, to a lesser degree, threats and denials, and explained 12 percent of the total variance. Loading on the third factor were two variables connoting positive affect: yield and reward. This dimension was labeled "reward"; it explained 9 percent of the total variance. As will be noted, the three factors combined to explain 79 percent of the variance in behavior received.

Using weighted summations of event-category frequencies, we operationalized foreign policy behavior, the variable ultimately to be explained in our framework, with three indicators:

(1) constructive diplomatic behavior
(2) nonmilitary conflict
(3) force

This triadic pattern suggests that decision makers structure their behavior by distinguishing between generally amiable actions and more hostile acts, while preserving the use of force as a demonstrable act of extreme disfavor.

A similar use of the factor analytic results regarding events targeted at (i.e., received by) states yields three indicators of foreign policy behavior stimuli, housed within the interstate component of the IBA framework:

(1) diplomatic behavior
(2) force
(3) reward

This dimensionalization implies that the more demonstrable acts of favor and disfavor are separable types of stimuli received by the state, whereas most conflictual and cooperative actions are more ambiguous and merge within a general factor labeled here as diplomacy.

The differing factor structures point to a communications theory perspective regarding behaviors targeted at states, and to a more traditional interpretation of actions as they are initiated. The latter tend to be structured according to the conflict-cooperation-force trichotomy of decision-making options; the cooperation category, however, seems to include some forms of conflict which are not decidedly negatively oriented. The former, actions received by states, conform to a structure of positive-negative-ambiguous messages in which only the most unambiguous messages are definitively accorded special status. To the extent that perceptual mechanisms reflect the structure of these incoming events, this triadic pattern will operate.

Also noteworthy, perhaps, are the different positions of particular event-types within these structures. Threats and denials, for example, appear to be received with a much more negative hue than that with which they are sent. Rewards and yields, initiated as normal constructive tools of diplomacy, seem to be received with especially positive status. Finally, the more subtle distinction between constructive and conflictual behavior, which is apparent in the structure of actions initiated, apparently becomes blurred within the reception structure, which distinguishes only strong acts of positive and negative valuation. These differences, while slight in comparison to the overall similarity of the patterns, may indicate subtle but important complexities within the action-reaction portion of our framework. Subsequent analyses will further explore this linkage.

NOTES

1. It is conceivable that an instrumental dimension—referring to the "how" in the "who does what to whom..." sequence—might be added. On the other hand, instrumental attributes are implicitly subsumed within the behavioral and substantial dimensions. In the interest of parsimony, we can consequently avoid adding yet another variable.

2. It is not our intention here to discuss the advantages and disadvantages of the utilization of event data. Nor will we discuss the problems of source coverage, reliability, and validity. For general treatments of these and related problems, see Azar et al. (1972a, 1972b), Sigler et al. (1972), Burgess and Lawton (1972), and Burrowes (1974).

3. We have accorded a significant amount of thought to the question of whether it is plausible to argue that different structures of events received and events sent can be usefully explained by reliance on leadership perception. Our feeling is that when decision makers/perceivers observe incoming events, they attempt to categorize them and draw inferences from events to behavioral dimensions in an effort to separate the meanings of events. The present factor analyses attempt to locate the possible ways states as aggregate entities manage to perceive and to structure that perception.

Chapter 5

Scientific Analyses of Foreign Policy Behavior

An Overview and Specification of Strategies

Previous chapters have chronicled the development of the Interstate Behavior Analysis Project framework from its conceptual underpinnings, to the actual construction and refinement of an analytical framework, to, finally, the assembly and collection of data sets in the various realms. It is obvious that the utility of the mass of empirical data depends upon the design and application of a series of appropriate—and increasingly sophisticated—methodologies for converting the framework into an actual model and generating empirically tested propositions. The failure to specify analytical strategies and conduct appropriate tests would relegate the IBA framework to the conceptual museum which houses so many of its predecessors. Thus, we maintain that analysis of the data should be the product of an organized, purposive analytical strategy in order to ascertain the relevance of the framework for the crucial tasks of explaining and eventually forecasting foreign policy.

This chapter sets forth the models and techniques of statistical inquiry which infuse the analytical phase of our research effort. We focus upon two broad realms:

(1) The model and statistical techniques which relate the data within the domain of the components—or independent variables—to the dimensions of foreign policy behavior.
(2) The model and statistical techniques which can be employed for the purpose of imposing controls for taking into account the mediating role of state typological characteristics.

Technical details will be provided in the appendix to this chapter; here, we provide an overview of the methodologies which will be employed in subsequent chapters. We shall treat the two methodological tasks independently and apply the selected solutions concurrently.

RELATING INDICATORS AND COMPONENTS TO FOREIGN BEHAVIOR

Given the existence of a voluminous and relatively comprehensive data set, we might have pursued one of two conventional paths of data analysis. The first entails the generation of massive outputs of correlation coefficients and a search for "significant" relationships between posited independent variables and foreign policy measures. The second route involves the identification of the dimensions which underlie the manifest indicators and either pinpoints those which display close associations with measures of foreign behavior or employs dimension scores—rather than indicators per se—to account for variation in foreign policy behavior.[1]

Since we have anchored our research in the context of an overarching framework, we avoided both of these options. The correlational approach would obviously highlight bivariate relationships between individual indicators and measures of foreign behavior output; it would simultaneously, however, ignore the impact of other variables both within and external to the indicator's general component. The painstaking specification of components would consequently be equivalent to a futile conceptual exercise. The dimensionalization approach features an analogous flaw, in that the conceptual categories are replaced by empirically determined clusters; this reduces the importance of unique indicators and inflates the role of general "factors." The framework suggests that both components (general conceptual arenas) and discrete variables (individual indicators within components) are pertinent to systematic analyses of foreign behavior. We therefore attempt to assess simultaneously the relevant impact of various components as well as the effects of individual independent variables.

Relative Potency Testing and Coleman Analysis

The concern with the *relative potency* of general conceptual components, which may be traced to the work of Rosenau (1966), is a recurring theme in international relations research. Frequently, the question revolves around the relative importance of internal versus external sources of foreign policy—or between comparative and international politics approaches to explaining foreign behavior (Rosenau and Hoggard, 1974; Rosenau and Ramsey, 1975; Singer, 1961; Sondermann, 1961). Various architects of foreign policy frameworks have refined this dichotomous issue into assessments of a number of distinct sources or clusters of foreign policy (see, e.g., Brecher et al., 1969; Coplin, 1974; Wilkinson, 1969). As noted earlier, we posit five sources (i.e., the components).

Prospective theoretical advances are dependent upon the assessment of relative potencies across general sources of foreign behavior. Theoretical development requires a reduction in the complexity of foreign policy explanations from the all-inclusive and comprehensive to a more manageable and focused set of explanatory factors. Exhaustive foreign policy theories must account for the influences of variables which are housed in all five of the components in the IBA framework; however, we must initially extract a parsimonious set of core propositions to provide a foundation for subsequent logical extensions which introduce more varied explanatory phenomena. The location of this core set within the larger "universe" of the five components of source factors is therefore a primary theoretical endeavor. Relative potency testing is one strategy for isolating a limited set of core foreign policy determinants.

Methodologically, relative potency tests advance research by delineating the set of independent variables which more robustly accounts for foreign policy patterns. It is not, however, the task of relative potency testing to identify either "correlates" or "empirical factors." Instead, the approach assumes that measurable phenomena within general variable realms combine to assign a given magnitude of explanatory power to each component. Variance is accounted for by amplifying measurements within the more potent components and, secondarily, by securing the additional explanatory power of less pivotal variable clusters when such complexity is warranted or desired. Relative potency tests indicate the relative merits of allocating further research attention to various sources of independent variables.

Utilizing portions of Rosenau's pre-theoretical framework, Rosenau and Hoggard (1974) and Rosenau and Ramsey (1975) have attempted to assess the relative potency of the domestic and external domains. This genre of research has juxtaposed the internal factors of size, economic development, and political accountability with the relational attributes of distance, homogeneity, and power. Employing relatively simple analytical techniques, Rosenau and his colleagues concluded that internal factors are dominant; the external (i.e., relational) cluster contributes much less to the explanation of conflictual and cooperative foreign behaviors.

Our framework reorganizes the internal factors of the Rosenau scheme. The internal factors of size, economic development, and political accountability are expanded and treated here as intervening or contextual variables, rather than as determinants per se. We assign static or structural attributes to a mediating variable cluster, while dynamic factors comprise the independent variable cluster. Relative potency tests are thus expanded to five sources of foreign behavior, modified to treat only dynamic variables, and conditioned by static state structural factors.

An emphasis on ascertaining the relative potencies of our sources of foreign behavior must be balanced, however, with the need to isolate relationships among discrete variables. In order to monitor patterns of foreign behavior and provide warning for such phenomena as impending crises, observable variables and specific relationships must be illuminated. Possession of the knowledge that "international politics" explains more than "comparative politics" (or that the global component is more potent than the societal) will enhance the quality of research and theory—but will contribute nothing to the more immediate tasks of monitoring or tracking foreign activity. For the latter purposes, we must unravel the unique effects of individual indicators within the general components.

The dual tasks of testing the relative potency of IBA framework source components and of specifying relationships among observable variables can be approached from more than one methodological vantage point. The essential problem is to determine a combination of indicators within a component and compare the relative strengths of these combinations in accounting for foreign behavior. We can highlight three potential strategies; two will be utilized in our subsequent analyses.

First, factor analysis is available for determining combinatory scores for the source components. In order to preserve the conceptual clarity of each component, separate factor analyses could be performed for each set of indicators. In this manner, a single factor is extracted from the data which are housed within a given component, providing a "factor score" for that source (see Corrado, 1975) and a weight for each indicator.

With a single dimension score for each source component (each of which represents a combination of observables), tests of their relative potencies in accounting for foreign behavior can be performed. The technique thus accomplishes the assigned task, but with a major drawback: Component (dimension) scores and indicator weights are derived from intercorrelations which are unrelated to foreign behavior; the scores consequently fail to maximize component potency or reveal effects of individual indicators.

A second approach—pioneered by Coleman et al. (1966) and Dye (1966)—remedied these problems. Relative potency is ascertained with reference to the ability of a set of indicators to account for foreign behavior, the dependent variable; individual indicator effects are obtained by regressing foreign behavior upon each set of indicators. Dye's technique requires that each component account for a different portion of the variance in foreign behavior (i.e., the portion—residuals—unexplained by the indicators of the other components); this minimizes the effects of all indicators and component potencies. Coleman et al. (1966), in their well-known study, *Equality of Educational Opportunity*, make a similar restriction in their technique, reducing the potency of one (of two) components. "Coleman analysis" can be modified, however, to assume that the combination of indicators within a block or component should be based upon the ideal of maximizing the explanatory power of that block. The dependent variable is regressed upon the indicators of each component and the (standardized) predictions serve to represent the combination of indicators; the beta weights index the effects of discrete variables. Relative potency between two or more components is ascertained by regressing the dependent variable upon the set of predictions, thus providing comparative betas for component combinations.

Coleman sought to explain educational achievement in terms of family background and school quality and to assess the relative potency of these two blocks of variables. We substitute foreign policy dimensions for the dependent variable; variable blocks which represent the interstate and societal components are posited to be the forces which account for foreign behavior. The empirical results for our "Coleman analysis" are presented in Chapter 6 for a two-component model (societal and interstate) and in Chapter 8 for a four-component model (psychological, societal, interstate, and global).

Central to Coleman's approach—and to that of many econometricians—is the concept of a "latent variable." To Coleman, *family* and *school* constitute unmeasurable variables which affect educational achievement. Indicators are housed within each cluster; they are not, however, functions of an underlying dimension or necessarily highly intercorrelated.[2] The set of indicators represents a conceptually distinct group of ex-

planatory variables which may be combined in order to assess
the effects of the conceptual category itself. The combination is
a latent variable and is determined by the indicator variables.[3]
Figure 5.1 depicts the directional nature of the postulated relationships.

The essential problem in latent variable analysis is the determination of weights to be attached to indicators for the purpose
of computing the unmeasured latent variables. Since a latent
variable combines the effects of indicators, it might represent
the value of the dependent variable as predicted by the single
block of indicators. This assumption allows for relative potency
tests, which in effect compare the abilities (beta weights) of individual latent variables to account for the dependent variable.
The effects of individual indicators are surmised on the basis of
their contribution to the latent variable, weighted by the potency of the latent variable.

"Coleman analysis" (with modified technique) appears to be
ideal in terms of IBA concerns. Latent variables are found
within the framework as source components; they constitute
blocks of conceptually related indicators. Latent variable
analysis permits relative potency tests and establishes indicator
relationships with the dependent variable.

The Partial Least Squares (PLS) Model

The single difficulty of applying Coleman analysis to the IBA
research task pertains to the treatment of the dependent variable
realm. As Figure 5.1 indicates, a single dependent variable is
provided for. Within our framework, however, the dependent
variable (foreign policy behavior) is operationalized with three
indicators (see Chapter 4): constructive diplomatic behavior;
nonmilitary conflict, and force. Coleman analysis can only treat
each one separately, thus necessitating three distinct analyses of
relative potency and individual variable effects.[4]

An alternative solution, the third analytic strategy to be
discussed, would entail the specification of a latent dependent
variable, foreign policy, which is constructed on the basis of the

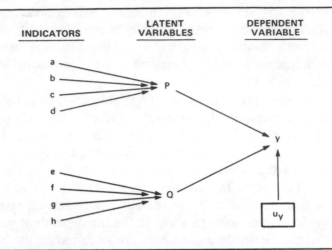

Figure 5.1: Latent Variable Analysis: Directional Nature of Relationships

three measures of foreign behavior. Variable y in Figure 5.1 would thereby become a combination of constructive diplomatic behavior, nonmilitary conflict, and force. This option has the advantage of providing an overall measure of relative potency for each of the independent latent variables. However, it also requires a modification of the Coleman strategy in order to accommodate this new conceptualization of the dependent variable realm. Fortunately, recent advances in econometrics provide explicitly for modifying Coleman's model for the purpose of incorporating a latent dependent variable: Partial Least Squares (PLS) is an approach to modeling latent variable relationships.[5]

The PLS model[6] is depicted in Figure 5.2. As in the Coleman model, the central concept of the PLS approach is a latent variable "specified in terms of the parameters of the model and the directly observed variables" (Wold, 1974: 70). However, the PLS model extends this concept to the dependent variable realm. The model thus relates only (1) latent variables with each other and (2) latent variables with their manifest counterparts. The model estimation differs from both Coleman analysis and typical econometric techniques:

As with conventional econometric models, the structural specification defines which variables are dependent and those which are independent in each estimated relationship. By contrast with conventional econometric models, the structural specification...relates *blocks* of variables, rather than single variables. The interactions among the variables in each block are left entirely unspecified, to be estimated without prior restriction...Each block can be thought of as representing a structural black-box [Adelman et al., 1975: 5].

A certain simplicity is achieved in that the latent variables are specified as linear combinations of the manifest variables and are linear in their interrelations as well.

The estimation problem becomes nonlinear because the predictor relations involve both unknown parameters and unknown variables (Wold, 1974: 71). This nonlinearity problem is solved through an iterated series of estimations spanning pieces of the whole model. However, the linearity of the model specification allows ordinary least squares to be applied to each predictor relation in it. Each such regression generates proxy estimates for a subset of the unknown parameters and latent variables; the estimates are employed in the succeeding step of the procedure to calculate new proxy estimates (Wold, 1974: 71). Thus the acronym PLS designates the procedure: It is partial in that the total model never encounters the observable; rather, parts of it separately and successively do so.

In Figure 5.2, endogenous (determined within the model) variables are represented by circles; squares symbolize the exogenous (unexplained or primitive) variables. There are three blocks of manifest variables in the model: p_i, q_i, and y_i.[7] Only observed variables are included within these three sets.

The latent variables P and Q are fully determined by a weighted sum of their respective components; P summarizes the forces as derived from observables p_1 to p_i while Q is derived from observables q_1 to q_j. The latent variable Y is a composite profile of observed variables y_1 to y_k. As an independent variable, this profile determines (stochastically) the values in set Y. As a dependent variable, Y is stochastically determined by P and Q forces. The model permits the estimation of the relative impact of general P and Q forces upon Y and also assesses the unique influence of discrete indicators which have been observed. Further details are provided in the appendix to this chapter.

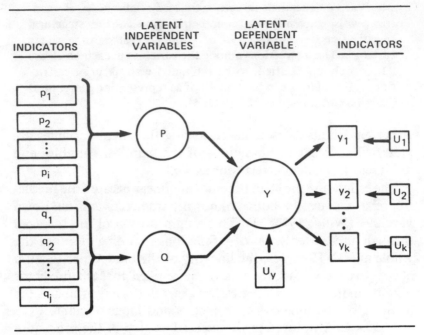

Figure 5.2: **Generalized PLS Model**

The PLS strategy effectively resolves the central problem which surfaces in the proposed extension of Coleman's model: How shall we determine the combination of manifest (i.e., observed) dependent variables in order to measure the latent dependent variable? The dictate in Coleman analysis regarding latent independent variables is that the combination is determined by maximizing the explained variance in the dependent variable; when this variable is an unknown compound, the dictate is indeterminate and it is impossible to estimate latent variables. It is therefore necessary to adopt a procedure which combines force, nonmilitary confict, and constructive diplomatic behavior for model estimation; the PLS approach accomplishes this task.

PLS assumes that the ultimate goal is to maximize the explanatory/predictive power of the model. The particular combination of manifest dependent variables which yields this situation is thus preferred over any other measurement of the depen-

dent variable. In terms of Figure 5.2, this means that Y is equal
to that combination (of observed foreign behavior variables)
which produces the maximum explanatory power of P and Q
(e.g., the latent variables representing the source components of
foreign behavior).

Since P and Q depend upon the measurement of Y, the process of estimating all of the latent variables is iterative in nature.
Each time that Y is adjusted in an effort to generate a better
data-to-model fit, P and Q are simultaneously adjusted. The
process continues until no further adjustment in Y will appreciably change the explanatory power of P and Q.[8]

The estimated latent dependent variable can be related to the
manifest variables, thereby providing a means for judging the
ability of the model to explain differentially each measure of
foreign behavior. In addition, the relationship between a
manifest independent variable and foreign behavior can be
ascertained by adjusting its contribution to the latent independent variable on the basis of the latter's relative potency.

Thus, the PLS model provides the following information:

(1) the relative potency of independent latent variables in account-
     ing for the dependent latent variable (the relative potency of
     interstate, societal, and other components in explaining foreign
     policy behavior generally)
(2) the ability of the model to account for foreign policy behavior
     generally
(3) the ability of the model to account for each manifest dependent
     variable (force, nonmilitary conflict, and constructive
     diplomacy)
(4) the direction and size of the effect upon foreign policy behavior
     of an individual manifest independent variable which is housed
     within a component.

These products satisfy the needs of IBA research: Relative
potency assessments are generated and individual indicator relationships are estimated, along with goodness-of-fit measures.
PLS testing is therefore given primacy over competing
strategies, with the single exception that the Coleman analysis

will be conducted in order to operationalize and test simplified versions of our model; the PLS model thus builds upon the less sophisticated—although satisfactory—procedure of conducting separate tests of foreign policy behavior.

CONTROLLING FOR TYPE OF STATE

The preceding section of the chapter outlined models which will handle questions pertaining to relative potency and indicator relationships. However, the proposed model does not as yet take into account the presumed effects of "moderating" variables which constitute the intervening variable cluster in the IBA framework. This section will identify the means by which the standard Coleman and PLS models may be altered in order to evaluate the impact of stable state structural characteristics upon indicator-behavior relationships.

Subrgouping Versus Moderated Regression

Variables which mediate between independent and dependent variables as conditioning factors, such as the state typological domain, are "moderators" of relationships. Moderators can be imposed upon models in two ways: through the subgrouping of the units of analysis or through moderated regression (James et al., 1977: 2). Both techniques have been widely employed in recent psychological literature (see, e.g., Blood and Mullet, 1977; Cohen and Cohen, 1975; Boehm, 1977; Cook and Campbell, 1976).

Moderator analysis is based upon the proposition that the nature and strength of a relationship between two variables are dependent upon the values of moderating factors. In the IBA framework, we assume that foreign behavior is related to societal unrest, for example, in a different fashion and to different degrees depending upon the values obtained for a state on its typological characteristics. For certain typological profiles, the relationship will be weak (or negative) while for others it will be strong (or positive). States with similar structural characteristics will have similar explanations for their foreign behaviors; analogously, dissimilar states are expected to exhibit dissimilar sources of foreign activities.

Subgrouping is the process of dividing the sample of cases into homogeneous classes, where states within groups are presumed to have the same moderator values and states in different groups have dissimilar values on the moderating variables. Each homogeneous subgroup is therefore composed of cases with similar intervariable relationships; relationships vary only across groupings. The subgrouping technique involves model estimation for each group and comparisons of results across groups. The effects of the moderator(s) are gleaned from this comparison.[9]

Moderated regression entails an attempt to build assumptions of moderator effects into the model itself. While subgrouping imposes no restrictions upon the nature of moderator effects, moderated regression involves assumptions regarding the relationship between the moderator(s), on the one hand, and the regression weight (or beta) relating independent and dependent variables, on the other. Specifically, moderated regression demands an explicit formulation of the function:

$$b = f(M),$$

where b is a regression weight relating an independent and a dependent variable and M is the moderator variable. Typically, a linear relationship is assumed,[10] resulting in an interactive relationship:

$$y = f(xM),$$

where y and x are the dependent and independent variables, respectively.

Each of the moderator treatments is plagued by difficulties in application. Subgrouping requires a sufficient number of cases within each group in order to perform statistical tests; the requirement becomes limiting when interval-level data are used (such as our four dimensions of state structure) and when more than one moderator is employed (the latter situation requires groupings which are homogeneous on all moderator variables). Moderated regression demands specific formulations (or models) of the effects of moderators upon regression parameters and could result in equations involving literally hundreds of interaction terms.

Control Methods in the Coleman and PLS Analyses

We utilize both methods of control for estimating the effects of stable state structural variables. In the application of Coleman analysis, the number of independent variables is sufficiently small to permit subgroup testing. The subgroups are defined on the basis of the results of the Q-factor analysis outlined earlier (see Chapter 3); although subgroup homogeneity does not approach perfection, the groupings provide sufficiently differentiated structural profiles to generate meaningful comparisons.

Moderated regression analysis was chosen as the control technique for the PLS model, which involves a large number of variables.[11] Models which relate typological dimensions to model parameters were specified (Rossa et al., 1980). The control mechanism (i.e., interaction terms) is allowed to enter the model at either of two points: the first (M_1) is the junction between manifest and latent independent variables; the second (M_2) is between the latent independent and latent dependent variables (Figure 5.3).

Since P and Q are unobservable, the choice between M_1 and M_2 is inconsequential. Conceptually, it may be advisable to view manifest variables as stimuli which define the foreign policy problems for decision makers, P and Q as structural representations of these problems, and Y as the resultant remedial actions. M_1, then, suggests that state typological characteristics affect the manner in which the stimuli or problems are structured by a particular state; given identical stimuli, different types of states structure their problems differently and therefore react differently. Conversely, states which receive dissimilar stimuli

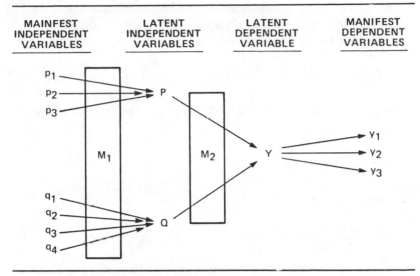

Figure 5.3: PLS Model: Location of Control

may, as a result of typological differences, nevertheless formulate identical problem structures and therefore act similarly.

Control M_2, on the other hand, suggests that all states structure stimuli in the same fashion but react to these structures according to the dictates of state characteristics. Because P and
Q are not observed, the two processes are indistinguishable.

Finally, the mediated regression control technique requires
models of moderator effects which permit the following:
(1) judgments regarding the importance of state typological
characteristics; (2) calculations of moderator effects for different components and/or indicators; and (3) derivations of
models specific to states. The first requirement is needed in
order to prevent a built-in bias in our models and allow for the
possibility that either the framework's assumption of mediating
structures or the chosen control model is wrong. The second requirement acknowledges that there is a possibility that
moderators may be less important to some relationships than to
others. The final requirement ensures that the model testing
results provide findings which are unique to states, corresponding to the uniqueness of state structural characteristics.

We provide for judging the importance of mediating variables by assuming that each parameter affected by moderators is determined by an equation of the form:

$$b_{yx} = c_{yx} + d_{yx}M, \tag{1}$$

where b is a regression weight, M the moderator, c an intercept, and d a weight. This changes equation:

$$y = a_{yx} + b_{yx}x \tag{2}$$

to equation:

$$y = a_{yx} + c_{yx}x + d_{yx}Mx \tag{3}$$

through substitution; x may have an unmediated effect upon y and, if $d = 0$, M may have no relevance.[12]

Differential treatment of components and indicators is a result of choosing between the alternative M_1 and M_2 controls in Figure 5.3; only if the moderators are placed to the right of F will overall moderator influence alone be ascertained. M_1 results in distinguishable moderator influences upon each indicator (manifest independent variable); M_2 imposes moderators upon each source component (latent independent variable).

Calculations of individual state results are possible in moderator analysis. Each b_{xy} in equation [1], which may have numerous independent variables, can be computed by reference to formula [2] after equation [3] is estimated. To the extent that the state structures affect parameters, each state will have a unique set of indicator-to-foreign policy relationships.

CONCLUSIONS

The unique requirements of IBA research include the following:

(1) conducting relative potency tests for source components

(2) measuring specific relationships between indicators and foreign policy behavior

(3) imposing control for the effects of state typological characteristics

In this chapter we have offered a nontechnical discussion of the methodological problems and decisions which will govern our analyses and produce the results of our empirical inquiry. We have found that Coleman analysis and the extension to PLS modeling are appropriate for specifying relative potencies and individual indicator effects upon foreign behavior. We have also decided to employ both subgrouping and moderated regression analysis in order to provide tests for the effects of state typological traits and state-specific parameter estimates. Subsequent chapters will discuss the empirical results.

APPENDIX TO CHAPTER 5—
LATENT VARIABLES, THE PLS MODEL, TYPOLOGICAL
CONTROL, AND INDIVIDUAL STATE RESULTS

Chapter 5 contains a nontechnical discussion of the methodological strategies of the IBA Project. The purpose of this appendix is to provide a discussion of the mathematics underlying our models of relative potency tests, indicator influences, and moderator controls. Chapter 5 is sufficient for acquiring an understanding of our empirical research findings; here, a technical presentation will provide more detailed methodological information.

LATENT VARIABLES

When a concept is proposed which encompasses a variety of observables without one of the latter adequately operationalizing the concept itself, concept measurement may take one of two forms. We may either assume that the observables are "caused" by the concept,

$$i_j = f_j(I) + e_{ji}, j = 1,n \tag{A1}$$

or that the concept is "caused" by the set of observables,

$$I = f(i_j, j = 1,n)$$ [A2]

Equation [A1] represents an assumed underlying dimension of observables and leads to the use of equation [A2] for the operationalization of the concept where f is determined by

$$f = g(f_j, j = 1,n)$$ [A3]

The set of $\{f_j, j = 1,n\}$ is estimated through pattern recognition techniques, such as factor analysis, which rely upon information concerning correlations among observables; the techniques seek to maximize the ability of I to account for $i_j, j = 1,n$.

When model [A2] is assumed to be valid, I is a latent variable and the result of observations. There is no necessary expectation that observables are correlated, as is implied in model [A1], and pattern recognition procedures are not appropriate; consequently, the criterion of maximizing correlations between I and $i_j, j = 1,n$, is not viable. Instead, we impose the criterion that f must maximize the explanatory ability of I regarding some dependent variable, y:

$$y = h(i_j, j = 1,n) + e$$ [A4]

and set $f = h$. I is then the estimated value of y obtained in model [A4].

Statistical models which are used in IBA research assume that operationalizations of concepts rely upon dimensionalization, equation [A1], through factor analysis. Entire components of the framework are latent variables, as in equation [A2], and regression analysis is used for model [A4] in order to estimate I (interstate), S (societal), and G (global), the independent latent variables, and F (foreign policy), the dependent latent variable.[13]

THE PLS MODEL

For the use of latent variables, the reader is referred to the formal presentation of the PLS model. Here, we define this model for two latent independent variables (societal and interstate) and a latent dependent variable (foreign policy). Coleman analysis is subsumed within the PLS model; only one manifest dependent variable is allowed, thus reducing the number of iterations to one and setting $k = r_k = 1$ in the following equations.

The PLS model is defined by a number of assumptions. First, let S, I, and F define sets:

$$S = \{S_n | 1 \leqslant n \leqslant N\}$$
$$I = \{I_j \ | 1 \leqslant j \leqslant J \}$$
$$F = \{F_k | 1 \leqslant k \leqslant K\}$$

Each element of each set is a variable and is standardized with a mean of zero and a standard deviation of one.

Let S*, I*, and F* represent scalers defined by:

(1) $S^* = c_1 \sum_{n}^{N} p_n S_n$

(2) $I^* = c_2 \sum_{j}^{J} q_j I_j$

(3) $F^* = c_3 \sum_{k}^{K} r_k F_k$

The terms c_1, c_2, and c_3 denote standardization functions, giving S*, I*, and F* unit variance and zero mean. The terms p_n, q_j, and r_k denote weights for given variables in each set.

The definitions are supplemented by the model's posited relationships. First, two of the above definitions are deterministic relationships—those defining S^* and I^*. Second, a set of stochastic relationships (numbering K) are posited:

(4) $F_k = r_k F^* + e_k$ $(1 \leqslant k \leqslant K)$

We assume that the error terms have means of zero and are linearly independent of F^*:

$E(e_k) = 0$ $r(e_k, F^*) = 0$ $(1 \leqslant k \leqslant K)$

We can thus predict:

(5) $E(F_k \mid F^*) = r_k$ F^* $(1 \leqslant k \leqslant K)$

The final relationship is the one between F^*, on the one hand, and S^* and I^*, on the other:

$F^* = a_1 S^* + a_2 I^* + u_1$

The residual is restricted, again, such that:

$E(u_1) = 0$ $r(u_1, F^*) = 0$

We thus predict:

$E(F^* \mid S^*, I^*) = a_1 S^* + a_+ I^*$

This concludes the definition of our model.

The PLS procedure is the method by which parameters p_n, $(n \leqslant 1 \leqslant N)$, $q_j (1 \leqslant j \leqslant J)$, $r_k (1 \leqslant k \leqslant K)$, a_1, and a_2 are estimated. The procedure is iterative with iteration $i = 1, 2, 3, \ldots$ converging in the limit to $i = \infty$ to the estimates of parameters. Each iteration includes a number of steps. Here we will describe one iteration.

In the first step, we calculate F^*. In the first iteration, weights $r_k (1 \leqslant k \leqslant K)$ are set equal to 1, using formula (3) above. After the first iteration, the weights will be supplied by a previous step.

Second, we employ Ordinary Least Squares Multiple Regression (OLS) to estimate $p_n(1 \leqslant n \leqslant N)$:

$$F^* = \sum_n^k (p_n S_n) + u_2$$

and likewise, to estimate $q_j(1 \leqslant j \leqslant J)$:

$$F^* = \sum_i^J (q_j I_j) + u_3$$

These weights are then used in formulae (1) and (2), respectively. Note that the weights used in constructing I* and S* are based upon each variable's predictive capacity.

The third step involves OLS multiple regression and estimates a_1 and a_2:

$$F^* = a_1 S^* + a_2 I^* + u_1$$

The term F* was computed in step one while S* and I* were computed in step two.

Finally, the fourth step involves the estimation of r_k ($1 \leqslant k \leqslant K$). The predicted estimated values of F*, called $\hat{F}^*$, are standardized and used to predict $F_k(1 \leqslant k \leqslant K)$. OLS simple regression is used, once for each F_k:

$$F_k = r_k \hat{F}^* + u_4 (1 \leqslant k \leqslant K)$$

With values $r_k(1 \leqslant k \leqslant K)$ firmly in hand, another iteration is possible.

The iterative process may cease when additional iterations do not "substantially" reduce u_x, the error terms in the model. One accepted criterion is:

$$|(u^{i+1} - u^i / u^i| 10^{-k}$$

where k equals about 5 (Wold and Areskoug, 1975: 3-6). A less stringent requirement will result in parameters with error in some decimal place; in our analyses, parameter error is restricted to the third decimal place ($k \cong 3$).

The estimates will be consistent, and thus maximally unbiased. They may not be efficient, for the residuals need not be normally distributed with constant variance. The parameters are therefore more meaningful than the R square values.

When only one independent latent variable is included in the PLS model, the result is a canonical regression model. When, furthermore, a single manifest dependent variable is present, the model reduces to simple OLS regression.

TYPOLOGICAL CONTROL

Three control models are utilized in IBA research in order to incorporate moderator effects. The first is defined by subgrouping such that:

$$y_j = a_m + \sum_i^k b_{im} \times_{ijm} + e_j, \, j = 1, N; \, m = 1, T \qquad [A5]$$

where m denotes the typological group (Q-factor group), i the independent variables, and j the state. Each subgroup is associated with a different set of parameters, estimated separately for each value of m (group number one to five).

The second model involves moderated regression in which, for each b_i in:

$$y_j = a + \sum_i^k b_i \times_{ji} + e_j \qquad [A6]$$

$$b_i = d_i + c_i E_j$$

$$c_j = p_i C_j$$

$$p_i = q_i R_j$$

$$q_i = r_i I_j$$

$$b_i = d_i + r_i I_j R_j C_j E_j$$

$$b_i = d_i + r_i T_j \qquad\qquad\qquad\qquad\qquad\qquad \text{[A7]}$$

where E, C, R, and I refer to dimensions of state structure; all relationships are assumed to be deterministic. Substituting in equation [A6] from equation [A7], we obtain:

$$y_j = a + \sum_i^k d_i \times_{ji} + \sum_i^k r_i T_j \times_{ji} + e_j \qquad\qquad \text{[A8]}$$

This is a multiplicative or interactive moderator influence model; it assumes that moderators interact to affect b_i and that no main effects (from moderator to regression weight) exist. Obviously, many alternative models are available. Various combinations of interactions and main effects are possible, while nonlinear and stochastic models are also possible. The model here reduces complexity, is the most parsimonious, and permits unmediated effects of $\times$ to emerge and possibly reduce the moderator's role.

The third model is a moderated regression analysis which alters model [A6] by assuming:

$$b_i = d_i + p_i C_j + c_i E_j + q_i R_j + r_i I_j \qquad\qquad \text{[A9]}$$

This is an additive moderator influence model, is also deterministic, and again allows for a direct effect of $\times$:

$$y_j = a + \sum_i^k d_i \times_{ji} + \sum_i^k p_i C_j \times_{ji} + \sum_i^k c_i E_j \times_{ji} + \sum_i^k q_i R_j \times_{ji} \qquad \text{[A10]}$$
$$+ \sum_i^k r_i I_j \times_{ji} + e_j$$

The model is less parsimonious than equation [A8] but permits the identification of the moderator influence of each structural dimension. Thus, each state typological dimension affects each indicator relationship in a unique fashion.

As noted in Chapter 5 (see Figure 5.3), moderator control can be imposed in one of two positions in a latent variable model when moderated regression analysis is used. When M_1 is the selected point of control, x_i in models [A8] and [A9] refers to manifest independent variables (i.e., operationalizations of societal, interstate, and global components). When M_2 is utilized, x_i in [A8] and [A9] refers to a latent dependent variable (a calculated combination of manifest variables within a component).

The choice of control location does not matter, since M_2 can be reformulated to an M_1 model. This can be illustrated with a single latent dependent variable, S, composed of two manifest variables, s_1 and s_2 and a single moderator, T:

$$(M_2) \quad F = b_1 ST$$
$$S = c_1 s_1 + c_2 s_2$$
$$F = b_1 c_1 s_1 T + b_1 c_2 s_2 T \qquad \text{[A11]}$$
$$= B_1 s_1 T + B_3 s_2 T$$

$$(M_1) \quad F = b_2 S$$
$$S = d_1 s_1 T + d_2 s_2 T$$
$$F = b_2 d_1 s_1 T + b_2 d_2 s_2 T$$
$$= B_2 s_1 T + B_4 s_2 T \qquad \text{[A12]}$$

B_1 and B_3 must be equivalent to B_2 and B_4, respectively.

RELATIVE POTENCY, INDICATOR EFFECTS, AND INDIVIDUAL STATE RESULTS

Relative potency is assessed in the Coleman and PLS models in terms of standardized regression coefficients which relate latent independent variables to foreign policy behavior. These beta weights indicate the relative impact upon foreign behavior of a change in the explanatory variable. When moderated regression analysis is employed to control for state typological characteristics, control technique M_1 leads to relative potency betas which are invariant across states; M_2, however, ties relative potency to state structure. Thus, M_1 and M_2 controls lead to different methods of assessing relative potency; one is universal and the other is case specific.

Indicator effects are evaluated in a similar fashion, depending upon control technique. When M_2 control is employed, indicators determine the latent independent variable in a universal set of relationships. M_1 control indicates that indicator weights in determining the latent variable will depend upon state characteristics.

Nevertheless, equations [A11] and [A12] should point to the similarity of control method results. No matter where moderators enter into the model, the basic relationship is that between indicators and foreign behavior; typological considerations simply mean that each and every indicator is uniquely related to foreign policy for each case (to the extent that the moderator is active). Thus, individual state results are produced by virtue of moderator influences, wherever they are actually imposed.

Individual state relative potencies (control M_2) are computed as follows: Given (standardized) latent variables S, I, and F and estimating equation:

$$F = b_1 I + b_2 S + e$$

with control (simplified to one moderation):

$$b_1 = a_1 = c_1 T \text{ and } b_2 = a_2 + c_2 T$$

then:

$$F = a_1 I + c_1 TI + a_2 S + c_2 TS$$

$$F = (a_1 + c_1 T)I + (a_2 + c_2 T)S$$

Terms in parentheses indicate the betas, or relative potencies, of I and S and are calculable *given the moderator value*, T. Thus, the relative potencies are state specific and calculable.

Individual state indicator weights are also calculable—although they are less straightforward as a result of standardization routines. In moderator model M_1, a manifest independent variable affects a latent variable in the following manner:

$$L = \frac{b\,(x-\bar{x})}{s_x} + \frac{d\,(Tx - \overline{T}x)}{s_{Tx}}$$

where L is the latent variable, $\times$ the manifest variable, and T the moderator variable. The dependent variable, y, is thus affected by $\times$:

$$
\begin{aligned}
y &= cL \\
&= c\left(\frac{b\,(x-\bar{x})}{s_x} + \frac{d\,(Tx - \overline{T}x)}{s_{Tx}}\right) \\
&= c\left(\frac{bx}{s_x} - \frac{b\bar{x}}{s_x} + \frac{dTx}{s_{Tx}} - \frac{d\overline{T}x}{s_{Tx}}\right) \\
&= c\left(\frac{b}{s_x} - \frac{b\bar{x}}{xs_x} + \frac{dT}{s_{Tx}} - \frac{d\overline{T}x}{xs_{Tx}}\right) x \\
&= c\left(\frac{b}{s_x} + \frac{dT}{s_{Tx}}\right) x - C\left(\frac{b\bar{x}}{s_x} + \frac{d\overline{T}x}{s_{Tx}}\right)
\end{aligned}
\qquad \text{[A13]}
$$

Thus, the regression weight relating x to y is:

$$= c\left(\frac{b}{s_x} + \frac{dT}{s_{Tx}}\right) \qquad \text{[A14]}$$

Equation [A14] varies with T. The other term in equation [A13] is a constant across states, including only parameters, variable means, and standard deviations of variables.[14] Given a calculable regression weight in equation [A14], a beta (standardization regression weight) is simply:

$$\beta_{yx} = \frac{c \left(\dfrac{b}{s_x} + \dfrac{dT}{s_{Tx}} \right) s_x}{s_y}$$

NOTES

1. Singer (1968) is a strong proponent of correlational analysis. Rummel (1967, 1972) popularized the alternative approach.

2. This is the common assumption in the factor analysis tradition of measurement. Measurement theories assume that a concept can be observed by reference to resultant indicators (Przeworski and Teune, 1972: 94-106; Kerlinger, 1964: 33-38; Gurr, 1972: 105-108). Indirect measurement theory was applied in the operationalization stage (see Chapter 3).

3. This reverses the causal direction of the indicator-concept relationship; see note 2 above and Jacobson (1973).

4. Of course, we again reject indirect measurement as a result of the independent nature of the three dimensions of foreign behavior.

5. See Joreskog and Wold (1980) and Wold (1975b); especially relevant are Wold (1974, 1975a), Wold and Areskoug (1975), and Adelman et al. (1975). The LISREL methodology (Joreskog, 1980, 1977, 1973) is appropriate when *maximum likelihood* data requirements can be met and indicators are always effects of latent variables (see Joreskog and Wold, 1980; Rossa, 1980); these conditions do not apply here. PLS makes no assumptions regarding data quality or "arrow scheme" (direction of relationship between latent variables and indicators) and is particularly appropriate when data analysis and modeling merge in quantitative study (see Wold, 1978a, 1978b, 1977a, 1977b, 1977c). This approach has been used by Noonan (1980) in educational reform research, Hui (1980) in marketing research, Kowalski et al. (1980) in chemical research, as well as others; see, e.g., the essays in Joreskog and Wold (1980).

6. In this chapter, PLS will subsequently refer to the particular model which will be described below. In earlier work, this model has been referred to as Nonlinear Iterative Partial Least Squares (NIPALS).

7. While the model here contains only two latent independent variables, it is generalizable to a larger number. Indeed, in the analysis reported in Chapter 8, four latent independent variables are employed.

8. The actual "adjustment" mechanism involves the changing of weights for manifest dependent variables on the basis of how well each is predicted by Y as predicted by P and Q. Technically, Y is the estimated value of the combination of manifest variables, not the combination per se. Y therefore represents a latent variable which combines P and Q, which are themselves combinations of variables; Y is the combined impact of all of the latent independent variables.

9. This is a "most similar systems" design in which the differentiation criteria are clearly specified; see Przeworski and Teune (1972).

10. Also, an intercept term is usually assumed, thereby permitting a nonmoderated effect. Usually, the intercept in the original regression is also assumed to be affected by the moderator, thereby allowing a direct effect on the part of the moderator itself (see the appendix to this chapter). It should also be noted that, typically, the effect of the moderator is assumed to be deterministic, meaning that the only possible moderator(s) is (are) in the equation.

11. PLS techniques to incorporate *latent moderators* are new (Rossa, 1980) and were unavailable when these analyses were performed.

12. Note that we do not allow M to directly affect y, since we assume that stable structures cannot affect foreign policy behavior.

13. In applying equation [A4] to measure a dependent latent variable, y is set equal to a combination of manifest dependent variables. The block of variables within F are the estimated latent independent variables, which become i_j ($j = 1$, n) in equation [A4]. Note that there is no latent dependent variable in Coleman analysis.

14. Note that each manifest variable produces a constant; the sum of constants across variables is the constant for the model.

Chapter 6

Testing a Preliminary Model of Societal and Interstate Determinants of Foreign Behavior

Up to this point we have discussed in some detail our framework for the comparative analysis of foreign policy behavior. We have also delineated the analytical strategies that we will pursue. As noted, the framework has three basic elements: a set of components into which the determinants of foreign policy are divided, a classificatory scheme for foreign policy actors, and a typology of foreign policy events. We have been careful to stress the point that a framework is not a causal model in any sense, but rather an organizational device designed to assist the analyst in integrating the various and disparate elements of a process. We have therefore proposed no discrete, testable hypotheses; nor have we indicated that anything resembling a "test" of the framework could be carried out.

In answering the question of relative potency in a way which specifies the precise conditions under which different determinants prevail, we hope to establish the groundwork for a series of studies which builds causal models of portions of the process which we attempt to specify in a general fashion below.

AUTHORS' NOTE: *Portions of this chapter are expanded versions of material which originally appeared in Hopple et al. (1977)*

Therefore, we view the issue of assessing the relative impact of portions of the conceptual framework as a necessary preliminary step in the development of sophisticated causal models. We will attempt to sketch some of these models at the end of our analysis.

Chapters 7 and 8 will report the results of complex analyses which deal with the question of the relative potency of various components of the framework. That, in a sense, will constitute the culmination of our work to date. The present chapter has a more modest goal. Here we will explore in a preliminary manner the relative potency of domestic versus external sources of foreign behavior, a question which has already received a considerable amount of attention in the literature on the comparative study of foreign policy. As noted in the preceding chapter, a debate has revolved around the question of which of these two realms has the greater impact in determining the composition of foreign behavior.

The most plausible solution at the outset is to avoid an arbitrary choice between the two vantage points. It can be posited that many foreign policy actions reflect the impact of both types of factors. It is nevertheless the task of foreign policy analysts to attempt to specify the conditions that enhance the impact of one of the sets of factors over the others.

As we noted at the outset of this study, the existence of an awesome array of factors requires research designs that attempt to impose coherence on this complex milieu of determinants. The construction of a framework is a vital task in a field of inquiry that features so many variables and interrelationships among variables. Hypotheses can then be extracted from the framework. These testable hypotheses can be employed to evaluate the consequences which are suggested by the framework. This strategy clearly differs from the ad hoc hypothesis-testing approach since propositions are derived directly from the organizational framework. The evaluation and modification of these findings can be expected to contribute to the gradual cumulation of knowledge in foreign policy research.

OPERATIONALIZATION

The research presented below operationalizes those portions of the Interstate Behavior Analysis framework that view foreign behavior as the dependent variable cluster, type of state as the intervening variable cluster, and societal and interstate factors as independent variables. More specifically, our expectation is that the amount of conflict behavior received by a state from its environment, the extent and nature of its involvement in the international system, and the level of societal instability, economic performance, and population growth rate characteristics all interact to produce varying levels and types of foreign behavior.

The extent to which societal factors have an impact on a state's foreign behavior has been the focus of various researchers. The relationship between domestic conflict behavior and foreign conflict behavior has been investigated from a variety of methodological perspectives (Rummel, 1963; Tanter, 1966; Wilkenfeld, 1968, 1969, 1973; Zinnes and Wilkenfeld, 1971; Hazlewood, 1973, 1975) and in differing regional and cross-national contexts (Burrowes and Spector, 1973; Collins, 1973; Liao, 1976; Wilkenfeld, 1975; Wilkenfeld et al., 1972).[1]

The most charitable judgment would be that this stream of inquiry has yielded inconclusive results. Only a few studies have discovered a nexus between internal and external conflict, and the findings generally account for a small portion of the measurable variance in foreign conflict behavior (Scolnick, 1974; Stein, 1976). Nevertheless, the suspicion persists that important relationships will be unearthed. The incorporation of a more extensive data base may yield some significant insights into the magnitude and nature of the linkage between internal and external conflict.

Both speculation and empirical research have focused on the extent to which economic factors impact upon the external aggressiveness of a society (Feierabend and Feierabend, 1969; Hazlewood, 1973; Katzenstein, 1976). The more dynamic aspects of the performance of a state's economy are expected to create a climate in which aggressive and conflictual foreign policy behaviors are more likely outcomes. It is again anticipated that the inclusion of this factor will generate noteworthy findings.

Also in the societal realm, population growth rate is expected to operate as an important force under certain circumstances. Prior research (Choucri, 1974; Choucri and North, 1975) has indicated the importance of taking into account various types of population pressures and their potential effects on policy outcomes.

The relationship between conflict received and conflict sent has been probed in prior work (Phillips, 1971, 1973, 1978; Wilkenfeld, 1975; Wilkenfeld et al., 1972). In fact, the notion that conflict begets conflict is one of the few propositions in the foreign policy literature that has been verified unambiguously. The more general hypothesis that action generates a reaction has also been tested (Holsti et al., 1968; Gamson and Modigliani, 1971; Kegley and Agnew, 1976). To the extent that this model accurately represents reality, the task of foreign policy makers (and of foreign policy analysts) would be considerably simplified. It is obvious, however, that only a portion—although a rather large portion—of the conflict behavior sent externally by a state can be attributed to the conflict behavior which it has received. The identification of other factors is a central goal of this chapter.

Finally, the level of participation in the international system, or international involvement, will be considered as an additional interstate factor. Here we are reasoning that the extent of participation in the international system will influence the types of foreign policy behaviors exhibited by the state.

With regard to the intervening or contextual element in the present analysis, the five state groupings which were delineated in Chapter 3 will be employed. That is, relationships between the sources of foreign behavior and behavior itself will be investigated within each of the five groups—*Western, closed, large developing, unstable,* and *poor.* To the extent that we have accurately identified those structural characteristics of states that provide a context for foreign behavior, our classification scheme should yield more reliable descriptions and more valid explanations.

In Chapter 4 we presented several analyses designed to conceptualize foreign behavior for purposes of empirical analysis. We employed the WEIS data set, and identified three types of foreign policy behavior sent—*constructive diplomatic, nonmilitary conflict,* and *force.* For purposes of the present analysis, only *constructive diplomatic* and *nonmilitary conflict* will be analyzed as dependent variables, since the small number of *force* events created statistical problems.[2] All three types of foreign behavior will be utilized as independent variables in this model.[3]

At this point, it may be helpful to present Figure 6.1 which provides a summary description of the research design for the present analysis.

ANALYSIS

We employed a relatively straightforward analytic strategy in order to evaluate the relationships between the two source variable components and foreign behavior. The basic approach involved the investigation of these relationships for the total set of 56 states, followed by an analysis within each of the five groups: *Western, closed, large developing, unstable,* and *poor.* Each of the five years (1966-1970) was analyzed separately, followed by an aggregated analysis in which all five years were combined.

Three distinct analyses were pursued. The first assesses the relationships between the interstate component and foreign behavior (e.g., behavior received and international involvement as related to behavior sent). The second investigates the relationships between elements of the societal component and

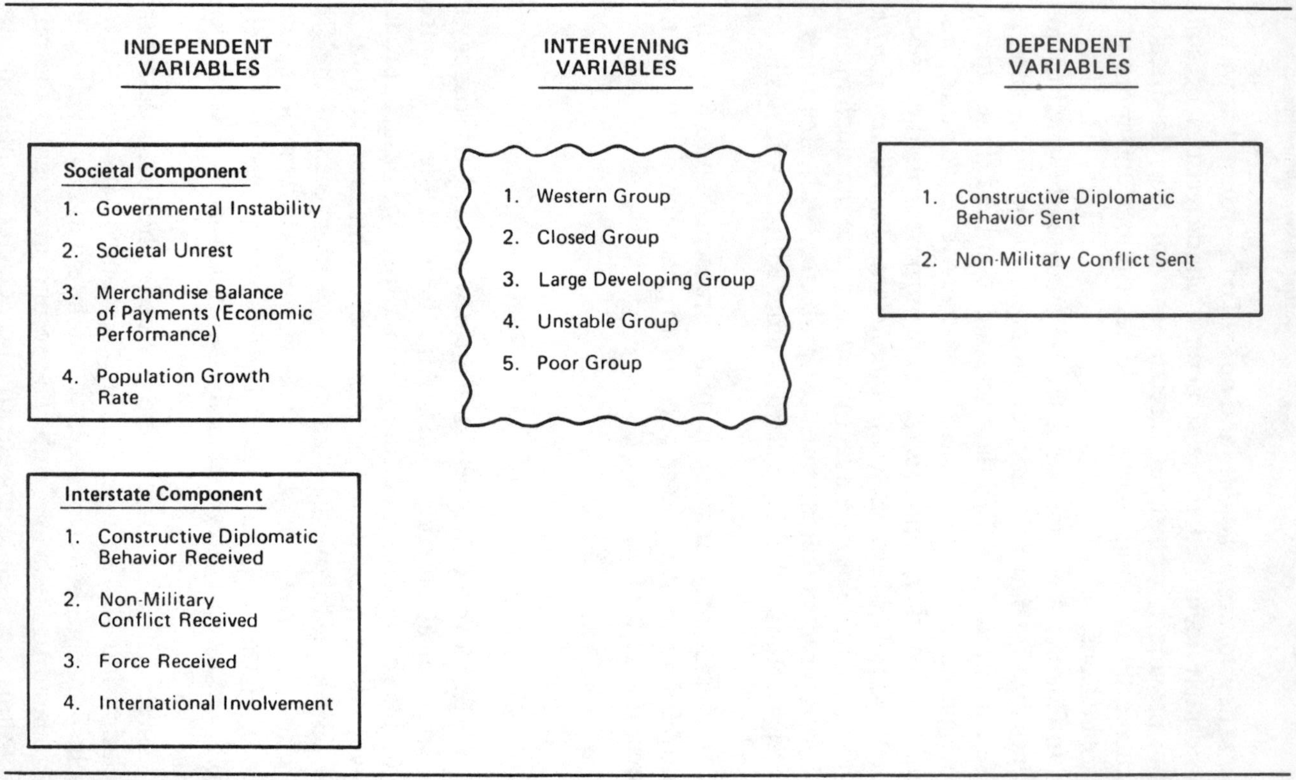

Figure 6.1: Research Design for Preliminary Coleman Analysis

INDEPENDENT VARIABLES

Societal Component

1. Governmental Instability
2. Societal Unrest
3. Merchandise Balance of Payments (Economic Performance)
4. Population Growth Rate

Interstate Component

1. Constructive Diplomatic Behavior Received
2. Non-Military Conflict Received
3. Force Received
4. International Involvement

INTERVENING VARIABLES

1. Western Group
2. Closed Group
3. Large Developing Group
4. Unstable Group
5. Poor Group

DEPENDENT VARIABLES

1. Constructive Diplomatic Behavior Sent
2. Non-Military Conflict Sent

foreign behavior. Finally, the predicted values generated by these two regression analyses were entered into a regression equation which predicted foreign behavior, in order to provide a preliminary estimate of the relative potency of the two clusters of determinants of foreign behavior.

Foreign Behavior as Predicted by the Interstate Component

It will be recalled that the foreign policy domain has been divided into two indices: constructive diplomatic behavior sent and nonmilitary conflict sent. The independent variables are diplomatic behavior received, nonmilitary conflict received, force received, and international involvement. The tables which follow present the results of stepwise multiple regression analyses for each of the dependent variables for the total group as well as for the five subgroups. The numbers in the columns are beta weights, with the final column presenting the proportion of variance explained (R^2). Asterisks indicate beta weight and R^2's which are significant at the .05 level.

Table 6.1 presents the multiple regression results for constructive diplomatic behavior. It can be noted at the outset that the percentages of variance explained are exceedingly high, ranging between 86 percent and 96 percent for the individual groups, and 92 percent for the total group. Furthermore, in each group, the amount of constructive diplomatic behavior received is the leading predictor of constructive diplomatic behavior sent. That is, not only does behavior received accurately predict to behavior sent, but there is an accurate matching of behavioral types in this domain.

These two findings depict a type of foreign policy behavior which, as its name signifies, measures the diplomatic exchanges among states. It is the types of behavior grouped here—yield, comment, consult, approve, promise, grant, reward, agree, request, propose, reject, deny, warn, and reduce relationships—which are characterized by a balanced type of behavior pattern between two or more states. This explains both the very accurate prediction and the fact that we discover virtually no

TABLE 6.1
Constructive Diplomatic Behavior as Predicted by
the Interstate Component

	Constructive Diplomatic Behavior	Non-Military Conflict	Force	International Involvement	R^2
	Total Group, Yearly N = 56				
1966	.66*	.18*	.09	.23*	.90*
1967	.80*	.09	.06	.07	.91*
1968	.70*	.16*	.09	.16*	.92*
1969	.81*	.03	.12*	.12*	.94*
1970	.74*	.11	.14*	.16*	.95*
Nation-Years Aggregated N = 280	.72*	.13*	.11*	.15*	.92*
	Western Group, Yearly N = 15				
1966	.62*	.18	.15	.15	.94*
1967	.88*	−.02	.10	.11	.98*
1968	.89*	−.26	.33*	.22*	.98*
1969	.85*	.05	.13	.03	.98*
1970	.77*	−	.20*	.13*	.98*
Nation-Years Aggregated N = 75	.69*	.12*	.17*	.13*	.96*
	Closed Group, Yearly N = 10				
1966	.67*	.42	−	−.11	.97*
1967	.81*	.19	.07	−.01	.98*
1968	.91*	.12	−.05	−	.97*
1969	93*	.13	−.07	.03	.97*
1970	.85	.59*	−.30	−.14	.98*
Nation-Years Aggregated N = 50	.83*	.19*	.09	−	.96*

NOTE: Numbers in first four columns are beta weights.
*Beta or R^2 significant at the .05 level.

Table 6.1 (Continued)

	Constructive Diplomatic Behavior	Non-Military Conflict	Force	International Involvement	R^2
	Large Developing Group, Yearly N = 8				
1966	1.09*	−.11	.04	−.12	.96*
1967	1.16*	−.21	−	−.07	.90*
1968	.62	.37	.18	−.06	.92
1969	.55	.20	.27	−.03	.87
1970	.98*	−.06	.09	.31	.92
Nation-Years Aggregated, N = 40	.86*	.03	.09	−	.86*
	Unstable Group, Yearly N = 8				
1966	−	1.28*	−.10	.43*	.97*
1967	.89	−.23	.10	−.15	.72
1968	.51	.57	.04	.16	.96*
1969	.95	−.17	.21	.05	.99*
1970	.30	.59	.26	.26*	.99*
Nation-Years Aggregated, N = 40	.70*	.15	.17*	.07	.87*
	Poor Group, Yearly N = 9				
1966	.74*	−.39	.66	−.16	.92*
1967	.85	−.40	.48	−.21	.87*
1968	.29	−	.49	−.28	.55
1969	1.05*	−.33	.19	−.07	.88*
1970	.91	−.08	.14	−.03	.94*
Nation-Years Aggregated, N = 45	.90*	−.11	.16	−.08	.87*

TABLE 6.2
Nonmilitary Conflict as Predicted by the Interstate Components

	Constructive Diplomatic Behavior	Non-Military Conflict	Force	International Involvement	R^2
Total Group, Yearly N = 56					
1966	.12	.63*	.05	−.05	.55*
1967	.36*	.16	.35*	−.02	.61*
1968	.35*	.54*	.05	−.13	.70*
1969	.62*	.49*	−.07	.33*	.83*
1970	.60*	.33*	−	−.20*	.75*
Nation-Years Aggregated N = 280	.39*	.45*	.09*	−.13*	.67*
Western Group, Yearly N = 15					
1966	−.05	.82	.20	−.04	.86*
1967	−	.88	.09	−.02	.90*
1968	.65*	−.17	.51*	.12	.87*
1969	.57	.46	.03	−.24	.89*
1970	.80	−.38	.57*	−.05	.81*
Nation-Years Aggregated, N = 75	.34*	.42*	.22*	−.10	.79*
Closed Group, Yearly N = 10					
1966	.48	.48	−	−.27	.65
1967	.22	.30	.26	.35	.68
1968	.67*	−.10	−.47	.73*	.91*
1969	.61	.49	−.26	.19	.90*
1970	.56*	.87*	−.34	−.08	.96*
Nation-Years Aggregated, N =50	.57*	.36*	−	−	.75*

NOTE: Numbers in first four columns are beta weights.
*Beta weights or R^2 significant at the .05 level.

Table 6.2 (Continued)

	Constructive Diplomatic Behavior	Non-Military Conflict	Force	International Involvement	R^2
	Large Developing Group, Yearly N = 8				
1966	.12	.59	.24	.26	.87
1967	1.36*	−.50	.12	−.11	.97*
1968	−.24	.87	.25	.43	.85
1969	.31	.89*	−.21	−.14	.98*
1970	.27	.45	−.12	.43	.72
Nation-Years Aggregated, N = 40	.36*	.44*	.11	.14	.74*
	Unstable Group, Yearly N = 8				
1966	−.29	1.41	.10	.60	.75
1967	−.34	.34	.61	−.17	.54
1968	−.15	.93*	.14	−	.85
1969	.19	.53	.27	−.04	.91
1970	.90*	.52	−.40	.13	.99*
Nation-Years Aggregated, N = 40	.23	.57*	.04	−.06	.69*
	Poor Group, Yearly N = 9				
1966	−	.30	.46	−.31	.56
1967	.85	−.30	.25	−.31	.63
1968	.29	−	.49	−.28	.55
1969	.85*	.25	−.24	−.56*	.91*
1970	.65	.26	.00	−.20	.88*
Nation-Years Aggregated, N = 45	.41*	.26	.14	−.29*	.63*

differences among the equations for the five groups. What we
have uncovered here is a universal characteristic of states which
transcends their wide differences on structural dimensions.

We turn now to the results in Table 6.2 for nonmilitary conflict. Here we can note that the percentages of variance explained range from 63 percent to 79 percent, while for the total group
it is 67 percent. While these figures are considerably lower than
the comparable results for constructive diplomatic behavior,
they are still quite substantial.

A close examination of Table 6.2 reveals a much less
homogeneous pattern than was discernible in Table 6.1. For
the individual groups, the type of explicit matching behavior
which we observed for constructive diplomatic behavior is not
as apparent for nonmilitary conflict. If we consider the aggregated results for each of the five types of states, we can note
that the relative contribution to explaining the variance in nonmilitary conflict sent is split between constructive diplomatic
behavior received and nonmilitary conflict received. Thus, if we
combine our findings for the two types of behavior at this point,
we can note that constructive diplomatic behavior reflects a
balanced interaction process among states, while the level of
nonmilitary conflict which states send tends to reflect a more
complex combination of factors.

With regard to the question of whether state type makes any
difference in terms of the patterns of relationships, the results
show a rather subtle distinction between the pattern for the
closed and *poor* states compared to that exhibited by the other
three groups. For the former two groups, nonmilitary conflict
behavior is best predicted by constructive diplomatic behavior
received. Apparently, among the leadership groups of these
states there is a tendency to react with foreign conflict behavior
to diplomatic situations. Referring back to Table 3.7, it is difficult to pinpoint similarities between the structural
characteristics of these two groups of states, with the noteworthy exception of their similar means on the governmental
dimension.

This leads us to concede that different processes within these groups lead to similar outcomes. This assumption is bolstered by the finding for the *poor* group of a significant negative beta for the indicator total involvement in the international system. A more complete explanation of these differences must await the analysis in the following chapter, which will utilize more complex statistical techniques in an effort to identify and characterize these more subtle relationships.

Aside from the one distinction identified above, an overview of the regression results for constructive diplomatic behavior sent and nonmilitary conflict sent reveals few if any distinctions among the behavior patterns exhibited by the different groups of states which we have identified. One conclusion might be that in this analysis we are encountering the action-reaction model of international politics, in which the different structural characteristics of states have relatively little effect on the distinctions in behavior patterns. Before we deal with this notion more fully, however, we should consider the results generated by the second portion of the model, the societal domain.

Foreign Behavior as Predicted by the Societal Component

Once again, we will investigate the foreign policy realm in terms of constructive diplomatic behavior sent and nonmilitary conflict sent. The predictor variables are governmental instability, societal unrest, merchandise trade balance, and population growth rate. As in the previous analyses, regression results will be presented for the total group, followed by those for the five subgroups.

Table 6.2 presents the multiple regression results for the equations predicting constructive diplomatic behavior sent. The percentages of variance explained are substantially lower than they were for the interstate component analysis, ranging between 14 percent and 34 percent for the individual groups, and 10 percent for the total group. It is in the context of these rather low percentages that we nonetheless find important distinctions

TABLE 6.3
Constructive Diplomatic Behavior as Predicted
by the Societal Components

	Governmental Instability	Societal Unrest	Merchandise Trade Balance	Population Growth Rate	R^2
	Total Group, Yearly N = 56				
1966	−.51	.33	.28*	−.02	.14
1967	.09	.32*	.30*	−.05	.23*
1968	−.08	.44*	.15	−.08	.28*
1969	.02	.21	.11	−.18	.13
1970	.05	.33*	.15	−.06	.14
Nation-Years Aggregated N = 280	−.22*	.24*	.21*	−.07	.10*
	Western Group, Yearly N = 15				
1966	−.23	.24	.39	.15	.38
1967	−.15	.46	.16	.05	.40
1968	−.17	.79*	.04	.24	.61*
1969	.16	.49	−.14	.10	.26
1970	−.25	.38	.29	.09	.29
Nation-Years Aggregated, N = 75	−.11	.44*	.18	.11	.31*
	Closed Group, Yearly N = 10				
1966	−	−	.64*	.12	.46
1967	.22	−	.73*	.27	.57
1968	.54	−.15	.77*	.88*	.77
1969	−.61	.70	.47	.41	.43
1970	−.22	.11	.34	.05	.12
Nation-Years Aggregated, N = 50	.10	−.05	.49*	.30*	.34*

NOTE: Numbers in first four columns are beta weights.
*Beta or R^2 significant at the .05 level.

Table 6.3 (Continued)

	Governmental Instability	Societal Unrest	Merchandise Trade Balance	Population Growth Rate	R^2
	Large Developing, Yearly N = 8				
1966	1.47	−.75	−.26	−.34	.72
1967	.70	.14	−.74	−.57	.92
1968	1.04	−	−.55	−1.09*	.83
1969	−.36	.07	.34	− .38	.34
1970	.38	−	−.08	.55	.51
Nation-Years Aggregated, N = 40	.31*	.05	−.18	−.20	.14
	Unstable Group, Yearly N = 8				
1966	.40	−.52	−.98*	.25	.89
1967	.34	.22	−.71	.69	.74
1968	.15	.58	−.34	−.27	.68
1969	−.13	.51	−.66	.16	.46
1970	−	.35	−.58	.10	.58
Nation-Years Aggregated, N = 40	−.01	−	−.65*	.12	.38*
	Poor Group, Yearly N = 9				
1966	−	−	.48	.04	.23
1967	.56	−	.10	−.05	.28
1968	−.47	−	−	.19	.20
1969	.57	.23	−.26	−	.40
1970	.63*	.77*	.04	−.84*	.88*
Nation-Years Aggregated, N = 45	.25	.27*	.02	−.09	.15

TABLE 6.4

Nonmilitary Conflict as Predicted by the Societal Component

	Governmental Instability	Societal Unrest	Merchandise Trade Balance	Population Growth Rate	R^2
Total Group, Yearly N = 56					
1966	−.06	−.08	−.08	−	.01
1967	.18	.20	.11	−.04	.09
1968	−.07	.30*	.07	−.08	.13
1969	.18	.07	.03	−.08	.06
1970	.12	.18	−.12	−.03	.07
Nation-Years Aggregated, N = 280	−	.10*	.01	−.04	.01
Western Group, Yearly N = 15					
1966	−.06	.60*	−.15	.44	.43
1967	.09	.52	−.10	.20	.25
1968	−.18	.65*	.06	.20	.44
1969	.39	.41	−.18	.30	.39
1970	−.23	.29	−.11	−.05	.07
Nation-Years Aggregated, N = 75	.02	.39*	−.04	.17	.17*
Closed Group, Yearly N = 10					
1966	−.12	.67	.94*	−.34	.81*
1967	.17	.23	.85*	.16	.68
1968	.35	−.05	.87*	.62	.74
1969	−	.18	.49	.10	.24
1970	−.39	.36	.55	−.24	.22
Nation-Years Aggregated, N = 50	−	.13	.57*	.07	.32*

NOTE: Numbers in first four columns are beta weights.
*Beta or R^2 significant at the .05 level.

Table 6.4 (Continued)

	Governmental Instability	Societal Unrest	Merchandise Trade Balance	Population Growth Rate	R^2
	Large Developing Group, Yearly N = 8				
1966	1.77*	−1.11	−.11	−.89	.82
1967	.60	.23	−.51	−.69	.84
1968	.79	.24	−.07	−.91	.79
1969	−	−.17	.33	−.26	.23
1970	.43	−	−	−.05	.11
Nation-Years Aggregated, N = 40	.30*	.09	−.04	−.39*	.21
	Unstable Group, Yearly N = 8				
1966	.81	−.77	−.92	.16	.82
1967	.90*	−1.02*	−.44	−.41	.90
1968	.16	.29	−.81*	−	.85
1069	.14	−.08	−.48	−	.30
1970	−	.28	−.62	.19	.56
Nation-Years Aggregated, N = 40	.32	−.30	−.74*	.11	.52*
	Poor Group, Yearly N = 9				
1966	.19	−	−.08	.27	.21
1967	−	−	−	−	−
1968	−.63	−.19	−.25	.13	.36
1969	.32	.35	−.73	−	.35
1970	.48	.76	−.26	−.70	.79
Nation-Years Aggregated, N = 45	.16	.15	−.28*	.07	.14

among the types of states which we have identified. Unlike the earlier interstate results, the overall R^2 of .10 conceals important between-group differences.

While the *Western*, *closed*, and *unstable* groups show significant multiple correlations, these results are generated by very different processes. In the case of the *Western* group, we find that the 31 percent of the variance explained is due largely to the existence of societal unrest (i.e., riots, antigovernment demonstrations, and general strikes). This group, composed for the most part of Western polyarchies, seems to be most sensitive to the types of spontaneous, society-based behaviors which are represented by these indicators. We have already noted that the Western states are among the most stable under investigation here, and we now have evidence that when events of this nature do occur, their impact is far greater than is the case in other types of states.

The *closed* group produces a multiple R^2 of .34; the key predictor variable is merchandise trade balance. As we noted earlier, merchandise trade balance is being employed here to assess the general state of the domestic economy. The positive impact of this factor on constructive diplomatic behavior sent contrasts sharply with the substantial negative impact on constructive diplomatic behavior sent for the *unstable* group (beta = $-$ .65, R^2 = .38). A more complex model will be necessary in order to explain these conflicting findings. We will, however, return to this issue later.

Examining the results for nonmilitary conflict sent, which appear in Table 6.4, we again find that the overall percentage of variance explained for the total group is negligible at 1 percent. This finding conceals important distinctions among the five groups; percentages of variance explained range from 14 percent to 52 percent. Interestingly, it is the same three groups—*Western*, *closed*, and *unstable*—which produce significant R^2's, and the patterns are substantially the same as those discovered earlier.

For the *Western* group, domestic conflict of the social unrest variety is the primary predictor of nonmilitary conflict. Neither this nor governmental instability appears with a significant beta on any of the equations for the other groups for which R^2 was significant. As indicated earlier, it appears that these Western democracies are more sensitive to manifestations of social unrest and are more apt to allow these events to permeate the realm of international behavior. It should be recalled, however, that this relationship accounts for only 17 percent of the variance explained; it is obvious that other factors are operating.

We once again discover that the *closed* and *unstable* groups show sharply different patterns, with merchandise trade balance having a positive impact on nonmilitary conflict sent for the *closed* group and a negative impact for the *unstable* group. Apparently, during periods of economic difficulties, as reflected by balance of trade deficits, the *closed* states turn inward, and there is a reduction in both their constructive diplomatic behavior and their nonmilitary conflict behavior. In contrast, the *unstable* states turn outward—as demonstrated by increases in both types of behavior during periods of economic difficulties. Different capability levels—as well as differences in the levels of development of the national economies—may be exerting differential impact on the behavior patterns of these states.

Interstate Versus Societal Predictors of Foreign Behavior

In the two preceding sections we have attempted to determine what portion of the variance in foreign behavior is attributable to various interstate and societal factors, considered separately. We also demonstrated that these rather complex relationships might be mediated by a classification scheme of foreign policy actors. We shall now assess the relative potency of the interstate component vis-à-vis the societal component.

Our strategy was to develop a single indicator for each of the two components, based on the combined effects of all variables within each cluster in terms of explaining foreign behavior. We preferred this option over the more conventional approach of producing a multiple regression equation consisting of four interstate variables and four societal variables. The former strategy will provide us with a summary measure of relative potency.[4]

Table 6.5 presents the multiple regression results for the combined effects on foreign behavior of both interstate and societal factors. It should be noted that the input values for the independent variables are the predicted values for constructive diplomatic behavior sent and nonmilitary conflict sent which were produced in stages one and two above. We will present only the results in their aggregated form for the entire five-year period.

In virtually all of the cases, the interstate realm is the key predictor of foreign policy behavior of both the constructive diplomatic and the nonmilitary conflict varieties. The conflict sent/conflict received process is so pervasive that it virtually overwhelms the subtle differences which we previously unearthed among the various types of states.

As we previously observed, constructive diplomatic behavior sent is generally better predicted by our model than nonmilitary conflict sent. To the extent that precise matching behavior is less evident for nonmilitary conflict sent, we can infer the greater impact of societal factors, although only for the *unstable* group does a statistically significant beta emerge.

CONCLUSION

This preliminary assessment of the relative explanatory power of domestic and interstate determinants unambiguously reveals the priority of the second cluster of factors. The findings offer striking support for the proposition that foreign behavior is a symmetrical phenomenon. While the action-reaction perspective applies to both diplomatic and conflict forms of behavior, the pattern emerges with more clarity in the case of constructive

TABLE 6.5
Interstate Versus Societal Predictors of Foreign Policy Behavior

	Interstate Component	Societal Component	R^2
Total Group			
Constructive Diplomatic Behavior	.95*	.01	.92*
Non-Military Conflict	.81*	.03	.67*
Western Group			
Constructive Diplomatic Behavior	.99*	−.01	.96*
Non-Military Conflict	.91*	−.04	.79*
Closed Group			
Constructive Diplomatic Behavior	.99*	−.01	.96*
Non-Military Conflict	.80*	.11	.76*
Large Developing Group			
Constructive Diplomatic Behavior	.96*	−.08	.87*
Non-Military Conflict	.82*	.10	.75*
Unstable Group			
Constructive Diplomatic Behavior	.88*	.09	.88*
Non-Military Conflict	.65*	.25*	.25*
Poor Group			
Constructive Diplomatic Behavior	.94*	−.02	.87*
Non-Military Conflict	.78*	.03	.64*

NOTE: Numbers in the first two columns are beta weight.
*Beta or R^2 significant at the .05 level.

diplomatic behavior. Apparently, the conflict-begets-conflict notion can be generalized to other types of interstate behavior.

Generally, domestic sources as measured here are not significant determinants of foreign policy behavior. When societal and interstate sources are considered simultaneously, internal factors remain significant only for the *unstable* group for the non-military conflict factor.

This initial effort to operationalize a comprehensive framework for the comparative analysis of foreign policy behavior has produced several noteworthy propositions:

(1) Interstate factors are generally more predictive of foreign policy behavior than societal factors; this finding is supported in the separate analyses of the two clusters and in the direct relative potency test.

(2) The strategy of classifying states is not as productive as we had originally expected. When interstate factors are posited to be predictors of foreign policy behavior, the *closed* and *poor* groups exhibit a similar pattern for nonmilitary conflict behavior. But it is probable that this similar outcome is the product of different processes within the two types. Generally, however, grouping states does not exert an impact of any discernible magnitude. In the case of societal determinants, distinctions among state groupings become more important. Especially interesting is the Western pattern: Spontaneous, unorganized violence and unrest are significant for constructive diplomatic behavior sent and, to a lesser extent, for nonmilitary conflict. Differences by type of state generally wash out when relative potency is assessed.

(3) Constructive diplomatic behavior sent is better predicted than nonmilitary conflict sent. The action-reaction model is more valid for characterizing such behaviors as "comment," "agree," and "request." Nonmilitary conflict actions—such as "threaten," "expel," and "seize"—are not predicted with equivalent accuracy. Part of the discrepancy may be attributable to the fact that diplomacy is a very structured process of interaction. Conflictual acts received are less routine and therefore offer more discretion to decision makers. It is significant that conflict behavior is not exclusively an action-reaction syndrome; however, the conflict received/conflict sent pattern does appear with sufficient frequency to suggest that foreign policy behavior is often a symmetrical process.

This, however, does not warrant the acceptance of a mechanistic stimulus-reponse model of foreign policy elites, other official decision makers, and—perhaps in some instances—the mass public. An elaborate decision process intervenes between events received and events sent. Psychological, political, societal, and external factors can be expected to impinge upon the process of decision-making.

The tentative, exploratory nature of this research must be recognized. Foreign behavior is a complex phenomenon. The elucidation of variable interrelationships will involve the construction of more refined models and the use of more sophisticated analytical techniques and strategies. While Chapter 7 will attempt to examine the impact of societal and interstate factors in a more detailed fashion, two other areas of inquiry should also be pursued. First of all, other determinants of foreign policy behavior must be measured and tested. In addition, relationships among the determinants of foreign policy must be explored. In the case of societal and interstate variables, the discrepancies between the societal analysis and the relative potency assessment may be attributable to the existence of a more complex model. Internal conditions may influence policies directed at the state; this model may have applied to the Rhodesian situation. Alternatively, foreign behavior received may affect societal conditions, as the impact of the Arab oil cartel has demonstrated.

NOTES

1. Researchers using the Dimensionality of Nations Project national attribute data have tested the strength of the relationship between diverse domestic factors and foreign conflict behavior; see Rummel (1968) and Phillips (1973). None of the domestic predictors in these studies accounts for an appreciable portion of the variance in foreign conflict behavior. For reviews of these general bodies of empirical literature, see Zinnes (1976a), Scolnick (1974), and Stein (1976).

2. The two factors were transformed (using the logarithm to the base 10) to correct for skewness.

3. It should be noted here that for the present analysis only, we do not distinguish between the different dimensionalizations of foreign behavior sent and received. These were explored in Chapter 4 and will be incorporated into later analyses reported in Chapters 7 and 8.

4. Stepwise regression analyses were also performed; the results involved more complex patterns, but the findings were essentially congruent with those patterns reported here.

Chapter 7

Testing a More Sophisticated Model
Societal, Interstate, and Global
Determinants of Foreign Behavior

In a previous chapter we discussed in some detail the analytic strategy—Partial Least Squares (PLS)—which will be employed in order to assess the relative potency of the components of the framework. A preliminary analysis—which was reported in the preceding chapter—presented the results of a relatively straightforward test of the relative importance of internal versus external determinants of foreign behavior. The present analysis, as depicted in Figure 7.1, examines the impact of the variables representing three components: societal, interstate, and global.[1] Figure 7.1 highlights the key variables of each of the components.

Regarding the societal component, we can observe that it remains as it was for the analysis reported in Chapter 6 (see Figure 6.1). That is, it incorporates indicators of domestic unrest and instability, economic performance, and population growth rate. While it is obvious that a large number of additional variables could be added to this list, our feeling is that these four capture

AUTHORS' NOTE: *Portions of this chapter constitute expanded versions of material which originally appeared in Wilkenfeld et al. (1979) and Rossa et al. (1980).*

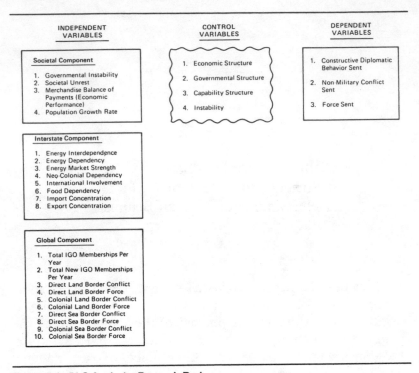

Figure 7.1: PLS Analysis: Research Design

the essence of the domestic scene from a societal perspective, particularly as it relates to foreign behavior. Additional variables would tend to be highly correlated with this set of indicators.

Turning to the interstate component, we note here some rather drastic changes in the composition of this cluster from the interstate component in Figure 6.1 of Chapter 6. First of all, we have greatly expanded (from one to eight) the number of indicators tapping interstate economic relations. These indicators (discussed in Chapter 2) take into consideration export and import flows, production and consumption within states, and commodity-specific relationships. Specifically, we examine interstate energy relationships, general trade relationships, food dependency and advantage, and import and export concentration (the generality of interstate economic relations). These indicators are designed to tap the essence of interstate relations in the economic sphere.

In addition to expanding the indicators of interstate economic relations, we made a critical decision concerning the action-reaction element of the interstate component. One of the thorniest problems which confront analysts who deal with the interstate realm is the manner in which the behavior received/behavior sent, or action-reaction element, should be treated. Clearly, such a process is at the core of interstate interactions, in the sense that most behaviors represent reactions to the behaviors of other states which constitute the state's operational environment. Nevertheless, one could convincingly argue in favor of excluding the action-reaction element on the grounds that it constitutes the overriding behavioral context within which other factors influence the process of determining foreign behavior outcomes. On the basis of an impressive volume of existing empirical studies, we can establish that behavior received explains a large proportion of behavior sent—ranging from 50 to 90 percent, depending upon the particular circumstances involved.[2] Yet such a figure is relatively meaningless, and consequently useless for policy analysis purposes, unless it is viewed as the context in which other factors from both the internal and external realms exert impact. The behavior received/behavior sent aspect will consequently be excluded from this analysis, in order to more closely observe the operation of these other factors.[3]

We must admit that we feel vaguely uncomfortable about excluding such an important and firmly established process. Indeed, it was only toward the end of the present research effort that we began to exclude systematically the action-reaction element from our analyses. Therefore, for the sake of comprehensiveness—both in terms of the current model and for purposes of comparison with the results of Chapter 6—we present a rather extensive appendix to the present chapter; the latter reports on a parallel analysis in which the action-reaction element was included within the interstate component. From time to time in the body of this chapter, we will offer comparisons between the main findings reported here and those resulting from inclusion of the action-reaction element.

The third element among the determinants of foreign behavior which is incorporated into this analysis is the global component. As we noted in Chapter 2, this component is composed of two sets of indicators. The first pertains to the number of overall and new international governmental organization memberships for each state; the latter are posited to be indicators of the degree of participation of the state in the international organizational system. The second set of variables concerns the extent of conflict in which bordering states are involved. Conflict exerts a spillover effect; a state which is surrounded by other states, some of which are immersed in conflict, may have a greater propensity to be pulled into certain types of conflict relationships and behaviors.

Finally, the classification of states, which was derived from the four dimensions of economic structure, capability, governmental structure, and instability, continues to function as the intervening variable domain. That is, we expect that the determinants of foreign behavior will have differing levels of impact, depending upon the type of state which experiences them. Foreign behavior itself is examined within three general domains: constructive diplomatic behavior, nonmilitary conflict, and force.

It is obvious that the number of independent variables in the analysis is quite large, relative to the number of control and dependent variables. One of the advantages of the PLS technique is that it is designed to overcome this specific problem, while it simultaneously capitalizes on all of the information which these variables can impart. We now turn to the actual analysis.

RESULTS

The results of the PLS analysis are presented in a series of tables, each of which builds upon the others; the results are designed to highlight the key indicators of foreign behavior in general and of conflict behavior in particular. As we pointed out above, the analysis initially identifies the parameters for the exogenous or manifest variables; the weights reflect each indicator's contribution to the latent variable's impact upon foreign behavior. The next step involves the introduction of the control for type of state, based on structural characteristics. This allows us to estimate a second set of parameters, between the societal, interstate, and global latent variables and foreign behavior in general. We then reduce the generality of the model considerably, and deal with two more specific questions: (1) What types of foreign behavior are best explained by the current model? and (2) What is the relative potency of each of the latent variables for each of the 56 states in the analysis? The last stage will entail the utilization of the full capability of the present analytic strategy, in that we will be able to assess the patterns of variability among the different states in the sample.

Latent Independent Variables Determined by the Manifest Independent Variables

Table 7.1 presents the parameters, or betas, resulting from the regressions of the computed latent variables on the three sets of manifest independent variables. The betas are weights which are used to aggregate the indicators within a latent independent variable cluster. It should be emphasized that the computation of these parameters is not analogous to a normal clustering technique; the betas here identify the relative contribution of those variables in each set in determining a latent variable which in turn most adequately explains the latent dependent variable—foreign behavior. This is quite a different operation from the normal process of index construction, which is undertaken independently of the question of the power of the index to explain a dependent variable. The difference, then, is between clustering, on the one hand, and a best-fitting operation, on the other. The utility of this approach for the related operations of early warning indicator construction and forecasting is obvious.

TABLE 7.1
Betas for Manifest Variables Regressed on Latent Variables

SOCIETAL COMPONENT		
Societal Unrest	.200	
Governmental Instability	−.033	
Population Growth Rate	−.011	
Economic Performance	.193	
Multiple R (R^2)	.297	(.088)
INTERSTATE COMPONENT		
International Involvement	.246	
Energy Dependency	−.261	
Energy Market Strength	−.106	
Energy Interdependency	−.016	
Food Dependency	−.029	
Export Concentration	−.048	
Import Concentration	.003	
Neo-Colonial Dependency	−.007	
Multiple R (R^2)	.388	(.151)
GLOBAL COMPONENT		
Total IGO Membership	.076	
New IGO Memberships	−.033	
Direct Land Border Conflict	.214	
Direct Land Border Force	.079	
Colonial Land Border Conflict	.180	
Colonial Land Border Force	−.038	
Direct Sea Border Conflict	.443	
Direct Sea Border Force	−.047	
Colonial Sea Border Conflict	.116	
Colonial Sea Border Force	−.065	
Multiple R (R^2)	.488	(.238)

We can note that among the societal variables, societal unrest and economic performance yield the highest betas, indicating their centrality to the societal latent variable. For the interstate latent variable, international involvement, energy dependency, and energy market strength stand out as critical in their impacts. Finally, the global latent variable is composed primarily of the four manifest variables representing conflict (rather than force) in direct and colonial land border countries and in direct and colonial sea border countries.

Societal unrest, generally viewed in *negative* terms by decision makers, and economic performance, which has *positive* connotations, have almost identical weights in determining the societal component, although their impacts are opposite in direction. Similarly, we can note that energy dependency tends to negate the effects of international involvement upon foreign behavior. Regarding the global latent variable, it should be emphasized that bordering conflict has a uniformly positive effect across the various types of borders; this impact is most strongly manifested in the case of direct borders. We shall refer to this specific indicator pattern below when we interpret the significance of state differences.

Foreign Behavior as Predicted by the Independent Latent Variables

We now expand the analysis to incorporate the control for states on the basis of their stable structural characteristics. Table 7.2 indicates the manner in which this control was introduced. In this regression, foreign behavior is regressed onto fifteen independent variables. A new set of betas is produced, indicating the relative weight to be assigned to each typologically controlled latent variable. These results indicate that the global and interstate latent variables are clearly the strongest when a control for capability is imposed. The global component also has some effect when controlling for economic structure, while the interstate component has additional (although more limited) strength when controlling for instability. The societal component, which shows comparatively little overall impact, appears to be most potent in its unmediated state, although some limited influence is observed for governmental structure and instability.

Overall, then, these findings show that for two of the components—the interstate and the global—the control for type of

TABLE 7.2

Betas for Foreign Behavior Regressed on Independent Variables
(control for structural characteristics)

COMPONENT	CONTROL	BETA
Societal	Uncontrolled	−.161
Societal	Economic Structure	.034
Societal	Capability	.025
Societal	Governmental Structure	−.117
Societal	Instability	−.119
Interstate	Uncontrolled	.120
Interstate	Economic Structure	.062
Interstate	Capability	.482
Interstate	Governmental Structure	.054
Interstate	Instability	.124
Global	Uncontrolled	−.043
Global	Economic Structure	.200
Global	Capability	.436
Global	Governmental Structure	−.040
Global	Instability	.096

$R^2 = .69$

state enhances the explanatory power of the variables. Further-more, there is a considerable variation among the three latent variables in terms of which structural characteristics are most important. As we shall see below, these and additional pieces of information will be meshed together to generate individual state profiles.

As Table 7.2 indicates, this set of fifteen variables explains 69 percent of the variation in foreign behavior. This rather impressive figure is even more striking when we recall that in the present analysis we have intentionally excluded the action-reaction element on the grounds that its overwhelming impact serves to mask the more subtle effects of the other determinants of foreign behavior. We have argued that the impact of these other variables is critical in that they intervene in the more routinized (as distinguished from routine) action-reaction processes. Here, then, we find strong evidence to support the independent effect of several other factors as determinants of foreign policy behavior.

Manifest Foreign Behavior Variables as Predicted by Latent Foreign Behavior

The above findings are further illuminated when we consider the first of the more specific questions which can be addressed by the present analysis: What types of foreign behavior are explained by the set of indicators incorporated into the present model? We have previously discussed the model as it terminated with the latent dependent variable, foreign behavior. Now, however, we can explore the links between this latent variable and the three manifest foreign behavior variables. By regressing each of these manifest variables on the predicted latent variable, we produce the results which are reported in Table 7.3

An examination of this table reveals that the model performs impressively in explaining the variation in constructive diplomatic behavior and in nonmilitary conflict. However, the force dimension, which is composed of only the most extreme forms of conflict behavior, is virtually unrelated to any of the indicators which we examine here. This finding offers striking evidence for the centrality of the action-reaction process for the most extreme forms of interstate conflict. In a parallel analysis (see the appendix to this chapter) in which the action-reaction aspect was retained in the model, the model as a whole explains 94 percent of the variance in general foreign behavior, with 50 percent of the type of conflict behavior designated as force accounted for. This contrasts sharply with the 1 percent of the variance in force explained here.

The process of accounting for these findings appears to be quite straightforward. Force actions, the most serious and consequential of the conflict actions which can be undertaken by states, are very much enmeshed in a stimulus-response or action-reaction type of mechanism. Once conflict between states reaches this level of intensity, it is unlikely that factors other than those directly related to the dynamics and rhythm of the conflict will be able to exert serious impact.

TABLE 7.3
Betas for Manifest Foreign Behavior Variables Regressed on
Foreign Behavior Latent Variable

Variable	Beta (=r)	R^2
Constructive Diplomatic Behavior	.847	.72
Non-Military Conflict	.684	.47
Force	.104	.01

On the other hand, constructive diplomatic behavior (mostly cooperative behaviors) and nonmilitary conflict (less serious conflict indicators) will be much more susceptible to the impact of the whole range of potential influences on state behavior. This differentiation among types of foreign behavior and the differing impacts of various classes of determinants are potentially significant to our conceptions of foreign behavior generally. Since the behavior of states in the international arena—even when dominated by conflict—is never undimensional, it is vital that both scholars and policy analysts be aware of the fact that not all behavior is subject to the same dynamic. To so treat it is to oversimplify reality and open oneself up to serious criticism (as a scholar) and to potential disaster (as a policy maker).

Individual State Profiles

We turn, finally, to the most "micro" of the analytic perspectives afforded by the PLS procedure: an examination of the individual state profiles upon which the above analyses are based. The procedure adopted here yields a measure of the relative potency for each of the three latent variables in predicting yearly levels of foreign policy behavior for each of the states involved.[4] Table 7.4 presents a listing of the relative potency scores for each state, averaged across the five-year period (1966-1970).[5] The variations which can be noted among the states in this list

TABLE 7.4
Average Relative Potency Scores by States (1966-1970)

	SOCIETAL	INTERSTATE	GLOBAL
USA	−.13	1.29	.48
Canada	−.12	.55	.16
Cuba	−.02	−.23	−.14
Brazil	−.23	.59	.12
Chile	−.30	.07	−.11
UK	−.11	.53	.16
Netherlands	−.15	.10	−.04
Belgium	−.18	.05	−.05
France	−.34	.80	.26
Spain	.08	.19	.03
Portugal	−.04	−.13	−.13
West Germany	−.15	.62	.19
East Germany	.02	.18	.07
Poland	.04	.30	.10
Hungary	−.12	.10	.00
Czechoslovakia	.01	.20	.08
Italy	−.22	.49	.10
Albania	−.02	−.54	−.30
Yugoslavia	−.08	.13	−.04
Greece	−.12	−.04	−.08
Cyprus	−.20	−.98	−.54
Bulgaria	−.04	−.02	−.06
Rumania	.05	.14	.02
USSR	.12	1.10	.46
Sweden	−.17	.18	.00
Denmark	−.21	−.18	−.16
Ghana	−.11	−.40	−.28
Nigeria	−.02	.07	−.07
Zaire	−.47	.21	−.01
Kenya	−.61	−.18	−.27
Ethiopia	−.01	−.38	−.27
South Africa	−.13	.11	−.06
Algeria	−.29	−.26	.03
Iran	−.24	.44	.09
Turkey	−.28	.34	−.03
Iraq	−.25	.20	.02
Egypt	−.32	.38	.04
Syria	−.56	.56	−.04
Lebanon	−.24	−.63	−.40
Jordan	−.08	−.53	−.30
Israel	−.20	−.18	−.16
Saudi Arabia	.10	−.04	−.04
Yemen	−.08	−.69	−.37
China	.05	.93	.32
South Korea	−.28	.17	−.08
Japan	−.32	.59	.12
India	−.19	.70	.10
Pakistan	−.17	.28	−.04

(Table 7.4 Continued)

Table 7.4 (Continued)

	SOCIETAL	INTERSTATE	GLOBAL
Thailand	−.21	.02	−.11
Cambodia	−.14	−.46	−.30
Laos	−.31	−.42	−.27
South Vietnam	−.41	.16	−.09
Malaysia	−.11	−.30	−.27
Philippines	−.27	−.10	−.22
Indonesia	−.10	.26	−.03
Australia	−.13	.36	.06

are attributable to differences in the values for these states on the four structural characteristics dimensions which constitute the control variables.

The relative potency scores show a pattern which is consistent with our earlier findings. That is, in virtually every case, the societal component is generally the weakest. The global component is occasionally significant, but virtually never to the exclusion of one of the other clusters.

In order to acquire more insight into the patterns which characterize these results, we decided to group those states which had unusually high scores in terms of the relative potency of one or more of the three latent variables. In the case of the global and societal latent variables, relative potency scores of ±.30 were considered to be high, while for the interstate component a score of ±.50 was used as the cutoff point.[6] Table 7.5 lists the states with high relative potency scores for each of the latent variables.

With regard to the global component, it should be recalled that the critical manifest variables which comprise the latent variable involve conflict actions which occur in bordering states. Six of the nine states with unusually high scores on the global component are members of the group of states which we have designated as *poor* (see Figure 3.1). As noted in Chapter 3, the outstanding characteristic of these states is the very low score for each on the capability dimension. Since the procedure in-

TABLE 7.5
States with Strong Relative Potency Scores

SOCIETAL		INTERSTATE		GLOBAL	
Kenya	−.61	USA	1.29	USA	.48
Syria	−.56	USSR	1.10	USSR	.46
Zaire	−.47	China	.93	China	.32
South Vietnam	−.41	France	.80	Albania	−.30
France	−.34	India	.70	Jordan	−.30
Egypt	−.32	West Germany	.62	Cambodia	−.32
Japan	−.32	Brazil	.59	Yemen	−.37
Laos	−.31	Japan	.59	Lebanon	−.40
Chile	−.30	Syria	.56	Cyprus	−.54
		Canada	.55		
		UK	.53		
		Jordan	−.53		
		Albania	−.54		
		Lebanon	−.63		
		Yemen	−.69		
		Cyprus	−.98		

NOTE: For the societal and global components, a cutpoint of ± .30 was used. For the interstate component, a cutpoint of ± .50 was used.

dicates that the global component was most potent in explaining foreign behavior when mediated by the effects of different levels of economic structure and capability, the present finding for the *poor* group is consistent. The *poor* group is marked by a lack of capabilities and low economic development, and reacts negatively to conflict in bordering states. China, the United States, and the Soviet Union are the top three states on the capability dimension and react positively to such conflict.

We have isolated, then, an interesting configuration of factors. The global component is most potent among those states which rank unusually high or low in terms of their capabilities. That is, the strongest and the weakest states appear to be particularly affected by conflict levels within bordering states. Those with extremely high capabilities will react to nearby conflict by increasing their activities, perhaps intervening in the fray in the hope of affecting the outcome. States with few resources, in contrast, will withdraw from the international political arena when faced with a conflict in the local environment. States in the middle ranges on the dimensions of capability and economic structure will be less constained in policy-making by the problems of their neighbors.

Concerning the interstate latent variable, we note a much larger number of states with high relative potency scores. Of the sixteen states, six are from the *Western* group, five are from the *poor* group, and three are from the *large developing* group. Generally, we find that once again the capability dimension is critical. All five of the *poor* states in this list have negative relative potency scores, while states with larger capabilities have positive scores. Referring again to the major manifest indicators within this latent variable, we find that strong states act in accordance with their relative position in the international economic hierarchy; for example, a large volume of trade and energy interdependence would indicate a strong position and frequent participation in international politics. States with fewer resources will match their foreign behavioral output volumes to the dominant pattern of economic interchange; activities increase when energy dependency or insufficient trade prevails, while energy self-sufficiency and a high volume of trade have the effect of reducing the need for external involvement.

Finally, we must deal with those states which exhibit high scores on the societal latent variable. It will be recalled that the latter was the only one of the three latent variables which did not exhibit a strong impact for the mediation by state type. That is, the societal latent variable operates directly on foreign behavior, with minimal impact attributable to the structural dimensions.

This finding is confirmed by the list of nine states which exhibit unusually high relative potency scores for the societal latent variable. Three are *Western*, three are *unstable*, and three are unclassifiable.[7] All indicate the same sign and rank high on the instability dimension (see Table 3.5). Apparently, stable governments do not strongly react to societal forces.

It is of some interest to note that the societal component as a whole is typified by a lack of strong positive relative potency. Neither societal unrest nor economic performance predicts to large increases in foreign behavior or foreign conflict; instead, both may lead to a decrease in such activity in unstable regimes.

An additional perspective for assessing the results entails an examination of those states for which the current model fits the data poorly. Here we refer to those states for which none of the three latent variables appears to be particularly potent. Fourteen states fall into this category. Seven are from the *closed* group: Spain, Portugal, East Germany, Hungary, Yugoslavia, Bulgaria, and Rumania. Four states are from the *Western* group: the Netherlands, Belgium, Sweden, and South Africa. Finally, three states—Greece, Nigeria, and Saudi Arabia—were unclassifiable in the scheme utilized here.

The unusually high number of members of the *closed* group—seven out of fourteen—is an interesting finding. Not only does this reveal a potentially important weakness in the present model; it also highlights the unique profile for the characteristics of the *closed* group. Regarding the first point—and in partial response to the second—it seems that the particular configuration of structural characteristics which typifies the *closed* group creates a situation in which the determinants of foreign behavior which have been incorporated into this model are not particularly relevant. The typological configuration for the *closed* group manifests the following pattern: strong on economic structure, extremely closed on the governmental dimension, relatively strong on capabilities, and high on stability. The explanation may be attributable to the fact that the *closed* group scored unusually low on the governmental and instability dimensions; our results show that these two dimensions, to the extent that they mediate the relationship at all, do so only weakly and only for the societal latent variable. Hence, the characteristics which serve to distinguish the *closed* group from the others turn out to be the ones which are least involved as potential mediating factors in the present model.

One of the questions which has not yet been considered concerns the meaning of these findings for the individual states
which are included in the analysis. At the outset, we emphasized
that our technique has the capability of producing findings
which can help us acquire insight into the dynamics of the processes within individual states. The relative potency scores
reported in Table 7.4 indicate the extent to which each state is
sensitive to various kinds of internal and external determinants.

As we have already noted, the interstate component is the
most important predictor of foreign behavior in general and of
foreign conflict in particular. That is, changes in this component, and particularly in the indicators of international involvement, energy dependency, and energy market strength (see
Table 7.1), will generate important variations in the level of
foreign behavior, primarily of the constructive diplomatic and
nonmilitary conflict varieties. Thus, since almost all of the 56
states in our sample conformed to this dominant pattern, the
three indicators identified above constitute key elements from
the perspective of a monitoring or tracking system.

We should not neglect those states for which the societal component is the most potent—or at least equal in importance to the
interstate cluster. Among the societal indicators, our findings
point to societal unrest and economic performance as those of
particular significance—and therefore as worthy of attention
from a monitoring vantage point. Fluctuations in these
variables from year to year can signal important changes in the
level of cooperative and conflictual behavior which the particular state exhibits.

Finally, although we isolated few cases in which the global
component was the most potent latent variable of the three, it
did occasionally show high potency scores. For those states for
which this was the case, particular attention should be accorded
to those indicators of conflict behavior (rather than force)
which involve neighboring states.

Given these general findings, the analyst can proceed to examine the individual state results. It should be emphasized that
this model does not fit all states equally well, as we have noted

above. In particular, the behavior of the *closed* group of states was poorly explained by the elements which constitute the present model. However, for those states for which foreign behavior is predicted accurately by this model, the findings reported above should be quite useful for developing some preliminary sets of indicator systems designed to aid both scholars and policy analysts in the tasks of anticipating—and therefore planning for—interstate behavior.

SUMMARY AND CONCLUSION

This analysis has involved an explicit attempt to measure the operation of a set of indicators as determinants of foreign behavior in general and of conflict behavior in particular. These indicators, which are derived from the societal, interstate, and global realms of a comprehensive framework, have been examined in the context of an econometric method which is designed to assess the relative potency of manifest variables in determining a set of latent independent variables; also central to this inquiry has been the determination of the relative potency of these latent independent variables in accounting for the foreign behavior of states.

We have seen that, in general, the interstate cluster is the most potent for most states, followed by the global and societal components. Type of state, as defined by the four stable characteristics of economic structure, capability, governmental structure, and instability, mediates the relationship between the interstate and global components and foreign behavior, while the operation of the societal realm is relatively unaffected by this mediation. Overall, the model explains 69 percent of the variance in foreign behavior, with constructive diplomatic behavior (primarily cooperative behaviors) and nonmilitary conflict explained most impressively. Finally, we have ascertained the relative potency of each of the latent variables for each of the 56 states in the study, thereby generating state-specific profiles.[8]

Among the more salient conclusions are those which concern the differences which relate to the types of determinants that contribute to explanations of the three different forms of foreign behavior identified: constructive diplomatic behavior, nonmilitary conflict, and force. The results reported here, when viewed together with the action-reaction results presented in the appendix to this chapter, suggest some significant distinctions. Constructive diplomatic behavior is almost totally a product of societal, interstate (economic), and global determinants. The addition of the action-reaction element did not enhance the 72 percent of the variance which the previous set of indicators had explained. Here, then, is clear evidence that the more routine, constructive, and cooperative types of behavior are dominated by situational factors rather than by those which evolve from patterns of interstate interactions.

Quite different are the conclusions pertaining to the two purely conflict behavior dimensions. Regarding force, we have observed a striking increase (from 1 to 50 percent) in our ability to explain this type of phenomenon after behavior received has been incorporated into the model. For this type of intense conflict behavior, the dynamics of the situation itself take precedence over other types of determinants. We have also seen (see Chapter 6) that type of state has very little impact upon this process. Clearly, at the very high levels of conflict behavior which are typified by the force dimension, there is very little maneuvering room left to the decision makers outside of the boundaries of the dynamics of the situation itself.

The model's ability to explain the variation in nonmilitary conflict also improved after the action-reaction element had been incorporated (from 47 to 61 percent). In this case, however, we are not starting from a base of almost zero, but rather from one where the other determinants have already explained almost half of the variance. While the addition of the action-reaction element does improve our ability to explain this type of behavior, it is clear that the determination of the level of nonmilitary conflict for a state is the most complex of the three behavioral processes described here; all potential determinants apparently exert influence.

To summarize, we have demonstrated that the indicators have clear implications in terms of accounting for the three very different types of foreign behavior. This general proposition leads to two major conclusions regarding the potential utility of these results:

(1) A clear differentiation among the types of foreign behavior is essential for understanding their very different dynamics. While finer breakdowns are of course conceivable, we nevertheless recommend that analysts employ these three dimensions of constructive diplomatic behavior, nonmilitary conflict, and force for purposes of monitoring and forecasting.

(2) A wide array of determinants or indicators should be monitored; the complex links between the latter and the different types of behavior should be fully understood and analyzed.

A legitimate question can be posed at this point. What is the value of the present findings in terms of the ultimate goal of developing sets of indicators for forecasting foreign behavior? While no single general answer can be given, we can definitively assert that the results here have singled out certain states—as profiled by their stable structural characteristics—which are susceptible to certain specified types of internal and external influences. We must, however, place these results in their proper perspective.

When we refer to the development of a forecasting capability which is based on the derivation of meaningful and measurable indicators for monitoring, we are alluding to two different types of indicators. The first type, which is based on overt behavioral changes and fluctuates on a daily or even hourly basis, provides a very useful type of information to the analyst who is charged with the responsibility for interpretation and response. Here we catalogue the process of detecting the potential precipitants of conflict. This type of indicator, and the monitoring which it entails, is beyond the scope of any university-based research project. We should, however, acknowledge its undeniable relevance (see Andriole and Young, 1977).

The second type of monitoring, which is exemplified by the present research, concentrates on the derivation of indicators which are capable of detecting significant changes in those determinants of foreign behavior which are measurable on a more long-term basis. Various types of individual, societal, economic, political, interstate, and systemic conditions are continually subject to change, although such change is perhaps best measured on a monthly, quarterly, or yearly basis, rather than for a much shorter span of time. Here, then, we refer to the identification and monitoring of the preconditions of confict at the interstate level. Indicators which can only be assessed on a yearly basis have often been neglected by those who are responsible for the formulation of policy outputs, on the grounds that they cannot afford the luxury of surveying developments from such a macro perspective. Correspondingly, academics have consequently been hesitant to offer these more long-range forecasting tools to the policy community.

It is, however, possible to envision a synthesis of the two sets of indicators, provided that proper coordination is undertaken. That is, the two types of indicators, reflecting very short-term, fluctuating phenomena as well as more long-term, fundamental changes in attributes, must be combined in a forecasting model which is sufficiently flexible to incorporate the strong points of each approach (Wilkenfeld and Hopple, 1977). We hope that the present effort has made a modest contribution to the eventual objective of a comprehensive, integrated system of indicators.

APPENDIX TO CHAPTER 7—PLS ANALYSIS: ACTION-REACTION FACTORS

This appendix, which will report on a second PLS analysis of the IBA framework, incorporates the action-reaction element.

That is, foreign behavior received will be included among the interstate indicators in our analysis of the relative potency of the determinants of foreign behavior. It will be recalled (see Chapter 4) that we undertook to cluster separately behavior received and behavior sent, on the assumption that they would dimensionalize differently. We have already noted that behavior sent dimensionalized into constructive diplomatic behavior, nonmilitary conflict, and force; these three dimensions constitute the dependent variables of our analyses. The three new independent variables, representing behavior sent, are diplomatic behavior (incorporating 19 of the 22 WEIS categories), force, and reward (incorporating yield and reward).

One other major difference is reflected in this analysis. While the analysis in the body of Chapter 7 incorporates the classificatory scheme for purposes of control in an additive manner, the present analysis does so in a multiplicative mode. While this change has profound effects on the manner in which the results for the individual states can be interpreted, for present purposes the modification should not create difficulties of interpretation and comparison. Our major objective in presenting this analysis in an appendix is to acknowledge the impact of the action-reaction element, most notably in terms of the impact of the interstate component relative to that of the societal and global components. For this purpose, it is not necessary to resolve the issue of how these findings are manifested in the context of individual state profiles.

Figure 7.2 presents a summary of the results derived from the three-component PLS analysis; the findings pertain to the entire set of 56 states for the years 1966-1970. Eight iterations were required to achieve stable parameter estimates. Beside each of the original 25 societal, interstate, and global variables in Figure 7.2 is the beta weight which determines its contribution to the appropriate latent variable. The number on the left indicates the direct effect of the variable, while the number in parentheses on the right is the beta weight as mediated by the typological dimension T. A further set of betas links the societal, interstate,

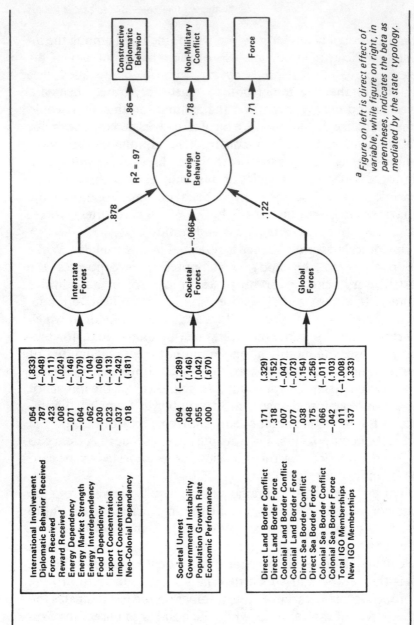

International Involvement	.054	(.833)
Diplomatic Behavior Received	.787	(−.048)
Force Received	.423	(−.111)
Reward Received	.008	(.024)
Energy Dependency	−.071	(−.146)
Energy Market Strength	−.064	(−.079)
Energy Interdependency	.062	(.104)
Food Dependency	−.030	(−.106)
Export Concentration	−.023	(−.413)
Import Concentration	−.037	(−.242)
Neo-Colonial Dependency	.018	(.181)

Societal Unrest	.094	(−1.289)
Governmental Instability	.048	(.146)
Population Growth Rate	.055	(.042)
Economic Performance	.000	(.670)

Direct Land Border Conflict	.171	(.329)
Direct Land Border Force	.318	(.152)
Colonial Land Border Conflict	.007	(−.047)
Colonial Land Border Force	−.077	(−.073)
Direct Sea Border Conflict	.038	(.154)
Direct Sea Border Force	.175	(.256)
Colonial Sea Border Conflict	.066	(−.011)
Colonial Sea Border Force	−.042	(.103)
Total IGO Memberships	.011	(−1.008)
New IGO Memberships	.137	(.333)

Interstate Forces
Societal Forces
Global Forces

Foreign Behavior

$R^2 = .97$

.878
−.066
.122

Constructive Diplomatic Behavior
Non-Military Conflict
Force

.86
.78
.71

[a] Figure on left is direct effect of variable, while figure on right, in parentheses, indicates the beta as mediated by the state typology.

Figure 7.2: Results of PLS Analysis: interstate, Societal, and Global Components[a]

196

and global latent variables to the foreign behavior latent variable. A multiple correlation coefficient indicates the combined impact of the three clusters of variables on the dependent variable. Finally, correlations (betas) link the predicted foreign behavior with each of the manifest dimensions of behavior.

Several noteworthy findings emerge. First, the overall model explains 94 percent of the variance in foreign behavior. In terms of the three behavioral dimensions, it explains 74 percent of the variance in constructive diplomatic behavior, 61 percent of the variance in nonmilitary conflict, and 50 percent of the variance in force. Clearly, the model does quite well in explaining foreign behavior, although the more routine actions, particularly of a diplomatic nature, are better explained than the force and conflict acts.

It is interesting to compare these results with those obtained above, where the action-reaction element was excluded. With regard to constructive diplomatic behavior, the model in this appendix produces an almost identical proportion of variance explained as does the analysis in the chapter, reinforcing the inference that this type of behavior is more subject to the influence of the array of determinants outside of the action-reaction context. The inclusion of action-reaction variables, then, does not appreciably affect our ability to explain the variance in constructive diplomatic behavior, which was already quite high at 72 percent.

On the other hand, the two purely conflict dimensions (nonmilitary conflict and force) show marked improvement in the percentage of variance explained. In particular, this applies to the force dimension, where only 1 percent of the variance is explained in the main analysis in the chapter; 50 percent of the variance is explained in the present analysis. Clearly, the action-reaction forces constitute an essential element of this type of behavior. The improvement in variance explained in nonmilitary conflict is more modest, from 47 percent to 61 percent. This indicates that behavior identified as nonmilitary conflict is the most complex in terms of the system of indicators which collectively determines its values. While the combined results of our models apparently indicate that constructive diplomatic behavior is the product almost exclusively of societal, interstate (economic), and global determinants, whereas force is almost solely the result of the behavior received/behavior sent dynamic, nonmilitary conflict is the consequence of a more complex mix of determinants.

The results clearly demonstrate the centrality of the interstate component in accounting for foreign behavior; the societal domain is obviously the least potent. When we compare these results with those reported earlier, we get a feel for the overwhelming impact of the action-reaction processes. It was for the purpose of avoiding the statistical consequences of this impact that the analysis presented in Chapter 7 was designed.

Within the interstate component, two variables are weighted very strongly and virtually dominate the block of variables: diplomatic behavior and force received. The direct (unmediated by type of state) effects of these two variables are much stronger than their mediated effects. Moreover, both are derived from the interstate component; rewards received, however, exerts little if any impact.

These results suggest that the reception of diplomatic and force behavior provides the most straightforward and valid explanation of foreign behavior patterns. When the control for the typological dimensions of states is taken into account, we discover that various interstate economic indicators, especially export sector dependency and international economic involvement, exert influence. The control for type of state is also important with the less powerful global and societal components. The overall summary generalization is that the reception of behavior is directly and strongly linked to foreign behavior whereas other indicators exert various levels of influence depending upon state characteristics; behavioral stimuli constitute universal determinants of action while other forces vary in impact by state type. This conclusion has been affirmed in previous research (Wilkenfeld, 1973, 1972; Zinnes and Wilkenfeld, 1971).

NOTES

1. Chapter 8 will be devoted to an independent analysis of the psychological component, while the political component must await subsequent analyses.

2. The analysis in Chapter 6 reports that behavior received explains an exceedingly high percentage of behavior sent. In studies of conflict patterns in the Middle East, Wilkenfeld et al. (1972) and Wilkenfeld (1975) found that the action-reaction component was the leading predictor variable for all Middle East conflict states, although a breakdown according to target was quite revealing in terms of the different processes at work. Phillips (1973) also found the action-reaction component to be of overwhelming significance in a study of conflict patterns for the entire international system in 1963.

3. Among the salient problems raised by the action-reaction approach is the utilization of the WEIS data for the operationalization of both behavior received and behavor sent. Bias in news coverage may seriously affect parameter estimation and artificially inflate such relationships, overestimating the potency, in this case, of behavior-received indicators. Burgess and Lawton (1972: 64) allude to the special problems of WEIS data in this regard.

A more troublesome criticism concerns the issue of aggregation. Because the "behavior-sent" and "behavior-received" indicators aggregate events which occur during a period of one year, it is impossible to state unequivocally that the events "received" occurred prior to the events "sent" by the state. A causal inference can therefore not be established in a definitive sense. Moreover, if event-causes-event sequences are assumed by the interaction model, the results reported above do not provide support for the thesis.

This issue cannot be dismissed, but it may be reinterpreted. Only when the action-reaction model is viewed from a discrete-event perspective does the problem become unmanageable. If the indices tap behavior which underlies the observed events, and if the behavior is perceived as important while events per se are relegated to an indicator role, then this criticism is no more applicable to indices than it is to transactions (e.g., trade) data. While this argument mitigates the critic's position, it neither resolves the basic issue (for trade data may also be suspect!) nor satisfies those who are concerned with time frames. At this point we assume that the problem of casual sequence is difficult, yet—in terms of the continuous reality perspective—not overwhelming.

4. The relative potency of a component (RPc) equals the sum of the five betas multiplied by their respective control dimensions. This score is the beta for the component as a whole. $RPc = \Sigma(beta\ ci \times control\ i)$, where c refers to global, interstate, and societal, and i refers to capability, instability, governmental, and economic. The betas are reported in Table 7.2. RPc is standardized, providing a relative potency interpretation by multiplying $RPc \times S_{FB}/Sc$, where FB = foreign behavior.

5. Computing an average beta across five years is not, strictly speaking, a proper statistical procedure. However, it does provide some insight into the patterns which are evident in these findings. Furthermore, it has been found (see Chapter 3) that the four structural characteristics dimensions are remarkably stable over this five-year period, thus reinforcing the stability of the present results.

6. The cutoff points were chosen on the basis of the standard deviations of the sets of relative potency scores for each of the three latent independent variables.

7. It will be recalled that 6 of the 56 states—Thailand, Ghana, Kenya, Greece, Saudi Arabia, and Nigeria—could not be classified into any of the five categories.

8. One must add a note of caution to guard against overzealous interpretations of these findings. When we refer to the societal latent variable, for example, and its strong impact on certain states, we must bear in mind that the latent variable is not the aggregation of all societal phenomena, or even of those societal indicators identified here, but only of those which are central in determining the latent variable. While we employ the terms *societal*, *interstate*, and *global*, the exact composition of these three broad indicators should be clearly recognized.

Chapter 8

Elite Values and Foreign Behavior
A Preliminary Analysis

The focus of the preceding two chapters has been on the entire sample of 56 states. Here we shall examine a subset of the total state sample in an effort to provide a preliminary assessment of the impact of the psychological component on the foreign behavior of states. Initially, however, we must review the strategy which was pursued in order to operationalize the psychological domain.

OVERVIEW

The empirical, normative, and prescriptive literature on leadership and politics is both voluminous and diffuse. Among the many prominent classical political philosophers who explored the interface between psychology and politics were Plato, Thucydides, and Machiavelli. In modern political science, Harold Lasswell (1930, 1948) has provided the impetus for subsequent empirical inquiry in the emergent subfield of political psychology. The mass of research which can be sub-

AUTHORS' NOTE: *Portions of the material appearing in this chapter constitute expanded versions of material which originally appeared in Hopple (1979, 1980).*

sumed under the rubrics of "elite studies" (see Marvick, 1977) and "psychopolitics" (see Greenstein, 1975; M. G. Hermann, 1977) represents an impressive monument to the pioneering efforts of such early twentieth-century micro-empiricists as Graham Wallas and Charles Merriam.

Chapter 2 provided a brief survey of the landscape in the realm of psychology and foreign policy analysis. Three distinct levels or foci of analysis can be pinpointed: psychodynamic factors, personality traits, and belief systems. O. Holsti (1976) presents a useful overview of research in one subfield of this area (cognitive process models) and simultaneously illustrates the incredible diversity which characterizes the entire realm of inquiry. The kaleidoscopic nature of existing research is obvious to anyone who is familiar with the literature; as O. Holsti (1976: 129) expresses it: "Diversity is the rule." This diversity is typical of all the following areas: theory, scope, categories and concepts, data, and analytic procedures. Table 8.1, which is reproduced in a slightly modified form from O. Holsti (1976: 131), reflects the variety which pervades the cognitive process approach to the analysis of foreign policy decision-making. Summaries for other approaches would reveal equivalent amounts of diversity. The more recent literature is surveyed in Hopple (1980).

The operationalization of the psychological component for the purpose of converting the IBA framework into a testable model involved the collection of foreign policy elite value data, as we pointed out in Chapter 2. We rejected the first two realms or levels for a variety of reasons.

In the case of psychodynamic or depth-psychological factors, access to data and numerous other obstacles surfaced immediately. This approach is especially inapplicable to cross-national or comparative research. Psychodynamic analysis has almost invariably involved the intensive examination of a single case. Even when the potential focus is a single leader, data are generally nonexistent, inaccessible, ambiguous, or contradictory; for only a small number of cases is the amount (and type) of material as available as that which was the basis for the land-

TABLE 8.1

Some "Cognitive Process" Approaches to Decision-Making[a]

DECISION MAKER AS[b]	STAGE OF DECISION MAKING[c]	THEORETICAL LITERATURE[b]	ILLUSTRATIVE CONSTRUCTS AND CONCEPTS	ILLUSTRATIVE STUDIES OF POLITICAL LEADERS
Believer	Sources of belief system	Political socialization Personality & politics	First independent political success	Barber (1972) Glad (1966) George and George (1956)
	Content of belief system	Political philosophy Ideology	Mind Set Image Operational code World view Decision premises	Operational code studies Brecher (1968) Cummins (1973) Stupak (1971)
	Structure of belief system	Cognitive psychology	Cognitive balance/congruity Cognitive complexity Cognitive rigidity/dogmatism Cognitive "maps"/style	Axelrod (1972b) M. Hermann (1972a) Osgood (1959) Schneidman (1961, 1963, 1969)
Perceiver	Identification of a problem	Psychology of perception Cognitive psychology	Definition of situation Perception/misperception Cognitive "set" Selective perception Focus on attention Stereotyping	Jervis (1968) Jervis (1976) Zinnes (1968) Zinnes et al. (1972)
Information Processor	Obtain information Production of solutions Evaluation of solutions	Cognitive consistency theories Theories of attitude change Information theory Communication theory	Search capacity Selective exposure Psycho-logic Tolerance of ambiguity Strategies for coping with discrepant information (various) Information overload Information processing capacity Satisficing/maximizing Tolerance of inconsistency	Abelson (1971) O. Holsti 1972) Jervis (1976)
Decision Maker/Strategist	Selection of a strategy	Game theory Decision theory Deterrence theory	Utility Risk taking Decision rules Manipulation of images End-means links Bounded rationality	Jervis (1970) Jervis (1976) Stassen (1972) Burgess (1968)
Learner	Subsequent learning and revisions (post-decision)	Learning theory Cognitive dissonance theory	Feedback "Lessons of history"	Jervis (1976) Lampton (1973) May (1973)

Left vertical note (spanning Believer rows): Pre-decision: conceptual baggage that DM bring to decision-making tasks

Right vertical note: Axelrod (1972); Bonham and Shapiro (1976); Shapiro and Bonham (1973); Steinbruner (1968, 1974)

a. Adapted from O. Holsti (1976: 131).
b. Columns one and three were suggested by, but differ greatly from, the framework provided by Axelrod (1972a).
c. Column two was drawn from Brim et al. (1962: 1).

mark George and George (1964) study of Woodrow Wilson. The lack of standards for reliability and validity, the apparent inability to translate depth-psychological constructs into operational measures, an array of inescapable problems relating to causal inference, and the controversies which are associated both with the approach in general and with specific psychodynamic theories are among the other pertinent difficulties.

Personality factors—conceived as single traits or viewed as more inclusive dimensions—generally are examined in an effort to ascertain "what the political consequences are for a nation of having a leader who has more or less of the trait under consideration" (M. G. Hermann, 1978: 55). Two troublesome issues intrude here.

The first concerns the selection of variables for analysis. A very partial list of discrete traits would include aggressiveness, self-confidence, nationalism, dogmatism, authoritarianism, cognitive complexity, level of self-esteem, achievement strivings, anxiety, field dependence, introversion/extroversion, and locus of control. All of these single characteristics have been examined empirically (e.g., Etheredge, 1978; M. G. Hermann, 1974, 1978) or represent prominent dimensions or "traits" of personality in psychology (see London and Exner, 1978). Given the potential number of traits and the lack of criteria for "sampling" items or determining which are most central, it would be impossible to conduct comparative research on such factors. The second difficulty concerns the impossibility of achieving direct access to most foreign policy elite members and the consequent need to make inferences of dubious validity from the available sources about personality traits.[1]

We described the belief systems approach in Chapter 2 and concluded that the Rokeach value scheme represents a coherent, parsimonious, and practicable route to operationalizing a key subsystem of the decision maker's belief system. Especially compelling was the relative ease with which data could be generated on a cross-national basis, given the existence of a readily available source with appropriate data for a significant number of states. The Foreign Broadcast Information Service (FBIS) *Daily Report* conformed to the criterion. We listed the 39 states which contained three or more speeches by heads of state and/or foreign ministers one or more times during the 1966-1970 time frame (see Table 2.1); these states constitute our value data "subsample" of the total set of 56 states.

We have already discussed the Rokeach belief systems framework and the role of the value subsystem in the belief system. The centrality of values in an individual's total cognitive system is a recurring theme in Rokeach's work.[2] If we consider the value concept in the context of Table 8.1, it is obvious that primordial values can be regarded as fundamental orientations or structuring tools. Values, in other words, perform vital screening functions for the individuals:

> The value screen of culture appraises and selectively perceives stimuli which act on it. Stimuli which are congenial are accepted and allowed to act on the social process. Those which are not tend to be screened out. Other stimuli are accepted, but they are shaped by the values of the culture before they act on the social process [Devine, 1972: 10].

A decision maker's values may be expected to shape his or her reactions and perceptions as a believer, perceiver, information processor, strategist, and learner. In the Rokeach scheme, values constitute a significant part of the *content* of a belief system and play a central role in determining the *structure* of such a system. Basic values can obviously shape the definition of situations and contribute to the process of selective perception. In the information-processing stage, values function as screens and thereby produce selective exposure. The value subsystem is presumably central to the selection of a strategy and is in fact implicitly highlighted in the cognitive processing model developed by Bonham and Shapiro (1973).

In order to determine the validity of the value scheme as applied to the comparative study of foreign policy, we could perform validity tests of one or more of the following types: content validity, criterion-related validity, and construct validity (Bohrnstedt, 1970). Two criterion-related validation strategies have been pursued in prior research. One entails the assessment of whether or not value rankings *discriminate* among subgroups; the other evaluates the relationship between values and *behaviors*.

The first approach is exemplified in a recent study of value rankings in the British House of Commons. Searing (1978: 75) focuses on the capacity of the technique to differentiate among politicians from different political camps. He compares a party's candidates with its parliamentary members and also compares Conservative and Labour members. The results offer striking support for the validity of the technique:

> Candidates are a faithful image of MPs from their own political camp. By contrast, Conservative and Labour members of Parliament are poles apart. They refer to one another as "the other side," and so they are: unlike the family resemblance between candidates and MPs, every value comparison save one produces differences which are statistically significant, usually at the .001 level [Searing, 1978: 76].

Relative ranks for the core political values of freedom and social equality show the expected differences; while 85 percent of the Conservative MPs rank freedom over social equality, 79 percent of the Labour members rank the latter value higher than freedom (Searing, 1978: 77).[3]

The value-behavior relationship is considered in detail in Rokeach (1973). Table 8.2 summarizes the major findings. Even a cursory examination of the tabular material generates three general conclusions.

(1) The behavior-value nexus is robust in magnitude. Of 360 correlations, 134 are statistically significant.

(2) The expected specific values exhibit strong relationships with given behaviors. Equality, for example, is the value which predicts to various forms of behavior in the areas of civil rights and discrimination.

(3) Certain values show an especially large number of significant relationships to the behavioral items. Among these are a comfortable life, equality, family security, national security, and salvation. The socioeconomic, political, and religious values of a comfortable life, equality, and salvation may be the most powerful overall determinants of both attitudes and behaviors,

as Rokeach (1973: 159) concludes. In contrast, the values freedom, inner harmony, self-respect, social recognition, true friendship, and wisdom exhibit no (in the case of the latter) or few potent correlations with behaviors.

VALIDITY: A PRELIMINARY ASSESSMENT

In assessing the validity of the value data which we generated from content analyses of FBIS *Daily Reports*, our major focus will be the predictive capacity of the values.[4] This issue is treated in some detail in the analysis sections of this chapter. A supplementary validation criterion involves the determination of the ability of the instrument to separate cases into meaningful clusters. As noted, Searing employs this method of validation and demonstrates that the value ranking procedure distinguishes unambiguously between members of different political parties and factions in the British House of Commons.

A summary descriptive profile of the value data set is presented in Table 8.3, where overall means for the eighteen values for all of the states and years in the data set are presented. Eight values have means above 1: a world of peace, freedom, national security, public security, progress, unity, ideology, and cooperation. Especially noteworthy is the mean of 4.54 for the value progress. The values with the lowest means are wisdom, social recognition, equality, and respect.

The aggregated descriptive statistics in Table 8.3 can be compared with the individual state means. Table 8.4 highlights the state value means for one year (1966) which are greater in magnitude than the overall mean for that value.[5] It is obvious that certain states are characterized by value patterns with an unusually high number of means above the overall "average" for the 1966 to 1970 span. Among these countries are the United States, Cuba, West Germany, East Germany, Hungary, Czechoslovakia, the Soviet Union, and the United Arab Republic.

Generally, all foreign policy elites in this particular sample emphasized the values which display high overall means (see

TABLE 8.2
Significant Value—Behavior Relationships: Diverse Content Areas

	CIVIL RIGHTS			RELIGION		POLITICS	HONEST BEHAVIOR		
	Join NAACP	Eye Contact with Blacks	Civil Rights Participation	Church Attendance (National)	Church Attendance (College)	Partisan Activism	Return Pencils	Male Prisoners	Female Prisoners
A comfortable life	●	●	●	●	●	●			●
An exciting life				●	●				●
A sense of accomplishment	●						●	●	●
A world at peace	●	●	●		●			●	
A world of beauty		●	●						
Equality						●		●	
Family security				●	●	●			●
Freedom									●
Happiness									
Inner harmony									
Mature love	●		●			●		●	
National security	●		●			●			●
Pleasure		●		●	●	●	●	●	●
Salvation				●	●			●	
Self-respect									
Social recognition									
True friendship									
Wisdom								●	●
Number of values	5	4	5	5	6	6	2	7	8

Table 8.2 (Continued)

	INTERPERSONAL CONFLICT	ACADEMIC PURSUITS	LIFE STYLE		OCCUPATIONAL ROLES AND CHOICES							Number of Behaviors
	Compatible Roommates	College Major	Hippies	Homosexuals	Professors	Police V. White	Police V. Black	Priests Laymen	Science, Artists, Business, Writers	Small Entre-preneurs	Salesmen	
A comfortable life		●	●		●		●	●	●	●	●	13
An exciting life	●		●		●					●		9
A sense of accomplishment			●		●	●	●			●		6
A world at peace	●	●	●		●			●	●	●	●	9
A world of beauty			●		●				●	●	●	10
Equality			●		●	●	●	●	●	●	●	12
Family security				●	●	●	●			●	●	10
Freedom										●	●	5
Happiness					●			●	●			6
Inner harmony												3
Mature love	●		●		●	●	●	●	●	●	●	8
National security			●		●	●	●	●		●	●	11
Pleasure	●		●		●			●		●	●	9
Salvation			●		●		●	●		●		11
Self-respect	●		●		●			●				5
Social recognition				●	●			●			●	3
True friendship					●			●				4
Wisdom												0
Number of values	5	2	11	2	15	5	7	11	6	12	10	134

SOURCE: Adapted from Rokeach (1973: 160-161).

TABLE 8.3
Value Means and Standard Deviations (1966-1970)

VALUE	MEAN	STANDARD DEVIATION
A comfortable life	.66	1.01
A world of peace	1.74	1.80
Equality	.34	.53
Freedom	1.60	1.36
Happiness	.47	.65
Governmental security	.65	.61
Honor	.47	.53
Justice	.63	.69
National security	2.32	1.64
Public security	1.19	1.01
Respect	.38	.36
Social recognition	.29	.43
Wisdom	.22	.51
Progress	4.54	4.16
Unity	1.52	1.30
Ideology	3.10	3.60
Cooperation	3.65	2.88
Support of government	.77	.85

Table 8.3). In other words, interstate variations are apparently not appreciable; instead of identifying distinct value ranking patterns, the procedure yields a single homogeneous profile for all states in the data set.[6] This suggests that the Rokeach value procedure is useful for delineating foreign policy value profiles which can be compared with patterns for other institutions within and across societies, but that foreign policy elites in different states tend to emphasize (and rank) values in a very similar fashion.

This question, however, has not been definitively answered. A preliminary exploration of the issue has been undertaken; the findings are presented in Table 8.5. The analysis of variance

TABLE 8.4
Value Means by State (1966)

STATE	1	2	3	4	5	6	7	8	9	10	11	12	13	14	15	16	17	18
United States	•	•	•	•			•		•		•		•	•			•	•
Cuba	•		•				•		•	•	•	•	•	•		•	•	•
Chile	•		•				•	•		•	•		•	•	•			•
France																		
West Germany	•	•	•	•	•			•	•					•		•		
East Germany		•	•		•		•	•	•	•	•		•	•	•	•	•	•
Poland									•				•				•	
Hungary	•				•		•	•	•	•	•		•	•	•		•	•
Czechoslovakia	•	•	•	•	•			•	•	•	•		•	•	•	•		•
Yugoslavia							•									•		
Greece							•		•									
Rumania	•	•	•		•	•		•	•	•	•		•	•	•	•		•
U.S.S.R.		•		•	•				•		•	•		•	•		•	
Ghana	•	•	•						•					•				•
Nigeria				•			•		•					•	•			•
Kenya					•				•									•
Algeria			•				•	•			•					•	•	
Turkey			•					•			•						•	
Iraq		•	•	•	•			•			•			•			•	
United Arab Republic	•	•	•	•	•		•	•	•		•			•	•	•	•	•
Syria			•	•										•	•			
Jordan					•	•	•	•	•				•	•				•
Israel																		
Saudi Arabia			•	•	•			•	•		•						•	
China								•	•		•			•	•	•	•	•
Japan		•								•	•		•					•
India		•															•	•
Pakistan		•				•	•											
Cambodia				•	•			•	•		•							
South Vietnam	•			•	•	•			•		•			•	•	•		•
Indonesia									•							•		•

NOTE: 1 = comfortable life; 2 = a world of peace; 3 = equality; 4 = freedom; 5 = happiness; 6 = governmental security; 7 = honor; 8 = justice; 9 = national security; 10 = public security; 11 = respect; 12 = societal recognition; 13 = wisdom; 14 = progress; 15 = unity; 16 = ideology; 17 = cooperation; 18 = support of government.
• Mean is greater than the average 1966-1970 mean (see Table 8.3).

results which appear in the table indicate that knowledge of the identity of the state is *generally* a more accurate prediction of values than knowledge of the year.

Logically, four outcomes are possible for this state-versus-year comparison. If both state and year are significant, the states remain different but changes which are attributable to "systemic" factors affect states "uniformly." If neither state nor year accounts for an appreciable percentage of variance, then states change over time but the variations are the product of measured internal and idiosyncratic forces. If the state

TABLE 8.5

State Versus Year: Variance Explained (1966-1970)

Value	STATE		YEAR		Unexplained Variance
	F-value	Eta^2	F-value	Eta^2	
A comfortable life	1.26	.35	3.31*	.10	.55
A world of peace	2.19*	.48	2.90*	.08	.44
Equality	2.42*	.51	1.03	.03	.46
Freedom	2.36*	.50	2.59*	.08	.42
Happiness	0.77	.25	9.87*	.24	.51
Governmental security	1.70*	.42	4.40*	.12	.46
Honor	7.87*	.77	0.91	.03	.20
Justice	2.26*	.49	0.82	.03	.48
National security	2.46*	.51	1.97	.06	.43
Public security	3.16*	.58	1.47	.04	.38
Respect	3.18*	.58	2.24	.07	.35
Social recognition	1.68*	.42	3.83*	.11	.47
Wisdom	0.67	.22	10.32*	.25	.53
Progress	2.77*	.54	2.49*	.07	.39
Unity	3.15*	.57	1.77	.05	.38
Ideology	5.94*	.72	1.70	.05	.23
Cooperation	5.70*	.71	1.11	.03	.26
Support of government	1.98*	.46	5.22*	.14	.40

*F-value significant at .05 level.

variable explains more of the measurable variance, then scores by state are stable and states differ. If the year variable is the more potent determinant, then states are similar and vary over time as a consequence of "systemic" (i.e., suprastate temporal context) factors.

In assessing the results, both the significance of the F-values and the magnitudes of the eta^2 correlations will be employed. Both criteria show that *state* is generally a more viable predictor than *year*. Fourteen of the eighteen state F-values are statistically significant while nine of the year F-values are significant; the state eta^2's are larger than the comparable year eta^2's in sixteen cases. The only exceptions to the latter configuration are happiness (equivalent eta^2's) and wisdom (.22 for state and .25 for year).

The most unambiguous supportive results are for those values for which state is significant while year is not: equality, honor, justice, national security, public security, respect, unity, ideology, and cooperation. At the other extreme, there are three instances when year exerts a significant impact while state is insignificant: a comfortable life, happiness, and wisdom. These three values fluctuate on a temporal basis and knowledge of the state is less helpful than for the other values (although the state variable explains 35 percent of the variance in a comfortable life, 25 percent in happiness, and 22 percent in wisdom). Both variables exert significant effects in six cases: a world of peace, freedom, governmental security, social recognition, progress, and support of government.

The third column in Table 8.5 presents the percentage of unexplained variance for each of the eighteen values. When the impact of state and year is taken into account, the unexplained variance ranges from 20 percent (honor) to 55 percent (a comfortable life). The mean percentage of unexplained variance is about 40 percent; on the average, knowledge of state and year accounts for 60 percent of the variance in the value data set.

ANALYSIS

In order to gauge the impact of articulated values on foreign behavior, we pursued an analytical strategy which is patterned after the Coleman strategy which was described conceptually in Chapter 5 and implemented in Chapter 6. We initially determined the discrete relationships between the dependent variable of foreign behavior and four predictor domains (i.e., the psychological, societal, interstate, and global components). Then the predicted values which were generated by these four regression analyses were entered into a regression equation which predicted foreign behavior; this provides a direct estimate of relative potency. As in Chapter 6, we conduct the tests both for the entire sample (i.e., the 39 states which appear in the value state sample one or more times between 1966 and 1970) and for the clusters which were identified in our Q-factor analysis of the state attribute data (see Chapter 3 on the Q-groups).

There is, however, one important modification in the research design. While we isolated five distinct groupings in our original analysis (i.e. *Western*, *closed*, *large developing*, *unstable*, and *poor*), here we report results for four groupings. Since the totals for the *large developing* and *poor* states were so low, we were unable to perform analyses of these clusters; as a result, we collapsed the two into a *Third World* category.[7] We thus present results for the *Western*, *closed*, *unstable*, and *Third World* categories.

While the analytical strategy in this chapter is based on the Coleman relative potency tests of Chapter 6, the substantive details of the research design are identical to those of the PLS analysis of Chapter 7. That is, we have adopted the three significant features which distinguish the PLS research design from the Coleman design: the removal of the behavior-received variables (diplomatic behavior, force, and reward), the introduction of other interstate variables, and the addition of the global component.[8] We thus have four independent variable realms (psychological, societal, interstate, and global) and three dependent variables (constructive diplomatic behavior sent, non-military conflict behavior sent, and force behavior sent). Figures 8.1 summarizes the overall research design.

Foreign Behavior as Predicted by the Individual Components

Regression results for each of the four components are presented in Tables 8.6, 8.7 and 8.8 (psychological), 8.10 (societal), 8.11 (interstate), and 8.12 (global). In each table, the numbers in the columns are beta weights; each table also presents the proportion of variance explained (R^2) for that particular component. Beta weights and R^2's which are statistically significant at the .05 level are identified by asterisks.

Perhaps the most striking finding for the prediction of constructive diplomatic behavior by the eighteen values (Table 8.6)

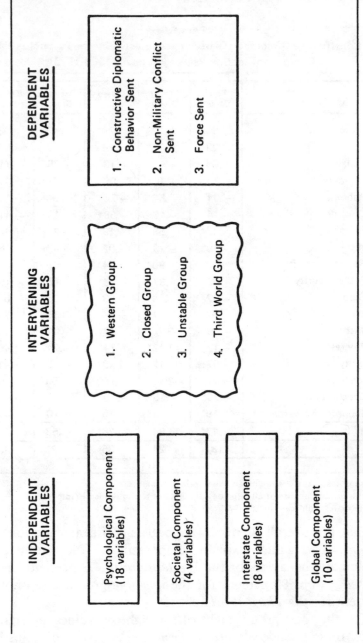

INDEPENDENT VARIABLES

Psychological Component (18 variables)

Societal Component (4 variables)

Interstate Component (8 variables)

Global Component (10 variables)

INTERVENING VARIABLES

1. Western Group
2. Closed Group
3. Unstable Group
4. Third World Group

DEPENDENT VARIABLES

1. Constructive Diplomatic Behavior Sent
2. Non-Military Conflict Sent
3. Force Sent

Figure 8.1: Value Data Analysis: Research Design

TABLE 8.6

Constructive Diplomatic Behavior as Predicted by the Psychological
Component (nation-years aggregated, 1966-1970)[a]

	Total Group	Western Group	Closed Group	Unstable Group	Third World[b]
A comfortable life	.09	3.18*	.74*	.43	.08
A world of peace	.23*	1.01*	.18	.60	−.52*
Equality	.09	−.51*	−.13	−.28	−.11
Freedom	.11	−.10	−.06	.49	.17
Happiness	−.04	.56*	−.36*	.04	−.18
Governmental security	−.14	−.46	−.58*	−.11	−.41*
Honor	.17*	.54	.18	−.21	.10
Justice	−.18*	−.23	.02	−.47	−.06
National security	.13	.80*	1.04*	.15	−
Public security	−.09	−.37	−.99*	.08	−.19
Respect	−.02	.04	.03	−.05	.02
Social recognition	.02	.17	−.29	1.19	.27
Wisdom	−.09	−3.76*	−.57*	−.01	.18
Progress	−.13	1.18*	−.74*	−.74	.46*
Unity	−.07	.12	1.18*	−.13	.41*
Ideology	−.01	−2.11*	−.14	.53	−.58*
Cooperation	−.20*	−.15	−.30	.29	−.01
Support of government	.19*	.75*	.19	−.70	−.43
R^2	.17*	.94*	.78*	.53	.39
N =	131	24	35	27	45

a. Numbers in the first eighteen rows are beta weights.
b. This group consists of all large developing, poor, and unclassifiable states.
*Beta or R^2 signficant at the .05 level.

is that the overall R^2 of .24 conceals significant variations by group. The values explain 93 percent of the variance in diplomatic behavior for the *Western* group, 73 percent for the *closed* group, 80 percent for the *unstable* group, and only 39 percent for the *Third World* cluster.

For the total group, eight of the eighteen values are significant; these include a world at peace, equality, honor, justice, national security, progress, ideology, and cooperation. Three of the betas are negative in direction; expressions about the values of justice, progress, and cooperation all tend to diminish acts of constructive diplomacy.

These overall results mask the kaleidoscopic patterns for the state clusters. Half of the values are significant for the *Western* group; especially noteworthy are the beta weights for wisdom ($+2.64$) and, to a lesser extent, a comfortable life (1.89).[9] In the case of the *closed* states, national security is the dominant value in relation to events of a constructive diplomatic nature. Interestingly, a concern with two internal values—public security and progress—depresses foreign behavior sent. Unity, however, correlates positively with external behavior. The most noteworthy finding for the *unstable* states is the negative relationship between articulations about progress and diplomatic behavior. Few of the relationships for the *Third World* category are substantively meaningful or statistically significant.

For nonmilitary conflict as predicted by the psychological component (Table 8.7), the same general finding emerges. The aggregate R^2 of .17 contrasts sharply with the fluctuating R^2's of .94 (*Western* group), .78 (*closed* group), .53 (*unstable* group), and .39 (*Third World* group). For both the *Western* and the *closed* states, the values are significant determinants of this particular form of foreign behavior.

Again, half of the eighteen values are significant for the *Western* states. As in Table 8.7, the largest single beta weight is wisdom (-3.76). Other large betas include a comfortable life (3.18) and ideology (-2.11). Within the *closed* group, national security (1.04) and unity (1.18) are the primary determinants of nonmilitary conflict. None of the results is significant for the *unstable* states, although social recognition exerts some impact (with a beta of 1.19). Five of the betas are significant within the *Third World* category, although the R^2 is insignificant.

Finally, we can consider the findings for force behavior (Table 8.8). Generally, the elite values are not significant predictors of this extreme form of foreign conflict. This finding con-

TABLE 8.7
Nonmilitary Conflict as Predicted by the Psychological Component
(nation-years aggregated, 1966-1970)[a]

	Total Group	Western Group	Closed Group	Unstable	Third World[b]
A comfortable life	.06	.90	.16	.11	.25
A world of peace	−.04	.15	.59*	−.44	−.30
Equality	.17*	−.29	.65*	−.03	−.23
Freedom	.02	.21	−.61*	.35	−.03
Happiness	−.10	.02	−.10	.21	−.08
Governmental security	−.09	−.14	−.28	−.26	−.20
Honor	.01	.97	−.07	−.91	−.30
Justice	−.05	−.95	.33	.71	.03
National security	.35*	.16	.60	1.13*	−.05
Public security	−.14	.95	.10	−.31	−.23
Respect	−.02	−.18	−.46	.35	.08
Social recognition	.12	−.73	−.14	.65	−.09
Wisdom	−.03	.27	−.24	−.98	.39
Progress	.04	−.01	−.16	−.78	−.18
Unity	−.08	−.48	−.23	−.50	.23
Ideology	−.04	.08	.30	.86	−.31
Cooperation	−.14	−.26	−.35	−.23	.28
Support of government	−.09	−.46	.40*	−.92	−.22
R^2	.19	.72	.76*	.50	.30
N =	131	24	35	27	45

a. Numbers in the first eighteen rows are beta weights.
b. This group consists of all large developing, poor, and unclassifiable states.
*Beta or R^2 significant at the .05 level.

forms to the pattern which was observed in the PLS analyses of Chapter 7 and its appendix, where it was discovered that force received accounts for force sent whereas the other variable realms exert almost no impact.

The one exception to this generalization is the *closed* group; the values account for a significant 76 percent of the variance in force behavior sent by the members of this cluster. The main

TABLE 8.8
Force as Predicted by the Psychological Component
(nation-years aggregated, 1966-1970)[a]

	Total Group	Western Group	Closed Group	Unstable	Third World[b]
A comfortable life	.15	1.89*	.58*	.87*	−.35
A world of peace	.20*	.52*	.18*	.25	−.18
Equality	.37*	−.31	−.16	−.39	.02
Freedom	−.15	1.20*	.01	.39	.37*
Happiness	−.09	.41*	−.36	.05	−.22
Governmental security	−.09	−.35	−.59*	−.50*	−.38*
Honor	.27*	1.26*	.24	−.23	.17
Justice	−.22	−	.05	−.44	−.18
National security	.19*	−.32	1.15*	.45	−.06
Public security	.07	−.19	−.86*	.40	−.21
Respect	.02	1.06*	−.01	.10	−.01
Social recognition	−.09	.62	−.37*	1.05*	.10
Wisdom	−.03	−2.64*	−.55*	−.52	.02
Progress	−.20*	.12	−.67*	−1.32*	.53*
Unity	−.15	.11	1.01*	−.21	.47*
Ideology	.32*	−.75	−.15	1.20*	−.44*
Cooperation	−.26*	−1.24*	−.36	.48	−.26
Support of government	−.01	−1.23*	.20	−.84	−.20
R^2	.24*	.93*	.73*	.80	.39
N =	131	24	35	27	45

a. Numbers in the first eighteen rows are beta weights.
b. This group consists of all large developing, poor, and unclassifiable states.
*Beta or R^2 significant at the .05 level.

contributors to this are a world of peace (.59), equality (.65), freedom (−.61), and support of government (.40). The positive relationship between the first two values and acts of force suggests that *closed* states may emphasize these values rhetorically as justifications for and rationalizations of force behaviors.[10]

The relationship between values which refer to internal states of affairs and foreign behavior is of interest because of its potential relevance to the internal-external nexus question. As we have pointed out several times in this study, extensive research has accrued on the subject of linkages between external and internal conflict. In a more general sense, scholars, journalists, and other students of public policy have frequently alluded to the putative nexus between internal politics and foreign policy. The alleged propensity for diverting attention from domestic fiascoes and crises by becoming embroiled in foreign adventures and imbroglios is a popular illustration of this general hypothesis. In a more academic context, the research on linkage politics is based on a recognition of the interplay (and even fusion) between domestic and foreign affairs (see Rosenau, 1969).

At least four of the eighteen values presumbly concern the internal dimension of politics: a comfortable life, happiness, public security, and progress. The relationships between these end-states and foreign behavior are depicted in Table 8.9; a P denotes a significant positive relationship and an N a significant negative relationship.

Much of the traditional conjectural speculation on the subject suggests that the relationships would be almost uniformly negative in direction, with an emphasis on an internal value reflecting a diminution in foreign behavior. Alternatively, the linkage politics perspective simply predicts that there will be robust interrelationships; the advocates of a "subsystem autonomy" interpretation would expect the general absence of relationships.

With respect to the latter controversy, the results offer support for neither position; 19 of the relationships are statistically significant and the other 21 fail to attain significance. Of the 19 significant beta weights, 11 are negative in direction and 8 are positive.

The patterns in Table 8.9 can be summarized in a series of propositions. First of all, there is a clear tendency for the value of a comfortable life to covary with increases in both constructive and nonmilitary conflict behaviors. Second, the other relationships are predominantly negative; this generalization is

TABLE 8.9

Internal Values and Foreign Behavior

	CONSTRUCTIVE DIPLOMATIC					NON-MILITARY CONFLICT				
	Total	Western	Closed	Unstable	Third World	Total	Western	Closed	Unstable	Third World
Comfortable life		P	P	P			P	P		N
Happiness			N	N	N			N		
Public security			N	N				N		
Progress	N		N	N	P		P	N		P

NOTE: P denotes a significant positive beta weight; N denotes a significant negative beta weight; a blank denotes a nonsignificant beta weight.

especially applicable to the *closed* states, where rhetorical emphases on happiness, public security, and progress all presage a decrease in external behavior and a turning inward process. Thus, articulations about prosperity and economic stability (the value of a comfortable life) predict increases in both general, primarily constructive and mildly conflictual foreign acts, undoubtedly reflecting the reality of economic interdependence in a world of sovereign states. This phenomenon, however, has not spilled over into domestic politics generally, at least for *closed* and, to a lesser extent, *unstable* states.

A final observation about the results for the value data is warranted. Debates about the explanatory potency of psychological factors become sterile exercises when it is recognized that the key questions concern *when* psychological forces exert an impact and *which* particular variables are relevant. Regarding the former issue, it is obvious that certain situations and variable configurations maximize the impact of psychological factors.[11] Among these are the organizational context, level in the hierarchy, decisional and situational attributes, and the type of state. The available evidence suggests that psychological source factors would exert maximal impact in *closed* states (because of concentration of power) and developing systems (because roles are less clearly institutionalized).

The prediction for closed systems is clearly supported in Tables 8.6, 8.7, and 8.8. However, the beta weights and R^2 values for the two "developing polity" categories are rarely large in size or significant. The two North clusters in terms of the North-South dimension—the *Western* and *closed* states—feature the majority of the noteworthy findings. This issue will be confronted again in the relative potency section of this chapter.

The results for the other three components can be dealt with in a more cursory fashion, since the preceding chapters have highlighted these three realms at some length. Turning to the results for the regression of the types of foreign behavior on the elements of the societal component, we should emphasize once again that the impact of the control for type of state is quite pronounced (see Table 8.10). As was the case for the value cluster, it is primarily the *Western* and *closed* groups which exhibit the strongest impact of societal factors, although the *unstable* group also deserves some attention. Among the societal indicators, societal unrest (riots, anti-government demonstrations, and general strikes) appears to be the most widely involved as a determinant of foreign behavior. In fact, for the *closed* group, where there are strong relationships for all three types of foreign behavior, societal unrest is the exclusive determinant.

Societal determinants exhibit greater diversity with respect to the *Western* and *unstable* clusters, especially in the greater role of economic performance; the latter is particularly important for constructive diplomatic behavior. Also, governmental instability exerts an effect on force behavior within the *Western* group. As we noted above, it is generally the case that force behavior is the least adequately explained of the three types of foreign behavior. This finding has remained relatively constant throughout our various analyses and will be commented on below.

The regression results for the three behavioral types on the interstate indicators are presented in Table 8.11. These results are surprisingly weak. With the exception of the *closed* group, neither the total group nor any of the other subgroups exhibits any consistent relationships of noteworthy magnitude. In the case of the *closed* group, all three types of behavior are well explained; the leading indicators are international involvement and the three energy-related indicators (energy dependency, energy market strength, and energy interdependence). Interestingly, while the *closed* group displays considerable immunity from the impact of internal economic conditions (see the results for the societal component discussed above), a variety of interstate economic factors affects all aspects of the foreign behavior of these states.[12]

Table 8.12 focuses on the regression results involving the variables which operationalized the global component. We again note the pattern identified earlier: There are important

TABLE 8.10

Foreign Behavior as Predicted by the Societal Component
(nation-years aggregated, 1966-1970)[a]

	Societal Unrest	Governmental Instability	Population Growth Rate	Ecomomic Performance	R^2
Total Group, N = 131					
Constructive Diplomatic	.55*	−.13*	−	.03	.31*
Non-Military Conflict	.17*	−.09	.09	.03	.03
Force	.14*	.10	.16*	−	.06
Western Group, N = 24					
Constructive Diplomatic	.22*	.12	.13	.80*	.87*
Non-Military Conflict	−.22	.21	.32	.27	.11
Force	.40*	.65*	.14	−.29	.63*
Closed Group, N = 35					
Constructive Diplomatic	.80*	−.10	.03	−.01	.61*
Non-Military Conflict	.76*	−.07	−.03	−.04	.55*
Force	.46*	−.23	.07	.01	.22*
Unstable Group, N = 27					
Constructive Diplomatic	.14	−.15	−.14	.63*	.62*
Non-Military Conflict	−.41*	−.04	−.26	.44*	.21
Force	.16	−.10	−.17	.17	.05
Third World, N = 45[b]					
Constructive Diplomatic	.04	−.19	−	.19	.08
Non-Military Conflict	.10	−.19	.07	.11	.05
Force	−.18	−.04	−.25*	.28	.16

a. Numbers in first four columns are beta weights.
b. This group consists of all large developing, poor, and unclassifiable states.
*Beta or R^2 significant at .05 level.

distinctions among the four subgroups of states, yielding rather
poor results for the total group. Force remains the least well explained of the behavioral types. Generally, degree of international involvement, as measured by fluctuations in IGO
memberships on a yearly basis, plays a lesser role than do in-

TABLE 8.11
Foreign Behavior as Predicted by the Interstate Component (nation-years aggregated, 1966-1970)[a]

	INTER-NATIONAL INVOLVEMENT	ENERGY DEPEN-DENCY	ENERGY MARKET STRENGTH	ENERGY INTER-DEPENDENCY	FOOD DEPENDENCY	EXPORT CONCEN-TRATION	IMPORT CONCEN-TRATION	NEO-COLONIAL DEPEN-EENCY	R²
Total Group, N = 131									
Constructive Diplomatic	.44*	.13	-.22*	.14	-.07	-.01	.12	—	.26
Non-Military Conflict	.17*	-.19*	-.31*	.23*	-.09	-.08	-.10	.13	.13
Force	-.08	-.03	-.09	.10	-.08	-.01	.29*	-.03	.08
Western Group, N = 24									
Constructive Diplomatic	.54*	.03	.03	-.08	-.09	-.06	-.01	-.32	.39
Non-Military Conflict	-.09	-.40	-.2C	-.37	-.33*	-.40*	-.31	-.14	.45
Force	-.19	.58*	.55	-.39	.03	.02	-.33	-.18	.31
Closed Group, N = 25									
Constructive Diplomatic	.36*	-31.70*	-7.3·*	29.10*	-.06	.30	.02	.08	.66*
Non-Military Conflict	.35*	-33.96*	-7.86*	31.12*	.01	.19	-.03	.06	.66*
Force	.21	-18.67*	-4.25*	17.02*	-.16	-.05	.35	-.09	.37*
Unstable Group, N = 27									
Constructive Diplomatic	.65*	-.01	-.16	.03	.12	-.03	.19	.06	.49
Non-Military Conflict	.51*	-.12	-.33	.30	.08	-.31	-.40	.39	.45
Force	-.11	-.24	-.03	-.04	.10	-.01	.37	-.14	.09
Third World, N = 45[b]									
Constructive Diplomatic	.57*	.16	-.40	.41	-.17	-.12	-.19	.32	.24
Non-Military Conflict	.42*	-.10	-.53*	.47*	-.25*	-.02	-.34	.43	.23
Force	-.14	-.13	-.27	.39	-.12	.02	.53*	.04	.31

a. Numbers in first eight columns are beta weights.

b. This group consists of all large developing, poor, and unclassifiable states.

*Beta or R² significant at the .05 level.

dicators of the extent of foreign conflict behavior involving neighboring states.

Relative Potency of the Psychological, Societal, Interstate, and Global Components

While Chapter 6 presented a simple two-component relative potency test, the assessment here involves four distinct components. We develop a single indicator for each of the components; the latter is based on the combined effects of all of the variables within the cluster on the dependent variable (i.e., the predicted values). Whereas the test in Chapter 6 yielded a single dominant conclusion—that the interstate component (which included the action-reaction variables) accounts for an overwhelming portion of the variance in a direct "contest" with the societal realm—the results shown in Table 8.13 are much more complex. This test, of course, differs from the earlier one in that it involves a modified sample of states (a subset of the sample in Chapter 6), a drastically modified interstate component (which exludes the action-reaction element), and two additonal components (psychological and global).

The dominance of the interstate component, observed in the earlier analyses, is not apparent here. In fact, if we view only the results for the four subgroups, we note a general primacy of internal over external factors as significant determinants of foreign behavior. The fact that the value or psychological data are significantly related to foreign behavior outputs for three of the four groups of states provides striking support for the necessity of operationalizing all of the major variable domains in foreign policy analysis.

Whereas the individual component results discussed earlier indicated that the value data set is important within the *Western* and *closed* groups, the relative potency assessment reveals that the values of foreign policy elites are significantly related to behavior within the *closed* and *Third World* clusters. Theoretically, three sets of conditions have been identified as ones which presumably maximize the impact of individual-level factors:

TABLE 8.12

Foreign Behavior as Predicted by the Global Component (nation-years aggregated, 1966-1970)[a]

	TOTAL IGO	NEW IGO	DLBC[b]	DLBF[b]	CLBC[b]	CLBF[b]	DSBC[b]	DSBF[b]	CSBC[b]	CSBF[b]	R²
Total Group, N = 131											
Constructive Diplomatic	.32*	.04	.03	.09	.70*	-.29*	.44*	-.15*	-.29*	.08	.44*
Non-Military Conflict	-.05	-.01	.25*	.01	.75*	.46	.44	.11	-.12	.07	.40
Force	.15*	-.08	-.15*	.41*	.11	-.09	-.07	.24*	-.05	-.17	.22
Western Group, N = 24											
Constructive Diplomatic	-.22*	-.18	.07	-.01	.06	1.32*	.09	.21*	-.41*	-.14	.93*
Non-Military Conflict	-.41*	-.09	.26	-.23	1.45*	-.62*	.19	.26*	-.42*	.25	.83*
Force	-.14	-.04	-.42	.74*	.55	-.32	-.06	-.05	-.39	.15	.38
Closed Group, N = 35											
Constructive Diplomatic	.20	-.04	.08	-.03	2.97*	-1.55*	.51*	-.29*	-1.54*	.40*	.77*
Non-Military Conflict	-.06	-.05	.15	-.03	3.25*	-1.62*	.54*	-.33*	-1.59*	.46*	.78*
Force	.27	-.29	-.01	-.04	1.20	-.79	.29	-.25	-.46	-.03	.28
Unstable Group, N = 27											
Constructive Diplomatic	.13	.06	.10*	.20*	-.18	.97*	.47*	-.25*	-.33*	.07	.96*
Non-Military Conflict	.25*	.29*	.11	.54*	1.71*	-1.39*	.55*	-.29*	-.34	-.47*	.88*
Force	.08	-.05	-.13	1.18*	-1.27*	-1.02	-.21*	-.19*	.27	.17	.91
Third World, N = 45											
Constructive Diplomatic	-.25*	-.17	.29	-.19	-.36	-.06	.73	.26	-.03	.07	.77*
Non-Military Conflict	-.30	-.17*	.28*	-.24	-.42	.19*	.43	.52*	.09	-.02	.67*
Force	-.03	-.04	-.10	.29	-.12	.05	-.33*	.80*	.12	-.61*	.43*

a. Numbers in first ten columns are beta weights.

b. Direct Land Borders Conflict (DLBC); Direct Land Border Force (DLBF); Colonial Land Borders Conflict (CLBC); Colonial Land Borders Force (CLBF); Direct Sea Borders Conflict (DSBC); Direct Sea Borders Force (DSBF); Colonial Sea Borders Conflict (CSBC); Colonial Sea Borders Force (CSBF).

*Beta or R² significant at the .05 level.

TABLE 8.13
Relative Potency of Predictors of Foreign Policy Behavior
(nation-years aggregated, 1966-1970)[a]

	Psychological	Societal	Interstate	Global	R^2
Total Group					
Constructive Diplomatic	.18*	.28*	.15*	.42*	.56*
Non-Military Conflict	.21*	.04	.15*	.49*	.46*
Force	.29*	.15*	.14*	.29*	.34*
Western Group					
Constructive Diplomatic	−.03	.58*	.01	.30	.61*
Non-Military Conflict	.07	−.05	.10	.72*	.61*
Force	.24	.29	.09	.31	.43*
Closed Group					
Constructive Diplomatic	.28*	.48*	.13	.20	.74*
Non-Military Conflict	.25*	.47*	.29	.15	.68*
Force	.55*	.16	.17	.07	.45*
Unstable Group					
Constructive Diplomatic	−.05	.09	−.01	.90*	.86*
Non-Military Conflict	.09	−.10	.30*	.50*	.56*
Force	.41*	.29	.04	.18	.26*
Third World[b]					
Constructive Diplomatic	.82*	−.09	.01	.21*	.59*
Non-Military Conflict	.62*	.11	.04	.23	.80*
Force	.21*	−.07	.05	.67*	.59*

a. Numbers in first four columns are beta weights.
b. This group consists of all large developing, poor, and unclassifiable states.
*Beta or R^2 significant at .05 level.

(1) level in the hierarchy (the higher the position, the greater the impact)
(2) type of situation (the less routine or more crisislike the context, the greater the impact)
(3) type of state (the more closed or developing the state, the greater the impact)

Empirically, the findings conform impressively to the predictions. Level in the hierarchy is a constant, since all of the decision makers are representatives of the highest stratum (head of state and foreign minister). The psychological beta weights are generally lowest for the Western (democratic or politically open) states, especially for the more routine constructive diplomatic and nonmilitary conflict forms of behavior.

Perhaps the most striking single finding in this set of results is the relationship between force acts and the psychological component. The beta weight for this component is statistically significant for the *closed* polities as well as for both the *unstable* and *Third World* groups. In the first two instances, in fact, the psychological forces are the sole determinants of the overall significance of the force equations. Given our previous inability to account for the domain of force behavior—aside from the pervasiveness of the action-reaction syndrome—this finding highlights the importance of incorporating additional factors into comparative foreign policy research designs. Aside from the research of M. G. Hermann (1978) and M. G. Hermann and C. F. Hermann (1979), no prior effort has been made to measure psychological phenomena on a cross-national basis in the context of a holistic analytical scheme which takes into account variables from different clusters. The results here are very encouraging since they enhance the variance explained so perceptibly for a previously "inexplicable" dimension of foreign behavior.

As a corollary to these findings, it should be noted that notwithstanding our increased ability to explain force behavior while at the same time excluding the action-reaction element, it remains true that of the three types of foreign behavior, force is lowest in terms of variance explained by this model. Table 8.13 reveals that constructive diplomatic behavior and nonmilitary conflict remain better explained by the elements of our model, although the gaps among the three domains have narrowed considerably. Overall, then, it is still apparent that the more routine and less conflictual forms of foreign behavior are better explained than are the more extreme forms of behavior.

As was the case in Chapter 7, we have once again performed a parallel analysis which incorporates the action-reaction elements within the interstate component. The results of this analysis are presented in the appendix to this chapter.

CONCLUSION

In a fundamental sense, this chapter has been designed to go beyond the prior examples of relative potency testing on psychological and other variable areas. Aside from the research of Rosenau (1968) and Stassen (1972) on individual versus role variables, few comparative, empirical analyses have dealt with this question.

Equally central to this chapter has been the explicit goal of providing a preliminary assessment of the validity of the value data set. The validation strategy which we have pursued here entails an emphasis on the behavioral relevance of the foreign policy-making elite values. Table 8.14, which can be compared with Rokeach's results as presented above in Table 8.2, summarizes the relevant findings. For the three forms of foreign behavior and the eighteen values, there are 69 significant relationships out of 270 possible entries in Table 8.14. If we disregard the force results—for which we discovered only seven significant betas—then there are 62 entries out of a possible total of 180. The first proportion is about 23 percent; the second is almost 35 percent. It is unlikely that these results are attributable exclusively to chance.

While the results are somewhat encouraging, we must also point out the potential problems with the data set. Aside from the obvious caveat that the direction of influence may be from behavior to value rather than the reverse, perhaps the most troublesome issue revolves around the question of inferring from the source (FBIS *Daily Reports* based on monitoring foreign broadcasts and speeches) to the realm of behavior.

This entire issue can be reduced to one basic contrast—between the representational and instrumental models of communication (see Pool, 1959). As O. Holsti (1976: 133) describes the dilemma:

> Analysts will be forced to rely on *documents that are in the first instance intended to convey information to the public, to legislatures, or to foreign governments.* As likely as not, they are also intended to persuade, justify, threaten, cajole, manipulate,

TABLE 8.14

Signigicant Value-Behavior Relationships: Foreign Behavior

	CONSTRUCTIVE DIPLOMATIC					NON-MILITARY CONFLICT					FORCE				
	Total	Western	Closed	Unstable	Third World	Total	Western	Closed	Unstable	Third World	Total	Western	Closed	Unstable	Third World
Comfortable life	●	●	●	●		●	●	●		●					
Peace	●●	●					●	●					●		
Equality	●	●					●				●		●		
Freedom		●●			●		●						●		
Gov't security	●●	●	●	●	●		●	●		●					
Happiness		●					●	●							
Honor						●●									
Justice	●		●			●		●							
Nat'l security	●●	●	●				●	●			●			●	
Public security			●												
Respect		●													
Social recognition	●	●	●	●	●										
Wisdom	●	●	●	●	●		●	●		●					
Progress		●	●	●	●		●	●		●					
Unity	●●	●	●		●		●	●		●					
Ideology															
Cooperation	●	●				●									
Support of gov't	●	●				●							●		

231

evoke sympathy and support, or otherwise influence the intended audience. Words may convey explicit or implicit clues about the author's "real" beliefs, attitudes, and opinions; they may also be intended to serve his practical goals of the moment [emphasis added].

This quotation provides a concise portrayal of the essence of the instrumental model, which involves "reading between the lines" in an attempt to determine what the message conveys, given its context and circumstances (Pool, 1959: 3). The representational model accepts articulations "at face value." Pool (1959: 209) concludes that every act of communication has representational and instrumental aspects.

Articulated values may be no more than rhetorical devices or meaningless shibboleths. In some instances, values may be used to deceive or obfuscate, as the relationship between force behavior and the value of peace for the *closed* group illustrates. To the extent that values are meaningless aphorisms, the utility of cross-national content analyses of public elite articulations is reduced to zero. Nevertheless, to the extent that elite value references are employed to confuse or mislead target(s), analysts can search for patterns of deception strategies. Even a pattern of lies can be of some importance in monitoring and predicting elite behavior.

A factor which complicates this problem is the finding that the nature of the audience influences both the decision maker's style of presentation and the substance of what is presented. Generally, statements for public consumption are less "truthful" than private statements (Bonham, 1975: 8). Empirical support is provided by Gilbert's (1975: 15) research on Secretary of State John Foster Dulles's perceptions of the People's Republic of China. In his statements to the general public, Dulles gave much higher assessments of Chinese hostility and strength; statements to the press ranked between those to the public and to Congress.

This implies that there is a validity-related hierarchy ranging from elite articulations directed at the mass public to an attentive or elite subgroup in the public (e.g., the press), to other actors within the political system (e.g., the legislature), to perhaps personal aides and confidants within the executive branch. Since the FBIS data consist of statements directed to the public and/or press, inescapable problems of image projection, manipulation, and distortion intrude.

Public statements, however, can impose constraints on a state's future freedom of action. Officially enunciated foreign policy doctrines exert this impact in at least two distinct ways: by contributing to expectations within the state and by influencing the basis upon which other actors make their decisions (Brodin, 1972: 105).

In addition, critics of content analyses of public documents may exaggerate the amount of distortion that occurs. We should recognize that manipulative (and distorting) communications, subtle cues, and direct messages are all lockstitched into the fabric of interstate interaction; instrumental and representational elements coexist. We should also distinguish between routine articulations and statements that occur during a crisis period; the former can be expected to provide more accurate and reliable profiles. The value approach assumes that each individual has (at least implicitly) a ranked scale of preferred terminal end-states. In a series of articulations over time, basic values will presumably be revealed.[13] Values are not consciously manipulated by the speaker, who of course is unaware that someone is planning to construct a profile of his or her value system.

Other validity criteria should be applied, but for both validity and policy-relevant purposes, the critical litmus test is the value-behavior relationship. As Marvick (1977: 124) asserts in his review of elite research:

> Those who attempt empirically grounded work have produced ingenious and thought-provoking findings about elite perspectives. At best, these specify the distinctive ways in which elite figures plausibly behave in real-life arenas—how they analyze problems, view strategies, treat rivals, use resources, and achieve

results. Evidence of actual elite behavior is seldom keyed to the evidence of elite beliefs.

This chapter presented a preliminary assessment of that relationship; future inquiry will attempt to pursue this issue in a more systematic fashion and further ascertain the reliability, validity, and explanatory/predictive utility of the foreign policy elite value data.

APPENDIX TO CHAPTER 8—VALUE DATA ANALYSIS: ACTION-REACTION RESULTS

The purpose of this appendix is to report results for analyses of the value data with the action-reaction or behavior-received variables included in the interstate component. Chapter 8 contains the findings for the subsample of states for which we amassed elite value data for the standard IBA 1966 to 1970 period; in that chapter (as in Chapter 7 on the PLS analysis for all 56 states and the three major components), we excluded the behavior-received variables. This appendix supplements Chapter 8, parallel to the manner in which this analysis was handled in the appendix to Chapter 7.

Table 8.15 presents the results for foreign behavior as predicted by the interstate component, which is operationalized here with eleven variables: the eight variables which appear in Chapter 8 and force received, reward received, and diplomatic behavior received. As in the less comprehensive interstate component analysis of Chapter 6, the behavior-received dimensions account for the overwhelming portion of the measurable variance in foreign behavior sent. Note that all but one of the R^2's is significant and that force behavior is predicted almost perfectly.

Looking across the entries for each form of behavior and type of group in Table 8.15, it becomes obvious that the incoming behavior indicators "wash out" or "suppress" the effects of the other interstate variables. Aside from scattered significant betas, the only exceptions to this configuration are the three energy measures for constructive diplomatic behavior which

TABLE 8.15

Foreign Behavior as Predicted by the Interstate Component, with Action-Reaction Variables (nation-years aggregated, 1966-1970)[a]

	INTER-NATIONAL INVOLVEMENT	ENERGY DEPENDENCY	ENERGY MARKET STRENGTH	ENERGY INTER-DEPENDENCY	FOOD DEPENDENCY	EXPORT CONCENTRATION	IMPORT CONCENTRATION	NEO-COLONIAL DEPENDENCY	FORCE RECEIVED	REWARD RECEIVED	DIPLO-MATIC BEHAVIOR RECEIVED	R²
Total Group, N = 131												
Constructive Diplomatic	.12*	-.01	–	.03	-.01	-.04*	.03	.01	-.08*	.09*	.91*	.93*
Non-Military Conflict	.04	-.13*	-.18*	.15*	-.04	-.09	-.23*	.13	.27*	.01	.45*	.47*
Force	-.01	-.01	–	-.01	-.02*	–	–	-.01	1.01*	-.05*	.01	.99*
Western Group, N = 24												
Constructive Diplomatic	.10	.02	.10	-.02	.02	.02	.10	-.07	-.14	.32*	.90*	.91*
Non-Military Conflict	-.19	-.43	-.22	-.30	-.30	-.37*	-.25	.05	.08	.04	.27	.51
Force	-.01	.01	.01	–	-.02*	.01	-.01	-.01	1.02*	-.02	-.03*	.99*
Closed Group, N = 25												
Constructive Diplomatic	.01	5.17*	1.19*	-4.74*	–	.02	-.01	–	-.13*	-.06*	1.18*	.99*
Non-Military Conflict	–	2.77	.61	-2.60	.05	-.11	-.03	-.02	-.23*	-.05	1.24*	.97*
Force	–	-.33	-.08	.30	–	–	–	-.01	1.15	.02	-.19*	.99*
Unstable Group, N = 27												
Constructive Diplomatic	.05	-.03	–	.01	.01	–	.05	-.04	-.15*	.21*	.81*	.99*
Non-Military Conflict	.24	-.06	-.24	.24	.02	-.18	-.31	.22	.47*	.69*	-.33	.75*
Force	-.01	-.01	.01	-.01	–	–	.01	.01	1.01*	–	-.04*	.99*
Third World, N = 45[b]												
Constructive Diplomatic	.42*	.06	-.26	.33*	.15	-.33*	.18	.10	-.23	.16	.72*	.63*
Non-Military Conflict	.32*	.03	-.32*	.28	-.19*	-.18*	-.20	.26	.09	.10	.64*	.72*
Force	.01	–	.05	-.08*	-.01	.04*	-.07	.02	1.01*	-.01	.01	.99*

a. Numbers in first eleven columns are beta weights.

b. This group consists of all large developing, poor, and unclassifiable states.

*Beta or R² significant at the .05 level.

TABLE 8.16

Relative Potency of Predictors of Foreign Policy Behavior, with
Action-Reaction Variables (nation-years aggregated, 1966-1970)

	Psychological	Societal	Interstate	Global	R^2
Total Group					
Constructive Diplomatic	.02	.05	.90*	.05	.93*
Non-Military Conflict	.13	−.07	.50*	.37*	.61*
Force	.02	−	1.01*	−.04*	.99*
Western Group					
Constructive Diplomatic	−	.23	.79*	−	.93*
Non-Military Conflict	.05	−.15	.36*	.65*	.69*
Force	.03	−.03	1.00*	−.01	.99*
Closed Group					
Constructive Diplomatic	−.01	.11	.90*	.03	.99*
Non-Military Conflict	.01	.16	.79*	.10	.91*
Force	.01	−.03	1.01*	−.02	.99*
Unstable Group					
Constructive Diplomatic	−.01	−	.87*	.13	.98*
Non-Military Conflict	.15	−.23	.59*	.23	.69*
Force	−.02	−.01	1.01*	−	.99*
Third World[b]					
Constructive Diplomatic	−.01	.11	.90*	.03	.99*
Non-Military Conflict	.01	.16	.79*	.10	.91*
Force	.01	−.03	1.00*	−.02	.99*

a. Numbers in first four columns are beta weights.
b. This group consists of all large developing, poor, and unclassifiable states.
*Beta or R^2 significant at .05 level.

emanate from the *closed* states (the same finding was reported
in Chapter 8) and international involvement within the *others*
cluster (for both constructive and nonmilitary conflict activity).

Table 8.16 lists the relative potency measures for the four
components with action-reaction factors incorporated into the
interstate realm. The table looks like an expanded replica of the
relative potency Coleman analysis of Chapter 6 (see Table 6.5).
In every case, the R^2 is significant; the percentages range from a
very respectable 61 percent to 99 percent. These results are attributable almost exclusively to the interstate domain, aside
from the global component in two cases (nonmilitary conflict
behavior for all states and within the *Western* group).

NOTES

1. This issue is discussed in detail in M. G. Hermann (1974), and O. Holsti (1976).

2. See especially Rokeach (1968a: Chapter 7; 1973: Chapter 8); see also Searing et al. (1973) for a discussion of the structuring principle in belief systems and public opinion research.

3. Expected differences also emerge for factional groups within parties; right-wing and progressive Conservatives and moderate and doctrinaire Labourites all tended to rank values in the predicted fashion. Searing (1978: 77) reports one illustrative example; the percentage ranking "public order" first, second, or third are (respectively): 71, 39, 12, and 3. Rokeach (1973) reports a variety of social structural value pattern differences within the United States (sex, social class, race, age, religion, and politics) and also presents cross-cultural comparisons for American, Canadian, Australian, and Israeli college men. Heterogeneous attitudes display expected and significant relationships with value configurations; among the attitudes are civil rights for the poor and black, black militancy, Vietnam, communism, student protest, religion, and church activism (Rokeach, 1973: 117). On the discriminating ability of values in the area of religion, see Rokeach (1969a, 1969b); for evidence concerning the domains of poverty and race relations, see Rokeach and Parker (1970).

4. The general research design and such specific procedures as state sample selection, coder training, and reliability assessment are discussed in Chapter 2.

5. See also Table 2.4.

6. This dominant profile was confirmed more systematically by intercorrelating the state rankings. For 1966, for example, the Spearman's rho correlations ranged from the .30s and .40s to the .60s and .70s. Furthermore, there were only a handful of negative relationships in the entire set of correlations and these were infinitesimal. While *frequencies* show marked variations, rankings are uniform.

7. While this new group is essentially a merger of the *large developing* and *poor* groups, it should be recalled that six states—Thailand, Ghana, Kenya, Greece, Saudi Arabia, and Nigeria—could not be classified on any of the factors which were extracted. Thailand appears in the value sample twice (1968, 1969), Ghana once (1966), Kenya once (1966), Greece twice (1966, 1967), and Nigeria three times (1966, 1967, 1969). With the exception of Greece, all of these states are clearly "developing" or "Third World" countries.

8. See Figure 7.1. The rationale for excluding the action-reaction element of the interstate component was identical to the reasoning which we discussed in Chapter 7. The appendix reports the results for an analysis which is parallel to the one in this chapter, except that the action-reaction or behavior-received variables are included in the interstate component.

9. The result for wisdom is unusual since that particular value appears rarely in the data set generally (see Tables 2.4 and 8.3); what this finding means is that on the infrequent occasions when a reference is made to wisdom in the speeches of Western leaders, it reduces the amount of constructive diplomatic behavior sent.

10. This foreshadows a critical issue which will be discussed in the conclusion of this chapter in the context of the instrumental versus representational debate: Are articulated elite values nothing more than rhetorical devices which are employed to deceive other actors and generally obfuscate reality? If we conceive of the values as a monitoring or forecasting tool rather than a scientific data set (i.e., a set of variables for

explaining foreign behavioral patterns), then it is important to recognize that states may say x and do y. That is, a positive relationship between the value a world of peace and acts of force may be *expected* (from an instrumental frame of reference) rather than *anomalous* (given a representational perspective).

11. See O. Holsti (1976: 127), Hopple (1980), and M. G. Hermann (1974, 1976, 1978) for a discussion of this issue.

12. The unusually large beta weights for energy dependency and energy interdependence means that even an occasional fluctuation in this area exerts a large effect on external behavior. Note that the direction of the effect for energy dependency is strongly negative (resulting in decreases in all forms of behavior), while the relationship in the case of energy interdependency is equally strong but in a positive direction.

13. This was true even for a diplomatic "prevaricator" such as Hitler; see White (1949) and Rokeach et al. (1970).

Chapter 9

Conclusion

The composite portrait which emerges from the foregoing chapters presupposes a process of inquiry which has been intentionally systematic. We have in effect pursued a set of research steps in a sequential fashion; boundary delineation and conceptualization and framework construction, refinement, operationalization, and testing have constituted the most salient of the distinct stages in our research. Larger questions of theory construction, analytical strategy, and policy relevance will be confronted in this final chapter. In the process, we will also attempt to assess the status of work in the scientific or comparative study of foreign policy behavior.

The IBA framework was designed to be comprehensive, comparative, operationalizable, and policy relevant. Since the last of the four criteria will be discussed in some detail below, our focus here will be limited to the first three. To the extent that it is feasible in the context of the current status of data and theory in the subfield of scientific foreign policy inquiry, the IBA framework is a comprehensive system of variable realms. Especially noteworthy was our success in operationalizing the psychological component on a genuinely cross-national basis. Equally pertinent, however, was our ultimate inability to generate any empirical, comparable measures for phenomena which are housed within the political component.

Our goal from the outset has been to avoid the polar extremes of positing an inordinately complex scheme of factors and specifying an empirically crude, totally unrepresentative set of operational measures. We have undoubtedly not achieved complete success. For example, critics could justifiably compare the relative richness of our interstate component with the comparatively "stark" character of the societal component. Such contrasts reflect the differential emphases of prior data-collection activities and the significant departures from randomness in the distributions of researcher interests and data availability.

We consciously attempted to prevent ease of access to data from dictating our choice of measures; when this structure has been violated in the past, the result has almost invariably been the generation of reams of meaningless computer output and the production of a series of unimpressive sets of factors, correlation coefficients, or beta weights. Our *prior* delineation of variable clusters and specific variables—based on the explicit adoption of a criterion of comprehensiveness—represented an effort to guard against the inductive/exploratory syndrome.

The criterion of comparability imposes the requirement that analysts eschew amorphous statements about "foreign policy in general" or "states in general." The variable clusters of state characteristics and foreign policy behavior both constitute typing schemes which serve to group phenomena within the broad domains of actors (states) and behavioral outputs (foreign policy). In a more fundamental sense, the comparative standard warns against generalizing from a case or a datum; we understand and explain phenomena on the basis of the identification of patterns and the delineation of generalizations about similarities and differences (both within groups and between groups). The *comparative method* is a basic form of scientific investigation, not a special feature of the comparative study of foreign policy.[1]

The operationalizability criterion requires a synthesis of careful planning and execution and the development of measures which reflect theoretically significant concepts. The application of this criterion to a research design which involves 56 states precluded the incorporation of certain theoretically signficant constructs such as bureaucratic politics. While the latter can be operationalized in case studies, it is difficult to imagine employing the concept in cross-national inquiry—unless we rely on indicators which are so indirect that the nexus between the latter and the concept becomes unacceptably tenuous.

THEORY CONSTRUCTION

The development of viable theories of foreign policy (or of international relations generally) remains an elusive goal. Part of the problem, of course, relates to the controversy that characterizes the concept of *theory* itself. As a philosophical-epistemological term, *theory* has been subjected to a regrettable amount of conceptual stretching; such conceptual imprecision pervades discussions of theorizing in all major subfields of the discipline of political science (see Rapoport, 1958).

A reasonably precise definition would equate *scientific theory* with an abstract, formal, simple, and rigorous *system* of statements. Some of the statements are a priori (the assumptions, premises, or *axioms*); others are logically implied from these and represent *theorems* which take the form of falsifiable statements about the real world. Theory, then, is a *deductively connected system of axioms and theorems*. This definition has attracted extensive support in the comparative study of foreign policy (McGowan, 1974, 1975, 1976: 226-227), in the parent subfield of international relations (Bobrow, 1972; Phillips, 1974; O. R. Young, 1972), and in the discipline generally (Popper, 1957; Rudner, 1966).

While philosophers have deified the deductive route to theory-building, practitioners generally discover that a purely deductive approach seldom "pays off." In order to conduct actual research, it becomes necessary to "descend" from the mists of pure deductivism. A reversion to unenlightened or absolute inductivism, however, is equally unrewarding. Mountains of data and chains of hypotheses accrue; cumulation remains additive rather than integrative (see Zinnes, 1976b).

We have attempted to move beyond this impasse by pursuing a strategy of "structured empiricism" or "sophisticated inductivism" in the interstices between what Brecher (1977: 60) calls "pure model-building or atomic empiricism." Our data collection and hypothesis-testing were thus anchored in the context of an overarching analytical framework; the framework served as the basis for generating testable causal models.

Beyond "structured empiricism," we foresee a phase of "dialogue" and interplay between deductive theorizing and further inductive work. This process is both mutually reinforcing (and cyclical) and dialectical in nature. As data sets are extended longitudinally and substantively while more hypotheses are added (accretion), deductive theory construction intervenes, achieves integration, and sets the stage for another round of data analysis and proposition synthesis.

ANALYTICAL STRATEGY SPECIFICATION

As Wold (1975a) emphasized in his overview description of the PLS strategy, the need is for an approach which permits modeling in *complex* situations with *soft* information. If we confront a complex problem or model rather than a simple one in a situation of scarce information (including theoretical information and empirical data), the notion of soft rather than hard modeling becomes pertinent.

The distinction refers to both the means and ends of modeling. Note that for every feature of the *means* of model-building listed below, foreign policy modelers are clearly at the "soft" end of the continuum:

(1) situations (controlled experiments versus nonexperimental observations)
(2) data (direct measurements with negligible observational errors versus indirect measurement)

(3) variables (nonrandom versus random)
(4) relationships (deterministic versus conditional expectations)
(5) residuals (specified versus unspecified distribution)

Wold (1975a) details the differences between the PLS and Maximum Likelihood methods. The key point is that the particular analytical strategy here is tailored to the state of data and theory in the comparative study of foreign policy. As more blocks of variables are added (such as the political) and as the present ones are modified and refined, we can continue to use the PLS method for model-estimation purposes. As our ability to specify exact relationships and measures increases, Maximum Likelihood approaches to latent variable models may be employed (Joreskog, 1980).

BEYOND RELATIVE POTENCY

The analytic portions of this volume have relied almost exclusively on a perspective which assesses the relative potency of various determinants of foreign behavior. Thus, while these analyses have been conducted in a rather sophisticated fashion, utilizing powerful analytic procedures, they nevertheless bring us only through the first stage of a comprehensive study of foreign policy behavior. In a sense, we have been engaged thus far in testing the framework itself. No attempt has been made here to develop more sophisticated causal models, building upon the results of the relative potency tests. Such models should now begin to stress the complex types of interrelationships among the clusters of determinants, as well as a variety of mediated relationships between the determinants of foreign policy and its various behavioral manifestations.

While the development of such models is beyond the scope of the present volume, the general perspectives which will guide such model construction have begun to emerge. These perspectives, dubbed "precondition-precipitant analysis" and "misperception analysis," will be outlined below.

The first perspective involves the crucial distinction between factors which can be viewed as constituting the basic underlying preconditions of foreign behavior and those factors or events which actually precipitate behavior. This distinction, originally developed by Eckstein (1972) and applied specifically to the phenomenon of internal war, can be modified for use at the interstate level of analysis as well. According to this perspective, precipitants are those events or conditions which give rise to specific acts. The preconditions are those circumstances which make it possible for the precipitants to cause behavior, i.e., they provide the necessary context for the precipitant-behavior causal sequence. There is a need, then, for the construction of sensitive models of the foreign behavior process which clearly identify and distinguish between these two realms.

The most significant contribution of this distinction is to shift attention from those aspects of a behavioral process which defy systematic analysis as a result of their uniqueness—precipitants—to those which are amenable to systematic inquiry. In other words, the precondition—precipitant distinction helps us to differentiate between conditions which may be controllable and manipulable, and those which are beyond the reach of the policy analyst and the policy maker.

The precondition-precipitant perspective may be particularly helpful in unraveling the complex interrelationships between the action-reaction element of our framework and the remaining determinants of foreign behavor. Action-reaction processes have traditionally been viewed from a precipitant perspective, whereas the remaining determinants of foreign behavior can be viewed as fluctuating sets of preconditions within which the action-reaction process operates. Models which bear this distinction in mind will have a greater chance of explaining these critical behavioral processes.

The second general perspective involves a reconceptualization of the notion of misperception. According to this formulation, misperception will not be understood in the traditional sense of a decision maker's cognitive screen causing him to misinterpret objective events. Rather, we speak here of the correct perception of overt events which do not, in turn, accurately reflect the intentions of the initiating state. Thus, a perfectly rational decision maker is likely to fall victim to this type of "misperception." In periods of intense conflict between states, and in the absence of direct communications between the parties, the only reality for decision makers is that which is reflected in the overt signals of their adversaries. Clearly, what is missing from this image or perception is the process which led to the overt act. This type of misperception can be defined as the *literal interpretation of events of complex origins.*

As we noted, a critical element in this process is any limitation on the ability of parties to communicate directly with each other concerning aspects of their conflict behavior. Generally, in-conflict situations the level of direct communications between adversaries decreases as the level of conflict increases. This being the case, we have the potential for an increase in the level of uncertainty concerning intentions, and therefore an increase in the possibility of divergence between perception and reality. Furthermore, the process appears to be escalatory in nature, and bold initiatives on the part of statesmen are often necessary to bring about their reversal. The Nixon/Kissinger breakthrough to China and the Sadat visit to Jerusalem constitute recent examples of this type of action.

This approach to misperception bears a direct relationship to some of the findings reported in this volume, and hence may form the basis for more complex causal models of the foreign behavior process. As noted throughout our discussions, the more extreme the level of conflict behavior we are examining, the less well the elements of the IBA framework do in accounting for these levels. We have noted that it is precisely in those situations of high conflict with limited communications that the type of misperception under discussion here is most likely to occur. It is in these types of situations that we find the direct action-reaction model, i.e., force received predicting to force sent, most potent. This, then, constitutes a second area in which more complex causal models should be developed and examined.

POLICY RELEVANCE

Policy relevance was adopted as one of our four evaluative criteria at the outset of the IBA Project. To the extent that social scientific inquiry is reliable, valid, and genuinely cumulative, it can, if properly focused, serve the informational needs of the policy maker. We have thus identified, operationalized, and ascertained the impact of several clusters of determinants of foreign policy behavior. Our research has provided very preliminary answers to such questions as the following:

(1) What are the major *determinants* of foreign policy?
(2) What are the *relationships* between these determinants and external behavior?
(3) What is the *relative impact* of these determinants on foreign behavior?
(4) What are the major *types of states* in the international arena?
(5) What are the central *dimensions of foreign behavior*?

Certainly, such results would have to be converted or "contextualized" before a real-world analyst would find them useful. The ability to provide state-specific findings is inherent in the IBA models and is essential to bridging the gap between basic and applied research, but has received relatively little attention in research findings. Instead, given the complexity of our basic research tasks, attention was focused less upon how the IBA framework might be made "relevant," and more upon how the framework might be conceived and tested. It was our conviction from the outset, however, that properly conducted basic social scientific research can (and should) constitute the foundation upon which applied research might be conducted. It is to this end that our research is ultimately aimed.

Perhaps an example of this basic-to-applied process should be highlighted here. Based at least in part upon IBA research, a computer-based system consisting of dynamic political indicators (one set of variables from one of the components) has been developed and tested retrospectively (see Andriole, 1976; Andriole and Young, 1977; Daly and Davies, 1978). The computer-based system, known as the Early Warning and Monitoring System (EWAMS), is currently based at the Defense Advanced Research Projects Agency Cybernetics Technology Office's (DARPA/CTO) Demonstration and Development Facility (DDF).

In order to supplement the data base of the EWAMS, the IBA data sets have been updated and expanded by the more applied Cross-National Crisis Indicators (CNCI) Project (see Hopple and Rossa, 1978). Other political, economic, region-specific, and real-time, expert-generated data will also be integrated into the Early Warning and Monitoring System. EWAMS is specifically designed to be user oriented, multisource, and multi-method in nature. Plans are currently being developed for transfer to a testbed location.

The EWAMS is an outgrowth of a variety of basic research endeavors. More recent developments and enhancements have been responses to the needs and suggestions of the applied community. The eventual goal is the transfer of a real-time monitoring and warning system to various elements in the policy arena.

Realistically, however, while there are traceable IBA contributions to the development of more applied, more "policy-relevant" early warning (or indications and warnings, as it is known in the government) analytical tools, we must assess the contributions as minor. Why? Part of the problem is rooted in our failure to understand what it means to be relevant or, more accurately, useful. Our research over the past several years has precipitated a renewed look at the nature of policy-relevant research. Indeed, it precipitated an analysis which took us back to Easton's 1969 address to the American Political Science Association in which he launched the so-called "post-behavioral revolution" (Easton, 1969).

Very succinctly, Easton's "credo of relevance" was designed to coax scientifically inclined basic researchers in academia into the applied area. Similarly, in 1970 at the annual meeting of the

International Studies Association, Snyder echoed Easton's credo and declared that behavioralists who study international politics and foreign policy also have an explicit obligation to put their knowledge to work (Snyder, 1970).

In the face of such challenges, in 1970 Singer characterized political science—and, therefore, the study of international politics and foreign policy—as "one of the more retarded" social sciences, hardly capable of producing policy-relevant "general theories" (Singer, 1970); and, in 1972, Whiting cautioned the policy-making community against the power of academic generalizations (Whiting, 1973). One year later one of us sat in front of Morton Halperin as he explained how the "scientists" could never really be relevant, at least not in the same sense as have the so-called "traditionalists."[2]

In the face of such "evidence," we have concluded that the "scientists" really have a relevance problem. We are now certain that those who scientifically study foreign policy and international politics will really have to make an effort to influence policy, and that the abstract search for empirical theory, the jargon, and the incomprehensible and misunderstood methodologies might very well remain permanently decoupled from real-world problems.

Yet at the same time we remain cognizant (via analysts such as Halperin and others) of the very real and often enormous impact which "traditional" work has exerted over the years upon many high-level policy makers. Indeed, who could possibly dispute the intellectual influence of analysts such as Hans Morgenthau, George Kennan, Thomas Schelling, Henry Kissinger, and Zbigniew Brzezinski? While the work of such men has rarely assisted policy makers in solving very specific decision-making problems, it continues to exert immeasurable impact upon the design and implementation of broad policy philosophies.

Interestingly enough, we discovered that only when the study of international politics and foreign policy passed from the traditional-qualitative to the scientific-quantitative stage did the question of relevance arise. Since so many scholars were convinced that scientific analyses were so "obviously" superior to traditional, "intuitive" ones, they naturally assumed that the new would be more influential than the old. Unfortunately, in their eagerness to elevate the "new and unique" to a special status, they neglected to identify key methodological differences and the impact that these differences would exert upon the quest for relevance. More to the point, they failed to realize that the traditional message was (and is) one which often seeks to influence policy and policy makers at the highest cognitive level. Concepts such as "realism," "balance of power," and "deterrence" were developed by traditionalists and internalized not by intelligence analysts responsible for the analysis of daily cable traffic, but by secretaries and assistant secretaries of state and, indeed, even presidents. The new quantitative work, we concluded, could not *and should not* appeal to high-level policy makers. We are now convinced that the frustration which launched the post-behavioral revolution as it applies to international politics and foreign policy was stimulated by a monumental misunderstanding of the nature of scientific analysis and the activites of high-, mid-, and low-level decision makers.

Of course, part of the problem can be traced to the nature of scientific research itself. It was (and remains) incomprehensible to even many of its producers. Highly jargonized and abstract, it is alien to most policy makers. But much more importantly, quantitative influence is limited because it is inappropriately aimed at high-level policy makers (who are disinterested in the results of a Markov analysis, or a PLS analysis). All of this, of course, serves to emphasize that the relevance which might flow from quantitative analyses such as ours will have to be less glamorous than that which impacts from the night tables of presidents.

So what of the relevance problem? Clearly, for those who seek high-level influence for their sophisticated scientific analyses, there will always be a relevance problem. Those who define relevance much more narrowly will have an easier time.

Let us return to the early warning, or indications and warnings, analysts mentioned above. While it is true that the IBA work has in an indirect way contributed to the development of a computer-based system that might satisfy some of their needs, our new perspective on relevance would find us examining more closely the activities of such analysts (who are by no means "policy" makers) and discovering that when they arrive at work in the morning, they usually grab a cup of coffee, light a cigarette, and begin the tedious task of examining the mound of intelligence information in front of them. They do not sit in on cabinet meetings; nor are they briefed on hostage situations. They are not concerned with theories of foreign policy behavior or interested in data collection. They are instead, people who must write coherent reports about what is happening in the world today, this morning, in one hour.

Certainly, there are governmental analysts who operate in less hectic environments. But they too are interested only in techniques and approaches that will help them with their contingency planning, long-range threat assessments, force posturing, and the like.

Again, traditional analyses of international politics and foreign policy can, and often do, find their way into policy-making circles; quantitative scientific analyses, such as the ones which appear in this volume, must be substantially modified, extended, translated, and properly targeted before they can be made at all useful.

All of this is not to suggest that quantitative social scientific analyses of foreign policy behavior cannot be made useful to real-world analysts, but rather that in their present form the above analyses are not immediately useful. Accordingly, we must conclude that in spite of our good intentions we have not yet satisfied the policy-relevance criterion. Hopefully, future work will enable us to better understand the nature of relevance and, when appropriate, conduct research which may be of genuine use to someone responsible for operational tasks.

Finally, we should mention that the quest for relevance should not dominate the scientific study of foreign policy. At this stage in the subfield's development such dominance would be exceedingly premature. Also, since the skills and perspective necessary for conducting potentially relevant research are specialized, it is not realistic to expect everyone to want to search for relevance. Many reseachers are best suited to the search for theory. Accordingly, if we are to develop useful insights into the sources and processes of foreign policy we should adhere to the logic of comparative advantages and productive divisions of labor.

THE COMPARATIVE STUDY OF FOREIGN POLICY

The promise of scientific foreign policy analysis has clearly been greater than the payoff (see Kegley, 1979). Much of the work has been pedestrian and ad hoc. Suggestions for future research are potentially infinite; our assessment will highlight four specific proposals.

The first is that the prevailing cross-national strategy should be supplemented by more most-similar systems designs. Regional interaction groups, for example, have not been studied sufficiently. There is a limit to the knowledge that can be produced when we study 50 or 60 states in all major geographic, sociocultural, and behavioral interaction regions.

Second, we should generally terminate data-collection operations and focus on the intensive *analysis* of available data sets. Rosecrance (1976) attributes the glaring lack of cumulativeness in international politics to the use of varying data bases, differing time periods and geographical contexts, noncomparable mathematical or manipulative procedures, and competing research paradigms. The fourth can certainly not be legislated out of existence or wished away; we can, however, orient research efforts around the IBA data base (which now exists for the ten-year period from 1966 to 1975 and could easily be updated) and a series of similar geographic contexts (cross-national, regional, dyadic).[3]

The third recommendation is to devote more emphasis to genuinely dynamic analysis. Our model, as it is currently conceived, completely ignores feedback processes. Using the 1966 to 1970 years as the base period, we could conduct time series analyses for the entire 1966 to 1975 period. Both change and stability in external behavior should be accounted for by holistic, dynamic causal models.

Finally, process analysis should receive priority on future research agendas. Source analysis is similar to a snapshot of an area; process analysis is indispensable for fleshing out the details of terrain on the foreign policy map. With the proliferation of both decision process frameworks and case studies (see Caldwell, 1977), the foundation has been provided. Perhaps the future will witness the synthesis of perspectives, an undertaking which Allison (1971) and Steinbruner (1974) have advocated.

In the future, we may expect some diminution in the avalanche of output in scientific foreign policy analysis as well as a narrowing of the focus. In a discussion of research on aggression in social psychology, Berkowitz (1978) contrasts the Hegelian view of the thesis/antithesis/synthesis pattern (a proposition is offered which generates opposing ideas and the contradiction is subsequently reconciled at a higher order of abstraction) with recent social psychological theorizing: Thesis leads to antithesis but the final result is a narrowing of the original conception rather than a broader synthesis. Perhaps this pattern will also characterize the comparative study of foreign policy movement. Initial enthusiasm stimulated an outpouring of conceptual and empirical work; the inevitable disappointments of the first and second waves may produce a decline in output and a redefined (and hopefully refined) focus of inquiry.

We may conclude on a note of cautious optimism. Conceptual, empirical, and methodological progress has certainly occurred. We can perceive the beginnings of theorizing. From the domain of framework construction, we can move on to continue the equally challenging and exciting tasks of sustained empirical inquiry and model construction and testing.

NOTES

1. See McGowan (1975) and Przeworski and Teune (1972). In a sense, our specific strategy was a most-similar concomitant variation design, since we selected the most active cases in the universe of actors. The design could also be viewed as a modified intersocietal survey approach, since the N of 56 represents over half of the polities in the system; the sample, however, is biased, not random.

2. Statements made during an interview of Morton Halperin by S. J. Andriole, November 1973.

3. The variables in the data base are described in detail in Hopple and Rossa (1978).

INTERSTATE BEHAVIOR ANALYSIS PROJECT LIST OF PUBLICATIONS

Research Reports

IBA Research Report 1: S. J. Andriole, J. Wilkenfeld, and G. W. Hopple, "A Framework for the Comparative Analysis of Foreign Policy Behavior."

IBA Research Report 2: G. W. Hopple, "The Psychological Component and the Comparative Study of Foreign Policy Behavior: Issues, Strategies, and Problems of Operationalization."

IBA Research Report 3: G. W. Hopple, "Internal Political Variables and the Comparative Study of Foreign Policy: A Framework for Research and Analysis."

IBA Research Report 4: G. W. Hopple, "The Societal Component and the Comparative Study of Foreign Policy."

IBA Research Report 5: S. J. Andriole, "Interstate Realities and the Conduct of Foreign Policy."

IBA Research Report 6: S. J. Andriole, "Global Systemic Variables and the Comparative Study of Foreign Policy."

IBA Research Report 7: J. Wilkenfeld, "Comparative Foreign Policy: A Typology of States." Presented at the Southwestern Political Science Association annual meeting, San Antonio, Texas, March 1975.

IBA Research Report 8: S. J. Andriole, "Conceptualizing the Dimensions of Interstate Behavior." Presented at the Southwestern Political Science Association annual meeting, San Antonio, Texas, March 1975.

IBA Research Report 9: S. J. Andriole, J. Wilkenfeld, and G. W. Hopple, "The Sources and Processes of Foreign Policy Behavior: A Panoramic Conceptualization." Presented at the International Studies Association annual meeting, Washington, DC, February 1975.

IBA Research Report 10: G. W. Hopple, "Public Opinion and the Comparative Study of Foreign Policy."

IBA Research Report 11: G. W. Hopple, "Comparative Foreign Policy: Determinants of Action and Reaction." Presented at the Southwestern Political Science Association annual meeting, San Antonio, Texas, March 1975.

IBA Research Report 12: S. J. Andriole, "Foreign Policies of Scarcity: Some Implications for Research and Analysis." Presented at the International Studies Association annual meeting, Washington, DC, February 1975.

IBA Research Report 13: G. W. Hopple, "The Comparative Study of Foreign Policy and the 'Data Gap' Problem: An Interim Report."

IBA Research Report 14: S. J. Andriole, "General Coding Instructions: Typology of States."

IBA Research Report 15: S. J. Andriole, "The Comparative Study of Foreign Policy: En Route to a Productive Conceptual Framework."

IBA Research Report 16: G. W. Hopple, "Psychological Sources of Foreign Policy Behavior: The Belief Systems Approach and Content Analysis."

IBA Research Report 17: J. Wilkenfeld and R. N. McCauley, "A Preliminary Factor Analytic Exploration of the State Attribute Domain."

IBA Research Report 18: G. W. Hopple, "Societal Factors in the Comparative Study of Interstate Behavior: An Operational Formulation."

IBA Research Report 19: R. N. McCauley, "Analytic Strategies in the Comparative Study of Interstate Behavior: Some Preliminary Thoughts."

IBA Research Report 20: G. W. Hopple, "International Behavior Analysis: The Interface Between the Conceptual and Operational Phases of Research."

IBA Research Report 21: G. W. Hopple, "Foreign Policy, Public Opinion, Social Science, and Policy-Relevance: Exploring the Linkages."

IBA Research Report 22: G. W. Hopple, "Events Data, the Bureaucratic Politics Perspective, and the Political Component."

IBA Research Report 23: J. Wilkenfeld, G. W. Hopple, S. J. Andriole, and R. N. McCauley, "Profiling States for Foreign Policy Analysis: Preliminary Findings." Presented at the American Political Science Association annual meeting, Chicago, September 1976.

IBA Research Report 24: P. J. Rossa, "A Q-Factor Analysis of the State Attribute Domain."

IBA Research Report 25: G. W. Hopple, J. Wilkenfeld, P. J. Rossa, and R. N. McCauley, "Frameworks and Analytic Strategies in the Study of Foreign Policy." Presented at the Southern Political Science Association annual meeting, Atlanta, November 1976.

IBA Research Report 26: P. J. Rossa, "Basic Assumptions and Analytical Frameworks in Explanations of Foreign Policy."

IBA Research Report 27: J. Wilkenfeld, G. W. Hopple, P. J. Rossa, and R. N. McCauley, "Action-Reaction, Societal, and Economic Explanations: Testing a Partial Model of Interstate Behavior." Presented at the International Studies Association annual meeting, St Louis, March 1977.

IBA Research Report 28: G. W. Hopple, P. J. Rossa, and J. Wilkenfeld, "Internal and External Inputs: Assessing the Relative Potency of Sources of Foreign Behavior." Presented at the Midwest Political Science Association annual meeting, Chicago, April 1977.

IBA Research Report 29: J. Wilkenfeld, "Interstate and Societal Perspectives on Conflict and Crisis in the Middle East." Presented at the American Political Science Association annual meeting, Washington, DC, September 1977.

IBA Research Report 30: P. J. Rossa and L. Fountain, "The Interstate Component: Data and Indices."

IBA Research Report 31: G. W. Hopple, "Psychological Sources of Foreign Policy Behavior: A New Approach."

IBA Research Report 32: L. Fountain and P. J. Rossa, "The Global Component: From the Conceptual to the Operational."

IBA Research Report 33: R. N. McCauley, "Analysis of International Behavior: Specification, Significance, and Critique."

Working Papers

IBA Working Paper 1: S. J. Andriole, "International Behavior Analysis and the Perennial Problems of Political Inquiry."

IBA Working Paper 2: G. W. Hopple, "The Psychological Component and the Comparative Study of Foreign Policy: The 'Relative Irrelevance' of Two Types of Sources."

IBA Working Paper 3: S. J. Andriole, "The Definition, Conceptualization, and Classification of Foreign Policy: Pacifying a Few Exasperating Analytical Issues."

IBA Working Paper 4: G. W. Hopple, "The Sources and Processes of International Behavior: An Explicit Conceptualization with a View Toward Analysis."

IBA Working Paper 5: S. J. Andriole, "The Information Needs of Foreign Policy-Makers and the IBA Project: Some First Thoughts."

IBA Working Paper 6: P. J. Rossa, "Typologizing: A Research Memorandum."

Data Packages*

IBA Data Package 1: J. Wilkenfeld, G. W. Hopple, and P. J. Rossa, "Structural Characteristics of States."

* All Interstate Behavior Analysis Project data sets are available from the International Relations Data Archive of the Interuniversity Consortium for Political and Social Research at the University of Michigan.

IBA Data Package 2: G. W. Hopple, J. Wilkenfeld, and P. J. Rossa, "Societal Determinants of Foreign Policy Behavior."

IBA Data Package 3: P. J. Rossa and L. Fountain, "Interstate Determinants of Foreign Policy Behavior: A Cross-National Data Set."

IBA Data Package 4: L. Fountain and P. J. Rossa, "The Global Realm: A Cross-National Data Set for Analyzing Foreign Policy Behavior.

IBA Data Package 5: G. W. Hopple, "Psychological Determinants of Foreign Policy Behavior: A Cross-National Data Set."

Books and Articles

Andriole, S. J., J. Wilkenfeld, and G. W. Hopple (1975) "A framework for the comparative analysis of foreign policy behavior." International Studies Quarterly 19, 2: 160-198.

Andriole, S. J. (1976) "Resource scarcity and foreign policy: implications for research and analysis." World Affairs 139, 1: 17-26.

Hopple, G. W., J. Wilkenfeld, P. J. Rossa, and R. N. McCauley (1977) "Societal and interstate determinants of foreign conflict." Jerusalem Journal of International Relations 2, 4: 30-66.

Wilkenfeld, J., G. W. Hopple, S. J. Andriole, and R. N. McCauley (1978) "Profiling states for foreign policy analysis." Comparative Political Studies 11, 1: 4-35.

Andriole, S. J. (1978) "The levels of analysis problem and the study of foreign, international, and global affairs: a review and critique and another final solution." International Interactions 2, 3: 113-133.

Wilkenfeld, J., G. W. Hopple, and P. J. Rossa (1979) "Sociopolitical indicators of conflict and cooperation," in J. D. Singer and M. D. Wallace (eds.) To Augur Well: Early Warning Indicators in World Politics. Beverly Hills, CA: Sage.

Hopple, G. W. (1979) "Elite values and foreign policy analysis: preliminary findings," in L. Falkowski (ed.) Psychological Models in International Politics. Boulder, CO: Westview.

Andriole, S. J. (1979) "Decision process models and the needs of policy-makers: thoughts on the foreign policy interface." Policy Sciences 11.

Hopple, G. W. (1980) Political Psychology and Biopolitics: Assessing and Predicting Elite Behavior in Foreign Policy Crises. Boulder, CO: Westview.

Wilkenfeld, J., G. W. Hopple, and P. J. Rossa (1980) "Bridging the image-reality gap: an empirical perspective," in N. Oren (ed.) Image and Reality in International Relations. Ramat Gan, Israel: Tur Hedove Press.

Wilkenfeld, J., G. W. Hopple, P. J. Rossa and S. J. Andriole (1980) Foreign Policy Behavior: The Interstate Behavior Analysis Model. Beverly Hills, CA: Sage.

Hopple, G. W., P. J. Rossa, and J. Wilkenfeld (1980) "Threat and misperception: assessing the overt behavior of states in conflict," in P. J. McGowan and C. W. Kegley, Jr. (eds.) Sage International Yearbook of Foreign Policy Studies, Vol. 5. Beverly Hills, CA: Sage.

Rossa, P. J., G. W. Hopple and J. Wilkenfeld (1980) "Crisis analysis: indicators and models." International Interactions 7, 2.

Rossa, P. J. (forthcoming) "Explaining international political behavior and conflict through Partial Least Squares modeling," in H. Wold and K. G. Joreskog (eds.) Systems Under Indirect Observation: Causality, Structure, Prediction. New York: Elsevier North-Holland.

REFERENCES

ABELSON, R. P. (1971) "The ideology machine." Presented at the annual meeting of the American Political Science Association, Chicago, September.

ABRAVANEL, H. and B. HUGHES (1973) "The relationship between public opinion and governmental foreign policy: a cross-national study," pp. 107-133 in P. J. McGowan (ed.) Sage International Yearbook of Foreign Policy Studies, Vol. I. Beverly Hills, CA: Sage.

ADELMAN, I., A. ABRAHAMSSON, B. ARESKOUG, L. O. LORENTSON, and J. WALLMYR (1975) "Applications of methods I-II to Adelman-Morris's data," in H. Wold (ed.) Modelling in Complex Situations with Soft Information. Presented at the Third World Congress of Econometrics, Toronto, Canada, August.

ALLISON, G. T. (1972) The Essence of Decision: Explaining the Cuban Missile Crisis. Boston: Little, Brown.

ALMOND, G. and G. B. POWELL (1966) Comparative Politics: A Developmental Approach. Boston: Little, Brown.

ANDRIOLE, S. J. (1976) Progress Report on the Development of an Integrated Crisis Warning System. Technical Report 76-19, McLean, VA: Decisions & Designs, Inc.

——— J. WILKENFELD, and G. W. HOPPLE (1975) "A framework for the comparative analysis of foreign policy behavior." International Studies Quarterly 19 (June): 160-189.

ANDRIOLE, S. J. and R. A. YOUNG (1977) "Toward the development of an integrated crisis warning system." International Studies Quarterly 21 (March): 107-150.

ARMSTRONG, J. A. (1965) "The domestic roots of Soviet foreign policy." International Affairs 61 (January): 37-40.

ART, R. J. and K. N. WALTZ (1971) The Use of Force, Boston: Little, Brown.

ASPATURIAN, V. V. (1972) "Soviet foreign policy," pp. 174-237 in R. C. Macridis (ed.) Foreign Policy in World Politics. Englewood Cliffs, NJ: Prentice-Hall.

263

AXELROD, R. (1972a) Framework for a General Theory of Cognition and Choice. Research Series No. 18. Berkeley: University of California, Institute of International Studies.

————— (1972b) "Psycho-algebra: a mathematical theory of cognition and choice with an application to the British Eastern Committee in 1918." Peace Research Society (International) 18: 113-131.

AZAR, E. E. (1971) "Analysis of international events." Peace Research Reviews 4 (November).

————— R. A. BRODY and C. A. McCLELLAND (1972a) International Event Interaction Analysis: Some Research Considerations. Beverly Hills, CA: Sage.

AZAR, E. E., S. H. COHEN, T. O. JUKAM, and J. M. McCORMICK (1972b). "The problem of source coverage in the use of international events data." International Studies Quarterly 16, 3: 373-388.

BANKS, A. S. (1972) "Patterns of domestic conflict: 1919-1939 and 1946-1966." Journal of Conflict Resolution 16 (March): 41-50.

————— (1971) Cross-Polity Time-Series Data. Cambridge, MA: MIT Press.

————— and P. M. GREGG (1965) "Grouping political systems: Q-factor analysis of a cross-polity survey." American Behavioral Scientist 9, 3: 3-6.

BARBER, J. D. (1972) The Presidential Character: Predicting Performance in the White House. Englewood Cliffs, NJ: Prentice-Hall.

BERGSTEN, C. F. and L. B. KRAUSE [eds.] (1975) World Politics and International Economics. Washington, DC: Brookings.

BERKOWITZ, L. (1978) "Whatever happened to the frustration-aggression hypothesis?" American Behavioral Scientist 21 (May/June): 691-708.

BHAGWATI, J. [ed.] (1967) International Trade. New York: Viking.

BISHOP, G. F., A. M. BARCLAY, and M. ROKEACH (1972) "Presidential preferences and freedom-equality value patterns in the 1968 American campaign." Journal of Social Psychology 88 (December): 207-212.

BLALOCK, H. M. (1972) Social Statistics. New York: McGraw-Hill.

BLONDEL, J. (1972) Comparing Political Systems. New York: Praeger.

BLOOD, M. R. and G. M. MULLET (1977) "Where have all the moderators gone? the perils of type II error." Technical Report 1, M-77-5 (Working Paper Series). Atlanta: College of Industrial Management, Georgia Institute of Technology. May.

BOBROW, D. B. (1972) "The relevance potential of different products," pp. 204-228 in R. Tanter and R. H. Ullman (eds.). Theory and Policy in International Relations. Princeton, NJ: Princeton University Press.

BODENHEIMER, S. (1971) "Dependency and imperialism: the roots of Latin American underdevelopment," in K. T. Fann and D. C. Hodges (eds.) Readings in U.S. Imperialism. Boston: Porter Sargent.

BOEHM, V. R. (1977) "Differential prediction: a methodological artifact?" Journal of Applied Psychology 62: 146-154.

BOHRNSTEDT, G. W. (1970) "Reliability and validity assessments in attitude measurement," pp. 80-99 in G. F. Summers (ed.) Attitude Measurement. Chicago: Rand McNally.

BONHAM, G. M. (1975) "Cognitive process models and the study of foreign policy decision-making." Presented at the annual meeting of the International Studies Association, Washington, DC, February.

——— and M. J. SHAPIRO (1976) "Explanation of the unexpected: the Syrian intervention in Jordan in 1970," in R. Axelrod (ed.) Structure of Decision: The Cognitive Maps of Political Elites. Princeton, NJ: Princeton University Press.

——— (1973) "Simulation in the development of a theory of foreign policy decision-making," pp. 55-71 in P. J. McGowan (ed.) Sage International Yearbook of Foreign Policy Studies, Vol. 1. Beverly Hills, CA: Sage.

BRADY, L. (1978) "The situation and foreign policy," in M. A. East et al. (eds.) Why Nations Act. Beverly Hills, CA: Sage.

——— (1974) "Bureaucratic politics and situational constraints in foreign policy." Presented at the annual meeting of the American Political Science Association, Chicago, September.

BRECHER, M. (1979) "State behavior in international crisis." Journal of Conflict Resolution (September): 445-480.

——— (1977) "Toward a theory of international crisis behavior: a preliminary report." International Studies Quarterly 21 (March): 39-74.

——— (1974a) Decisions in Israel's Foreign Policy. New Haven, CT: Yale University Press.

———(1974b) "Inputs and decisions for war and peace: the Israel experience." International Studies Quarterly 18 (June): 131-177.

——— (1974c) "Research findings and theory building in foreign policy behavior," in P. J. McGowan (ed.) Sage International Yearbook of Foreign Policy Studies, Vol. II: 49-122.

———— (1973) "Images, process, and feedback in foreign policy: Israel's decision on German reparations." American Political Science Review 67 (March): 73-102.

———— (1972) The Foreign Policy System of Israel. New Haven, CT: Yale University Press.

———— (1968) India and World Politics: Krishna Menon's View of the World. New York: Praeger.

———— B. STEINBERG, and J. STEIN (1969) "A framework for research on foreign policy behavior." Journal of Conflict Resolution 13 (March): 75-101.

BRIM, O., D. C. GLASS, D. E. LAVIN, and N. GOODMAN (1962) Personality and Decision Processes. Palo Alto, CA: Stanford University Press.

BRODIN, K. (1972) "Belief systems, doctrines, and foreign policy." Cooperation and Conflict 7: 97-112.

BROWN, L. (1974) World Without Borders. New York: Viking.

BURGESS, P. M. (1968) Elite Images and Foreign Policy Outcomes: A Study of Norway. Columbus: Ohio State University Press.

———— and R. W. LAWTON (1972) Indicators of International Behavior: An Assessment of Events Data Research. Beverly Hills, CA: Sage.

BURROWES, R. (1964) "Mirror, mirror, on the wall...A comparison of event data sources," in J. N. Rosenau (ed.) Comparing Foreign Policies. Beverly Hills, CA: Sage.

———— and B. SPECTOR (1973) "The strength and direction of relationships between domestic and external conflict and cooperation: Syria, 1961-67," pp. 294-321 in J. Wilkenfeld (ed.) Conflict Behavior and Linkage Politics. New York: David McKay.

BUTWELL, R. (1969) "Contemporary international relations and development," in R. Butwell (ed.) Foreign Policy and the Developing Nations. Lexington: University of Kentucky Press.

CALDWELL, D. (1977) "Bureaucratic foreign policy-making." American Behavioral Scientist 21 (September/October): 87-110.

CAMPBELL, J. T. and L. S. CAIN (1965) "Public opinion and the outbreak of war." Journal of Conflict Resolution 9 (September): 318-328.

CASANOVA, P. G. (1966) "Internal and external politics of developing countries," pp. 131-49 in R. B. Farrell (ed.) Approaches to Comparative and International Politics. Evanston, IL: Northwestern University Press.

CHOUCRI, N. (1974) Population Dynamics and International Violence. Lexington, MA: D. C. Heath.

——— and R. NORTH (1975) Nations in Conflict: National Growth and International Violence. San Francisco: Freeman.

———(1969) "Pressure, competition, tension, threat: toward a theory of international conflict." Presented at the annual meeting of the American Political Science Association, New York, September.

COHEN, B. C. (1973) The Public's Impact on Foreign Policy. Boston: Little, Brown.

——— (1957) The Political Process and Foreign Policy: The Making of the Japanese Peace Settlement. Princeton, NJ: Princeton University Press.

COHEN, J. and P. COHEN (1975) Applied Multiple Regression/Correlation Analysis for the Behavioral Sciences. New York: John Wiley.

COLEMAN, J. S., E. Q. CAMPBELL, C. J. HOBSON, J. McPARTLAND, A. M. MOOD, F. D. WEINFELD, and R. L. YORK (1966) Equality of Educational Opportunity. Washington, DC: Department of Health, Education, and Welfare.

COLLINS, J. N. (1973) "Foreign conflict behavior and domestic disorder in Africa," pp. 251-293 in J. Wilkenfeld (ed.) Conflict Behavior and Linkage Politics. New York: David McKay.

CONVERSE, P. E. (1964) "The nature of belief systems in mass publics," pp. 206-261 in D. Apter (ed.) Ideology and Discontent. New York: Macmillan.

COOK, T. D. and D. T. CAMPBELL (1976) "The design and conduct of quasi-experiments and true experiments in field settings," in M. D. Dunnette (ed.) Handbook of Industrial and Organizational Psychology. Chicago: Rand McNally.

COOPER, R. N. (1968) The Economics of Interdependence. New York: McGraw-Hill.

COPLIN, W. D. (1974) Introduction to International Politics: A Theoretical Overview. Chicago: Rand McNally.

CORRADO, R. (1975) "Nationalism and communalism in Wales." Ethnicity 2: 360-381.

COSER, L. A. (1956) The Function of Social Conflict. New York: Macmillan.

COSTELLO, T. W. (1970) "Psychological aspects: the soft side of policy formation." Policy Sciences 1: 161-168.

CUMMINS, H. W. (1973) "Value structure and political leadership," in V. Davis and M. A. East (eds.) Sage Professional Papers in International Studies. Beverly Hills, CA: Sage.

CUTRIGHT, P. (1963) "National political development: measurement and analysis." American Sociological Review 28: 253-264.

DAHL, R. A. (1970) Modern Political Analysis. Englewood Cliffs, NJ: Prentice-Hall.

DALLIN, A. (1969) "Soviet foreign policy and domestic politics: a framework for analysis." Journal of International Affairs 23: 250-265.

DALY, J. A. and T. R. DAVIES (1978) The Early Warning and Monitoring System: A Progress Report. Technical Report. McLean, VA: Decisions & Designs, Inc.

DEUTSCH, K. W. and J. D. SINGER (1964) "Multipolar power systems and international stability." World Politics 16 (April): 390-406.

DEVINE, D. J. (1972) The Political Culture of the United States. Boston: Little, Brown.

DYE, T. R. (1966) Politics, Economics, and the Public. Chicago: Rand McNally.

EAST, M. H. (1973) "Size and foreign policy behavior: a test of two models." World Politics 24 (July): 556-576.

——— (1972) "Status discrepancy and violence in the international system: an empirical analysis," pp. 299-316 in J. N. Rosenau et al. (eds.) The Analysis of International Politics. New York: Macmillan.

——— and P. M. GREGG (1967) "Factors influencing cooperation and conflict in the international system." International Studies Quarterly 11 (September): 244-269.

EAST, M. H. and C. F. HERMANN (1974) "Do nation-types account for foreign policy behavior?" pp. 269-303 in J. N. Rosenau (ed.) Comparing Foreign Policies: Theories, Findings, and Methods. Beverly Hills, CA: Sage.

EAST, M. A., S. A. SALMORE, and C. F. HERMANN [eds.] (1978) Why Nations Act: Theoretical Perspectives for Comparative Foreign Policy Studies. Beverly Hills, CA: Sage.

EASTON, D. (1969) "The new revolution in political science." American Political Science Review (December): 1051-1061.

ECKHARDT, W. (1967) "Can this be the conscience of a conservative? The value analysis approach to political choice." Journal of Human Relations 15: 443-456.

——— (1965) "War propaganda, welfare values, and political ideologies." Journal of Conflict Resolution 9: 345-358.

ECKSTEIN, H. (1972) "On the etiology of internal wars," in I. K. Feierabend et al. (eds.) Anger, Violence, and Politics. Englewood Cliffs, NJ: Prentice-Hall.

———— (1962) Internal War: The Problem of Anticipation. Report Submitted to the Research Group on Psychology and the Social Sciences. Washington, DC: Smithsonian Institute.

EHRLICH, P. and A. EHRLICH (1974) The End of Affluence. New York: Ballantine.

ELEY, J. W. and J. H. PETERSEN (1973) "Economic interests and American foreign policy allocations, 1960-1969," pp. 161-187 in P. J. McGowan (ed.) Sage International Yearbook of Foreign Policy Studies Vol. 3. Beverly Hills, CA: Sage.

EPSTEIN, E. N. (1965) "Effects of the Cuban crisis upon attitudes toward war and peace." Psychological reports 17: 424-426.

ETHEREDGE, L. S. (1978) "Personality effects on American foreign policy, 1898-1968: a test of interpersonal generalization theory." American Political Science Review 72 (Junc): 434-451.

FANN, K. T. and D. C. HODGES [eds.] (1971) Readings in U.S. Imperialism. Boston: Porter Sargent.

FARRELL, R. B. (1966) "Foreign politics of open and closed societies," in R. B. Farrell (ed.) Approaches to Comparative and International Politics. Evanston, IL: Northwestern University Press.

FEIERABEND, I. K. and R. L. FEIERABEND (1969) "Level of development and international behavior," pp. 135-188 in R. Butwell (ed.) Foreign Policy and the Developing Nations. Lexington: University of Kentucky Press.

FRANKEL, J. (1963) The Making of Foreign Policy. New York: Oxford University Press.

GALTUNG, J. (1969) "Foreign policy orientation as a function of social position," in J. N. Rosenau (ed.) International Politics and Foreign Policy. New York: Macmillan.

———— (1967) "Social position, party identification and foreign policy orientation: a Norwegian case study," pp. 161-193 in J. N. Rosenau (ed.) Domestic Sources of Foreign Policy. New York: Macmillan.

———— (1964) "A structural theory of aggression." Journal of Peace Research 2: 95-119.

GAMSON, W. A. and A. MODIGLIANI (1971) Untangling the Cold War: A Strategy for Testing Rival Theories. Boston: Little, Brown.

GEORGE, A. L. (1969) "The 'operational code': a neglected approach to the study of political leaders and decision-making." International Studies Quarterly 13: 190-222.

—— and J. L. GEORGE (1964) Woodrow Wilson and Colonel House: A Personality Study. New York: Dover.

GILBERT, J. D. (1975) "John Foster Dulles' perceptions of the People's Republic of China: an assessment of accuracy." Presented at the annual meeting of the Southwestern Political Science Association, San Antonio, Texas, March.

GILLESPIE, J. V. (1971) "Introduction: studies on democratization," pp. 375-381 in J. V. Gillespie and B. A. Nesvold (eds.) Macro-Quantitative Analysis. Beverly Hills, CA: Sage.

GILPIN, R. (1975) "Three models of the future," in C. F. Bergsten and L. B. Krause (eds.) World Politics and International Economics. Washington, DC: Brookings.

GLAD, B. (1966) Charles Evans Hughes and the Illusion of Innocence: A Study in American Diplomacy. Urbana: University of Illinois Press.

GOOD, R. (1962) "State-building as a determinant of foreign policy process in the new states," in L. W. Martin (ed.) Neutralism and Nonalignment. New York: Praeger.

GREENSTEIN, F. I. (1975) Personality and Politics. Chicago: Markham.

GROSS, F. (1954) Foreign Policy Analysis. New York: Philosophical Library.

GURR, T. R. (1972) Politimetrics. Englewood Cliffs, NJ: Prentice-Hall.

—— (1970) Why Men Rebel. Princeton, NJ: Princeton University Press.

HAAS, M. (1973) "Societal development and international conflict," in J. Wilkenfeld (ed.) Conflict Behavior and Linkage Politics. New York: David McKay.

—— (1970) "Dimensional analysis in cross-national research." Comparative Political Studies 3 (April): 3-35.

—— (1968) "Social change and national aggressiveness, 1900-1960," in J. D. Singer (ed.) Quantitative International Politics. New York: Macmillan.

—— (1965) "Societal approaches to the study of war." Journal of Peace Research 4: 307-323.

HALLE, N. H. (1966) "Social position and foreign policy attitudes." Journal of Peace Research 3: 46-74.

HAZLEWOOD, L. A. (1975) "Diversion mechanisms and encapsulation processes: the domestic conflict-foreign conflict hypothesis reconsidered," pp. 213-244 in P. J. McGowan (ed.) Sage International Yearbook of Foreign Policy Studies, Vol. III. Beverly Hills, CA: Sage.

——— (1973) "Externalizing systemic stress: international conflict as adaptive behavior," pp. 148-190 in J. Wilkenfeld (ed.) Conflict Behavior and Linkage Politics. New York: David McKay.

HELLMANN, D. C. (1969) Japanese Domestic Politics and Foreign Policy. Berkeley: University of California Press.

HERMANN, C. F. (1978) "Decision structure and process influences on foreign policy," in M.A. East et al. (eds.) Why Nations Act. Beverly Hills, CA: Sage.

——— [ed.] (1972) International Crises: Insights from Behavioral Research. New York: Macmillan.

——— (1971) "What is a foreign policy event?" pp. 295-321 in W. F. Hanrieder (ed.) Comparative Foreign Policy: Theoretical Essays. New York: David McKay.

——— (1969) "International Crisis as a Situational Variable," pp. 409-421 in J. N. Rosenau (ed.) International Politics and Foreign Policy: A Reader in Research and Theory. New York: Macmillan.

——— M. A. EAST, M. G. HERMANN, B. G. SALMORE, and S. A. SALMORE (1973) CREON: A Foreign Events Data Set. Beverly Hills, CA: Sage.

HERMANN, M. G. (1978) "Effects of personal characteristics of political leaders on foreign policy," pp. 49-68 in M. A. East et al. (eds.) Why Nations Act. Beverly Hills, CA: Sage.

——— [ed.] (1977) A Psychological Examination of Political Leaders. New York: Macmillan.

——— (1976) "When leader personality will affect foreign policy: some propositions," in J. N. Rosenau (ed.) In Search of Global Patterns. New York: Macmillan.

——— (1974) "Leader personality and foreign policy behavior," pp. 201-234 in J. N. Rosenau (ed.) Comparing Foreign Policies: Theories, Findings, Methods. Beverly Hills, CA: Sage.

——— (1972a) "Effects of leader personality on national foreign policy behavior: a theoretical discussion," Ohio State University. (mimeo)

———(1972b) "How leaders process information and the effect on foreign policy." Presented at the annual meeting of the American Political Science Association, Washington, September.

——— and C. M. HERMANN (1979) "The interaction of situations, political regimes, decision configurations, and leader personalities in interpreting foreign policy." Presented at the XIth World Congress, International Political Science Association, Moscow.

HOFFMAN, S. (1962) "Restraints and choices in American foreign policy." Daedulus 91 (Fall): 688-704.

HOLSTI, K. J. (1977) International Politics. Englewood Cliffs, NJ: Prentice-Hall.

HOLSTI, O. (1976) "Foreign policy decision makers viewed psychologically: 'cognitive process' approaches," pp. 120-144 in J. N. Rosenau (ed.) In Search of Global Patterns. New York: Macmillan.

—— (1972) Crisis, Escalation, War. London: McGill-Queen's University Press.

—— (1967) "Cognitive dynamics and images of the enemy," pp. 25-96 in D. J. Finlay et al. (eds.) Enemies in Politics. Chicago: Rand McNally.

—— R. C. NORTH and R. A. BRODY (1968) "Perception and action in the 1914 crisis: insights and evidence," pp. 160-186 in J. D. Singer (ed.) Quantitative International Politics. New York: Macmillan.

HOPPLE, G. W. (1980) Political Psychology and Biopolitics: Assessing and Predicting Elite Behavior in Foreign Policy Crises. Boulder, CO: Westview.

—— (1979) "Elite values and foreign policy analysis: preliminary findings," in L. Falkowski (ed.) Psychological Models in International Politics. Boulder, CO: Westview.

—— and P. J. ROSSA (1978) "Final Report of the Cross-National Crisis Indicators Project." College Park: University of Maryland.

HOPPLE, G. W., J. WILKENFELD, P. J. ROSSA, and R. N. McCAULEY (1977) "Societal and interstate determinants of foreign conflict." Jerusalem Journal of International Relations 2, 4: 30-66.

HUI, B. S. (1980) "On building PLS models with interdependent relations," in K. G. Joreskog and H. Wold (eds.) Systems Under Indirect Observation: Causality-Structure-Prediction. New York: Elsevier North-Holland.

International Studies Quarterly, Special Issue (1977) "International crisis: progress and prospects for applied forecasting and management." 21, 1.

JACOBSON, A. L. (1973) "Measuring intrasocietal conflict." Sociological Methods and Research 4 (May): 440-461.

JAMES, L. R., K. E. CORAY, and R. G. DEMAREE (1977) "Moderator analysis based on subgrouping: problems arising from the use of standardized variables." Techical Report 77-21. Fort Worth: Texas Christian University, Institute of Behavioral Research.

JENSEN, L. (1969) "Postwar democratic polities: national-international linkages in the defense policy of the defeated states," pp. 304-323 in J. N. Rosenau (ed.) Linkage Politics. New York: Macmillan.

JERVIS, R. (1976) Perception and Misperception in International Politics. Princeton, NJ: Princeton University Press.

——— (1970) The Logic of Images in International Relations. Princeton, NJ: Princeton University Press.

——— (1968) "Hypotheses on misperception." World Politics 20 (April): 454-479.

JONES, S. D. and J. D. SINGER (1972) Beyond Conjecture in International Politics: Abstracts of Data-Based Research. Itasca, IL: Peacock.

JORESKOG, K. G. (1980) "The LISREL approach to causal model building in the social sciences," in K. G. Joreskog and H. Wold (eds.) Systems Under Indirect Observation: Causality-Structure-Prediction. New York: Elsevier North-Holland.

——— (1977) "Structural equation models in the social sciences: specification, estimation, and testing," in R. P. Krishnaiah (ed.) Applications of Statistics. New York: Elsevier North-Holland.

——— (1973) "A general method for estimating a linear structural equation system," in A. S. Goldberger and O. D. Duncan (eds.) Structural Equation Systems in the Social Sciences. New York: Seminar.

——— and H. WOLD (1980) "The ML and PLS techniques for modeling with latent variables: comparative aspects," in K. G. Jorsekog and H. Wold (eds.) Systems Under Indirect Observation: Causality-Structure-Prediction. New York: Elsevier North-Holland.

KAPLAN, M. A. (1957) System and Process in International Politics. New York: John Wiley.

KATZ, F. E. and F. V. PIRET (1964) "Circuitous participation in politics." American Journal of Sociology 69: 367-373.

KATZENSTEIN, P. J. (1976) "International relations and domestic structures: foreign economic policies of advanced industrial states." International Organization 30 (Winter): 1-45.

KEAN, J. G. and P. J. McGOWAN (1973) "National attributes and foreign policy participation: a path analysis," pp. 219-251 in P. J. McGowan (ed.) Sage International Yearbook of Foreign Policy Studies. Vol. 1. Beverly Hills, CA: Sage.

KEGLEY, C. W. Jr. (1979) "The comparative study of foreign policy: paradigm lost?" Prepared for the conference on the Future of International Studies and the ISA, Columbia, South Carolina.

―――― (1973) A General Empirical Typology of Foreign Policy Behavior. Beverly Hills, CA: Sage.

―――― and A. C. AGNEW (1976) "Reciprocity and symmetry in interstate interactions: an attribute of dyadic foreign policy behavior?" Presented at the annual meeting of the American Political Science Association, Chicago, September.

KEGLEY, C. W. Jr., M. R. RICHARDSON, and C. RICHTER (1978) "Conflicts at home and abroad: an empirical extension." Journal of Politics 40: 742-751.

KELMAN, H. C. and A. H. BLOOM (1973) "Assumptive frameworks in international politics," pp. 261-295 in J. N. Knutson (ed.) Handbook of Political Psychology. San Francisco: Jossey-Bass.

KENDALL, M. and A. STUART (1958) The Advanced Theory of Statistics. Vol. 3. New York: Hafner.

KERLINGER, F. N. (1964) Foundations of Behavioral Research. New York: Holt, Rinehart & Winston.

KOWALSKI, B. R., R. GERLACH, and H. WOLD (1980) "Chemical systems under indirect observation," in K. G. Joreskog and H.Wold (eds.) Systems Under Indirect Observation: Causality-Structure-Prediction. New York: Elsevier North-Holland.

LAMPTON, D. M. (1973) "The U.S. image of Peking in three international crises." Western Political Quarterly 26: 28-50.

LASKI, H. (1944) "The parliamentary and presidential systems." Public Administration Review 4 (Autumn): 349-357.

―――― (1935) The State in Theory and Practice. New York: Viking.

LASSWELL, H. D. (1948) Power and Personality. New York: Viking.

―――― (1930) Psychopathology and Politics. Chicago: University of Chicago Press.

LENTNER, H. H. (1974) Foreign Policy Analysis. Columbus, OH: Charles E. Merrill.

LIAO, K. (1976) "Linkage politics in China: internal mobilization and articulated external hostility in the Cultural Revolution, 1967-1969." World Politics 28 (July): 590-610.

LIJPHART, A. (1968) "Typologies of democratic systems." Comparative Political Studies 1: 3-34.

LIPSET, S. M. (1959) "Some social requisites of democracy." American Political Science Review 53: 69-105.

LONDON, H. and J. E. EXNER, Jr. [eds.] (1978) Dimensions of Personality. New York: John Wiley.

LONDON, K. (1949) How Foreign Policy Is Made. New York: Van Nostrand.

LUTTBEG, N. R. [ed.] (1974) Public Opinion and Public Policy: Models of Political Linkage. Homewood, IL: Irwin.

MACRIDIS, R. C. [ed.] (1972) Foreign Policy in World Politics. Englewood Cliffs, NJ: Prentice-Hall.

MARVICK, D. (1977) "Elite politics: values and institutions." American Behavioral Scientist 21 (September/October): 111-134.

MAY, E. R. (1973) "Lessons" of the Past: The Use and Misuse of History in American Foreign Policy. New York: Oxford University Press.

MAYER, K. (1967) "Migration, cultural tensions, and foreign relations: Switzerland." Journal of Conflict Resolution 11 (June): 139-152.

McCLELLAND, C. A. (1968) "Access to Berlin: the quantity and variety of events, 1948-1963," in J. D. Singer (ed.) Quantitative International Politics. New York: Macmillan.

——— and G. HOGGARD (1969) "Conflict patterns in the interactions among nations," pp. 711-724 in J. N. Rosenau (ed.) International Politics and Foreign Policy. New York: Macmillan.

McCLELLAND, C. A. and R. A. YOUNG (1969) World Event/Interaction Survey Handbook and Codebook. WEIS Technical Report 1. Los Angeles: University of Southern California.

McCLOSKY, H. (1967) "Personality and attitude correlates of foreign policy orientation," pp. 161-193 in J. N. Rosenau (ed.)Domestic Sources of Foreign Policy. New York: Macmillan.

McGOWAN, P. J. (1976) "The future of comparative studies: an evangelical plea," pp. 217-234 in J. N. Rosenau (ed.) In Search of Global Patterns. New York: Macmillan.

——— (1975) "Meaningful comparisons in the study of foreign policy: a methodological discussion of objectives, techniques and research designs," pp. 52-87 in C. W. Kegley, Jr. et al. (eds.) International Events and the Comparative Analysis of Foreign Policy. Columbia: University of South Carolina Press.

——— (1974) "Problems in the construction of positive theories of foreign policy," pp. 25-44 in J. N. Rosenau (ed.) Comparing Foreign Policies: Theories, Findings, Methods. Beverly Hills, CA: Sage.

———— and H. B. SHAPIRO (1973) The Comparative Study of Foreign Policy: A Survey of Scientific Findings. Beverly Hills, CA: Sage.

McLELLAN, D. S. (1969) "Comparative 'operational codes' of recent U.S. secretaries of state: Dean Acheson." Presented at the annual meeting of the American Political Science Association, New York, September.

MEEHAN, E. J. (1971) "The concept 'foreign policy'," pp. 265-294 in W.F. Hanrieder (ed.) Comparative Foreign Policy: Theoretical Essays. New York: David McKay.

MERKL, P. H. (1971) "Politico-cultural restraints on West German foreign policy: sense of trust, identity, and agency." Comparative Political Studies 3 (January): 443-468.

MERRITT, R. L. (1972) "Public opinion and foreign policy." Policy Studies Journal 1 (Winter): 86-91.

MIDLARSKY, M. I. (1974) "Power, uncertainty, and the onset of international violence." Journal of Conflict Resolution (September): 395-431.

MODELSKI, G. (1962) A Theory of Foreign Policy. New York: Praeger.

MOORE, D. W. (1974) "National attributes and national typologies: a look at the Rosenau genotypes," pp. 251-267 in J. N. Rosenau (ed.) Comparing Foreign Policies. Beverly Hills, CA: Sage.

MORGENTHAU, H. J. (1948) Politics Among Nations. New York: Knopf.

MORSE, E. L. (1971) The Comparative Study of Foreign Policy: Notes on Theorizing. Princeton, NJ: Princeton University, Center for International Studies.

MUNTON, D. (1973) "Comparative foreign policy: fads, fantasies, orthodoxies, perversities." Presented at the ICFP Conference on the Future of Comparative Foreign Policy Analysis, Ojai, June.

NESVOLD, B. A. (1971) "Scalogram analysis of political violence," pp. 167-186 in J. V. Gillespie and B. A. Nesvold (eds.) Macro-Quantitative Analysis. Beverly Hills, CA: Sage.

NEWCOMBE, H. and A. NEWCOMBE (1972) Peace Research Around the World. Oakville, Ontario: Canadian Peace Research Institute.

NOONAN, R. (1980) "Toward a multivariate design for evaluation of educational reforms: an application of Partial Least Squares," in K. G. Joreskog and H. Wold (eds.) Systems Under Indirect Observation: Causality-Structure-Prediction. New York: Elsevier North-Holland.

NYE, J. S. (1972) Peace in Parts. Boston: Little, Brown.

O'LEARY, M. K. (1969) "Linkages between domestic and international politics in underdeveloped nations," pp. 324-346 in J. N. Rosenau (ed.) Linkage Politics. New York: Macmillan.

ORGANSKI, A. F. K. (1958) World Politics. New York: Knopf.

OSGOOD, C. E. (1959) "The representational model and relevant research methods," in I. de Sola Pool (ed.) Trends in Content Analysis. Urbana: University of Illinois Press.

PAIGE, G. D. (1977) "On values and science: the Korean decision reconsidered." American Political Science Review (December): 1603-1609.

——— (1968) The Korean Decision: June 24-30, 1950. New York: Macmillan.

PAPP, D. S. (1975) "Nixon, Brezhnev, Ford, and Watergate: the effects of a domestic crisis on Soviet-American relations." Presented at the Southwest Political Science Association annual meeting, San Antonio, Texas, March.

PETERSON, S. (1971) "International events, foreign policy-making, elite attitudes and mass opinion: a correlational analysis." Presented at the annual meeting of the International Studies Association, March.

PHILLIPS, W. R. (1978) "Prior behavior as an explanation of foreign policy," in M. A. East et al. (eds.) Why Nations Act. Beverly Hills, CA: Sage.

——— (1974) "Where have all the theories gone?" World Politics 26 (January): 155-188.

——— (1973) "The conflict environment of nations: a study of conflict inputs to nations in 1963," pp. 124-147 in J. Wilkenfeld (ed.) Conflict Behavior and Linkage Politics. New York: David McKay.

——— (1971) "The dynamics of behavioral action and reaction in international conflict." Peace Research Society Papers 17: 31-46.

——— and D. R. HALL (1970) "The importance of governmental structure as a taxonomic scheme for nations." Comparative Political Studies 3 (April): 63-89.

PLOSS, J. (1963) "The uncertainty of Soviet foreign policy." World Politics 15 (April): 455-64.

POOL, I. S. (1959) Trends in Content Analysis. Urbana: University of Illinois Press.

POPPER, K. R. (1957) The Logic of Scientific Discovery. London: Routledge & Kegan Paul.

PRZEWORSKI, A. and H. TEUNE (1972) The Logic of Comparative Social Inquiry. New York: John Wiley.

PUCHALA, D. J. (1971) "International transactions and regional integration," in L. Lindberg and S. Scheingold (eds.) Regional Integration: Theory and Research. Cambridge, MA: Harvard University Press.

RAPOPORT, A. (1958) "Various Meanings of Theory." American Political Science Review (December): 972-988.

REINTON, P. O. (1967) "International structure and international integration: the case of Latin America." Journal of Peace Research 4: 334-365.

RIGGS, F. (1950) Pressures on Congress: A Study of the Repeal of Chinese Exclusion. New York: King's Own.

RIKER, W. H. (1957) "Events and situations." Journal of Philosophy 54 (January): 57-70.

ROBERTS, C. M. (1974) "Foreign policy under a paralyzed presidency." Foreign Affairs 52 (July): 665-689.

ROKEACH, M. [ed.] (1979) Understanding Human Values: Individual and Social. New York: Macmillan.

——— (1975) "Value images of science and the values of science." Washington State University. (mimeo)

——— (1973) The Nature of Human Values. New York: Macmillan.

——— (1969a) "Religious values and social compassion." Review of Religious Research 11: 24-38.

——— (1969b) "Value systems in religion." Review of Religious Research 11: 3-23.

——— (1968-1969) "The role of values in public opinion research." Public Opinion Quarterly 32 (Winter): 547-559.

——— (1968a) Beliefs, Attitudes, and Values: A Theory of Organization and Change. San Francisco: Jossey-Bass.

——— (1968b) "A theory of organization and change within value-attitude systems." Journal of Social Issues 24 (January): 13-33.

——— (1960) The Open and Closed Mind: Investigations into the Nature of Belief Systems and Personality Systems. New York: Basic Books.

——— R. HOMANT, and L. PENNER (1970) "A value analysis of the disputed Federalist Papers." Journal of Personality and Social Psychology 16 (October): 245-250.

ROKEACH, M. and S. PARKER (1970) "Values as social indicators of poverty and race relations in America." Annals of the American Academy of Political and Social Science 388: 97-111.

ROSECRANCE, R. (1976) "The failures of quantitative analysis: possible causes and cures," pp. 174-180 in J. N. Rosenau (ed.) In Search of Global Patterns. New York: Macmillan.

——— (1966) "Bipolarity, multipolarity, and the future." Journal of Conflict Resolution 10 (September): 314-327.

ROSENAU, J. N. [ed.] (1976) In Search of Global Patterns. New York: Macmillan.

——— (1973) "Theorizing across systems: linkage politics revisited," in J. Wilkenfeld (ed.) Conflict Behavior and Linkage Politics. New York: David McKay.

——— (1971) "The external enviroment as a variable in foreign policy analysis," pp. 145-163 in J. N. Rosenau et al. (eds.) The Analysis of International Politics. New York: Macmillan.

——— (1969) [ed.] Linkage Politics. New York: Macmillan.

——— (1968) "Private preferences and political responsibilities: the relative potency of individual and role variables in the behavior of United States Senators," in J. D. Singer (ed.) Quantitative International Politics. New York: Macmillan.

——— (1967) "Foreign policy as an issue area," in J. N. Rosenau (ed.) Domestic Sources of Foreign Policy. New York: Macmillan.

——— (1966) "Pre-theories and theories of foreign policy," in R. B. Farrell (ed.) Approaches to Comparative and International Politics. Evanston: Northwestern University Press.

——— (1961) Public Opinion and Foreign Policy: An Operational Formulation. New York: Random House.

——— P. N. BURGESS, and C. F. HERMANN (1973) "The adaptation of foreign policy research: a case study of an anti-case study project." International Studies Quarterly 17 (March): 119-144.

ROSENAU, J. N. and G. HOGGARD (1974) "Foreign policy behavior in dyadic relationships: testing a pre-theoretical extension," in J. N. Rosenau (ed.) Comparing Foreign Policies: Theories, Findings, and Methods. Beverly Hills, CA: Sage.

ROSENAU, J. N. and G. RAMSEY (1975) "External vs. internal sources of foreign policy behavior," pp. 245-262 in P. J. McGowan (ed.) Sage International Yearbook of Foreign Policy Studies, Vol. III. Beverly Hills, CA: Sage.

ROSI, E. J. (1965) "Mass and attentive opinion on nuclear weapons tests and fallout, 1954-1963." Public Opinion Quarterly 29: 280-297.

ROSSA, P. J. (1980) "Explaining international political behavior and conflict through Partial Least Squares modeling," in K. G. Joreskog and H. Wold (eds.) Systems Under Indirect Observation: Causality-Structure-Prediction. New York: Elsevier North-Holland.

——— G. W. HOPPLE, and J. WILKENFELD (1980) "Crisis analysis: indicators and models." International Interations 7, 2: 121-161.

RUDNER, R. (1966) Philosophy of Social Science. Englewood Cliffs, NJ: Prentice-Hall.

RUMMEL, R. J. (1972) The Dimensions of Nations. Beverly Hills, CA: Sage.

——— (1970) Applied Factor Analysis. Evanston, IL: Northwestern University Press.

——— (1969) "Indicators of cross-national and international patterns." American Political Science Review 68, 1: 127-147.

——— (1968) "The relationship between national attributes and foreign conflict behavior," pp. 187-214 in J. D. Singer (ed.) Quantitative International Politics. New York: Macmillan.

——— (1967) "Understanding factor analysis." Journal of Conflict Resolution 21 (December): 444-480.

——— (1963) "Dimensions of conflict behavior within and between nations." General Systems Yearbook 8: 1-50.

RUSSETT, B. M. (1968a) "Delineating international regions," pp. 317-352 in J. D. Singer (ed.) Quantitative International Politics. New York: Macmillan.

——— (1968b) "Is there a long-run trend toward concentration in the international system?" Comparative Political Studies 1 (April): 103-122.

——— (1968c) "Regional Trading Patterns, 1938-1963." International Studies Quarterly (December): 360-379.

———(1967) International Regions and the International System. Chicago: Rand McNally.

——— (1966) "Discovering voting groups in the United Nations." American Political Science Review 60 (June): 327-339.

—— H. R. ALKER, Jr., K. W. DEUTSCH, and H. D. LASSWELL (1964) World Handbook of Political and Social Indicators. New Haven, CT: Yale University Press.

RUSSETT, B. M. and C. LAMB (1969) "Global patterns of diplomatic exchange, 1963-1964." Journal of Peace Research 1: 37-55.

SALMORE, S. A. (1972) "Foreign policy and national attributes: a multi-variate analysis." Ph.D. dissertation, Princeton University.

——— and C. F. HERMANN (1969) "The effect of size, development, and accountability on foreign policy." Papers of the Peace Research Society (International): 15-30.

SALMORE, S. A. and D. E. MUNTON (1974) "Classifying foreign policy behaviors: an empirically based typology," in J. N. Rosenau (ed.) Comparing Foreign Policy. Beverly Hills, CA: Sage.

SANTOS, T. D. (1971) "The structure of dependence," in K. T. Fann and D. C. Hodges (eds.) Readings in U.S. Imperialism. Boston: Porter Sargent.

SAWYER, J. (1967) "Dimensions of nations: size, wealth and politics." American Journal of Sociology (September): 145-172.

SCHWARTZ, J. J. and W. R. KEECH (1968) "Group influence on the policy process in the Soviet Union." American Political Science Review 62 (September): 840-851.

SCHWARTZ, M. (1975) The Foreign Policy of the USSR: Domestic Factors. Belmont, CA: Dickenson.

SCOLNICK, J. M. (1974) "An appraisal of studies of the linkage between domestic and international conflict." Comparative Political Studies 6 (January): 485-509.

SEARING, D. D. (1978) "Measuring politicians' values: administration and assessment of a ranking technique in the British House of Commons." American Political Science Review 72 (March): 65-79.

——— J. J. SCHWARTZ, and A. E. LIND (1973) "The structuring principle: political socialization and belief systems." American Political Science Review 67 (June): 423-437.

SHAPIRO, H. B. and M. K. O'LEARY (1974) "The systematic study of issues in international relations." PRINCE Research Studies 14 (March).

SHAPIRO, M. J. and G. M. BONHAM (1973) "Cognitive process and foreign policy decision-making." International Studies Quarterly 17, 2: 147-174.

SHNEIDMAN, E. S. (1969) "Logic content analysis: an explication of styles of concludifying," pp. 261-279 in G. Gerbner et al. (eds.) The Analysis of Communcation Content. New York: John Wiley.

——— (1963) "Plan II: the logic of politics," pp. 178-199 in L. Arons and M. A. May (eds.) Television and Human Behavior. Englewood Cliffs, NJ: Prentice-Hall.

——— (1961) "A psychological analysis of political thinking: the Kennedy-Nixon 'great debates' and the Kennedy-Khrushchev 'grim debates.'" Harvard University. (mimeo)

SIGLER, J. H., J. O. FIELD, and M. L. ADELMAN (1972) Applications of Event Data Anaysis. Beverly Hills, CA: Sage.

SIMMEL, G. (1955) Conflict. New York: Macmillan.

SINGER, J. D. (1979a) The Correlates of War: I. New York: Macmillan.

——— (1979b) Explaining War. Beverly Hills, CA: Sage.

——— (1972) "The 'Correlates of War' Project: interim report and rationale." World Politics 24: 243-270.

——— (1970) "Knowledge, practice, and the social sciences in internatoinal politics," quoted in N. Palmer (ed.) A Design for International Relations Research: Scope, Theory, Methods, and Relevance. Philadelphia: American Academy of Political and Social Science, Monograph 10 (October): 139-145.

——— [ed.] (1968) Quantitative International Politics. New York: Macmillan.

——— (1961) "The levels of analysis problem in international relations," in K. Knorr and S. Verba (eds.) The International System: Theoretical Essays. Princeton, NJ: Princeton University Press.

——— and J. E. RAY (1973) "Measuring the concentration of power in the international system." Sociological Methods and Research 1: 403-437.

SINGER, J. D. and M. SMALL (1972) The Wages of War, 1816-1965: A Statistical Handbook. New York: John Wiley.

——— (1968) "Alliance aggregation and the onset of war, 1815-1945," pp. 247-284 in J. D. Singer (ed.) Quantitative International Politics. New York: Macmillan.

SINGER, J. D. and M. D. WALLACE [eds.] (1979) To Augur Well: Early Warning Indicators in World Politics. Beverly Hills, CA: Sage.

SMALL, M. and J. D. SINGER (1969) "Formal alliances, 1815-1945: an extension of the basic data." Journal of Peace Research: 6: 257-282.

SNYDER, R. (1970) "Address to the International Studies Association/West," quoted in R. Lieber (1972) Theory and World Politics. Cambridge, MA: Winthrop.

——— H. W. BRUCK, and B. SAPIN [eds.] (1962) Foreign Policy Decision Making: An Approach to the Study of International Politics. New York: Macmillan.

SONDERMANN, F. A. (1961) "The linkage between foreign policy and international politics," in J. N. Rosenau (ed.) International Politics and Foreign Policy. New York: Macmillan.

SPROUT, H. and M. SPROUT (1971) Toward a Politics of the Planet Earth. New York: Van Nostrand.

STARR, H. and B. A. MOST (1976) "The substance and study of borders in international relations research." International Studies Quarterly 20 (December): 581-620.

STASSEN, G. H. (1972) "Individual preference versus role-constraint in policy making: Senatorial response to Secretaries Acheson and Dulles." World Politics 25 (October):. 96-119.

STEIN, A. A. (1976) "Conflict and cohesion: a review of the literature." Journal of Conflict Resolution 20 (March): 143-172.

STEINBRUNER, J. D. (1974) The Cybernetic Theory of Decision: New Dimensions of Political Authority. Princeton, NJ: Princeton University Press.

——— (1968) "The mind and the milieu of policy-makers: a case study of the MLF." Ph.D. dissertation, MIT.

STEWART, P. D. (1969) "Soviet interest groups and the policy process: the repeal of production education." World Politics 22 (October): 29-50.

STUPAK, R. J. (1971) "Dean Rusk on international relations: an analysis of his philosophical perceptions." Australian Outlook 25, 3: 13-28.

TANTER, R. (1966) "Dimensions of conflict behavior within and between nations, 1958-60." Journal of Conflict Resolution (March): 41-64.

VAN DYKE, V. (1966) "The optimum scope of political science," pp. 1-17 in J. C. Charlesworth (ed.) A Design for Political Science: Scope, Objectives, and Methods. Philadelphia: American Academy of Political and Social Science.

VASQUEZ, J. A. (1976) "Statistical findings in international politics: a data-based assessment," International Studies Quarterly 20, 2: 171-218.

WALLACE, M. D. (1973) War and Rank Among Nations. Lexington, MA: D. C. Heath.

WALTZ, K. N. (1967) Foreign Policy and Democratic Politics: The American and British Experience. Boston: Little, Brown.

——— (1964) "The stability of a bipolar world." Daedalus 93 (Summer): 892-907.

————— (1959) Man, The State and War. New York: Columbia University Press.

WEINSTEIN, F. B. (1972) "The uses of foreign policy in Indonesia: an approach to the analysis of foreign policy in the less developed countries." World Politics 24 (April): 256-281.

WHITE, R. K. (1951) Value-Analysis: The Nature and Use of the Method. Glen Gardner, NJ: Libertarian.

————— (1949) "Hitler, Roosevelt, and the nature of war propaganda." Journal of Abnormal and Social Psychology 44: 157-174.

WHITING, A. (1973) Personal correspondence with S. J. Andriole.

WILKENFELD, J. (1975) "A time-series perspective on conflict in the Middle East," pp. 177-212 in P. J. McGowan (ed.) Sage International Yearbook of Foreign Policy Studies, Vol. III. Beverly Hills, CA: Sage.

————— (1973) "Domestic and foreign conflict," pp. 107-123 in J. Wilkenfeld (ed.) Conflict Behavior and Linkage Politics. New York: David McKay.

————— (1972) "Models for the analysis of foreign conflict behavior of states," in B. M. Russett (ed.) Peace, War, and Numbers. Beverly Hills, CA: Sage.

————— (1969) "Some further findings regarding the domestic and foreign conflict behavior of nations." Journal of Peace Research 2: 147-56.

————— (1968) "Domestic and foreign conflict behavior of nations." Journal of Peace Research 1: 56-69.

————— and G. W. HOPPLE (1977) "Cross-national crisis indicators." Research proposal submitted to and funded by the Cybernetics Technology Office of the Defense Advanced Research Projects Agency. College Park: University of Maryland.

————— S. J. ANDRIOLE, and R. N. McCAULEY (1978) "Profiling states for foreign policy analysis. Comparative Political Studies 11 (April): 4-35.

WILKENFELD, J., G. W. HOPPLE, and P. J. ROSSA (1979) "Sociopolitical indicators of conflict and cooperation," in J. D. Singer and M. D. Wallace (eds.) To Augur Well: Early Warning Indicators in World Politcs. Beverly Hills, CA: Sage.

WILKENFELD, J., V. L. LUSSIER, and D. TAHTINEN (1972) "Conflict interactions in the Middle East, 1949-1967." Journal of Conflict Resolution 16 (June): 135-154.

WILKINSON, D. O. (1969) Comparative Foreign Policy: Framework and Methods. Belmont, CA: Dickenson.

WINHAM, G. R. (1970) "Developing theories of foreign policy making: a case study of foreign aid." Journal of Politics 32 (February): 41-70.

WOLD, H. (1978a) "Model construction and evaluation when theoretical knowledge is scarce: an example of the use of Partial Least Squares." Uppsala, Sweden: University of Uppsala, Department of Statistics.

——— (1978b) "Ways and means of multidisciplinary studies," in The Search for Absolute Values in a Changing World. New York: International Cultural Foundation, Inc.

——— (1977a) "On the transition from pattern recognition to model building," in R. Henn and O. Moeschin (eds.) Mathematical Economics and Game Theory: Essays in Honor of Oskar Morgenstern. Berlin. Springer.

——— (1977b) "Open path models with latent variables," in H. Albach et al. (eds.) Kvantitative Wirtschaftsforschung. Wilhelm Krelle Zum 60. Geburtstag. Tuebingen: Mohr.

——— (1977c) "Soft modeling: intermediate between traditional model building and data analysis." Vol. 6: Mathematical Statistics. Warsaw, Poland: Banach.

——— (1975a) "From hard to soft modelling," in H. Wold (ed.) "Modelling in complex situations with soft information." Presented at the Third World Congress of Econometrics, Toronto, Canada, August.

——— [ed.] (1975b) "Modelling in complex situations with soft information." Presented at the Third World Congress of Econometrics, Toronto, Canada, August.

——— (1974) "Causal flows with latent variables: partings of the ways in light of NIPALS modelling." European Economic Review 5 (June): 67-86.

——— and B. ARESKOUG (1975) "Methods II: path models with latent variables as proxies for blocks of manifest variables," in H. Wold (ed.). "Modelling in complex situations with soft information." Presented at the Third World Congress of Econometrics, Toronto, Canada, August.

YOUNG, O. R. (1972) "The perils of Odysseus: on constructing theories of international relations," pp. 179-203 in R. Tanter and R. H. Ullman (eds.) Theory and Policy in International Relations. Princeton, NJ: Princeton University Press.

YOUNG, R. A. (1975) "A classification of nations according to foreign policy output," in E. Azar and J. Ben-Dak (eds.) International Interactions: Theory and Practice of Events Analysis. London: Gordon & Breach.

ZINNES, D. A. (1976a) Contemporary Theory in International Relations. New York: Macmillan.

———— (1976b) "The problem of cumulation," pp. 161-166 in J. N. Rosenau (ed.) In Search of Global Patterns. New York: Macmillan.

———— (1966) "A comparison of hostile behavior of decision-makers in simulate and historical data." World Politics 18 (April): 474-502.

———— and J. WILKENFELD (1971) "An analysis of foreign conflict behavior of nations," in W. F. Hanrieder (ed.) Comparative Foreign Policy. New York: David McKay.

ZINNES, D. A., J. L. ZINNES, and R. D. McCLURE (1972) "Hostility in diplomatic communication: a study of the 1914 crisis," pp. 132-162 in C. F. Hermann (ed.) International Crises. New York: Macmillan.

ABOUT THE AUTHORS

JONATHAN WILKENFELD is Associate Professor of Government and Politics at the University of Maryland. He has held visiting appointments at the Hebrew University of Jerusalem and Johns Hopkins University, School of Advanced International Studies. From 1975 to 1980 he served as Editor of *International Studies Quarterly*. His publications include work on conflict analysis and the comparative analysis of foreign policy. His most recent articles appear in the *Sage International Yearbook of Foreign Policy Studies, Comparative Political Studies, Jerusalem Journal of International Relations, International Studies Quarterly*, as well as in a number of edited anthologies.

GERALD W. HOPPLE is Director, Technical Research and Development, at the International Public Policy Research Corporation (IPPRC), a private research firm in McLean, Virginia. He is also a faculty member at George Mason University and was previously on the faculty at the University of Maryland, where he received his Ph.D. in Political Science in 1975. Dr Hopple is the author of *Political Psychology and Biopolitics: Assessing and Predicting Elite Behavior in Foreign Policy Crises* (Westview Press, 1980) and the coauthor and coeditor of *Expert-Generated Data: Applications in International Affairs* (Westview Press, 1980). A specialist in crisis analysis, political psychology, and comparative foreign policy, he is also the author or coauthor of a number of articles and book chapters.

PAUL J. ROSSA is a Research Analyst at the International Public Policy Research Corporation, and specializes in the application of quantitative research methods to the study of international politics and conflict. He was formerly the Senior Research Assistant of two research projects at the University of Maryland under the direction of the Crisis Management Program of the Cybernetics Technology Office within the Defense Advanced Research Projects Agency. Mr. Rossa received his B.A. in 1974 from Northwestern University, his M.A. in 1976 from the University of Pittsburgh, and continued Ph.D. studies at the University of Maryland. Mr. Rossa has contributed articles to edited volumes by J. D. Singer and M. D. Wallace, H. Wold and K. Joreskog, and P. J. McGowan and C. W. Kegley, and has published in journals such as *International Interactions* and *Jerusalem Journal of International Relations*.

STEPHEN J. ANDRIOLE is the President of International Information Systems, Incorporated. He is formerly the Director of the Defense Advanced Research Projects Agency's Cybernetics Technology Office, where he was also a Program Manager. He has taught international relations, national security analysis, and methodology at the University of Maryland as an Assistant Professor and at the Johns Hopkins School of Advanced International Studies; he was also a Research Analyst and Project Manager at Decisions and Designs, Incorporated. He is a frequent contributor to professional journals in the national security, quantitative international relations, and command and control areas. His most recent publications have appeared in *Policy Sciences, Futures: The Journal of Forecasting and Planning, Journal of Defense Research, Air Force Magazine, Defense Management Journal, International Interactions*, and *Jerusalem Journal of International Relations*.